HEALTH IN COLONIAL GHANA: DISEASE, MEDICINE, AND SOCIO-ECONOMIC CHANGE, 1900–1955

by

K. David Patterson

P
CROSSROADS
E
S
S

International Standard Book Number 0-918456-42-8

Crossroads Press
Epstein Building, Brandeis University
Waltham, Massachusetts 02254

Crossroads Press is a subsidiary
of the African Studies Association

Printed in the United States of America

To the Memory of

Gerald W. Hartwig

1935-1980

CONTENTS

PREFACE

A new interest in problems of disease and medicine is broadening the scope of historical research on African societies. Scholars should, and do, attack the complex historical problems of health conditions and medical systems from a variety of perspectives. I take an essentially epidemiological view, focusing on infectious diseases. My objectives are to describe changes in the epidemiological environment confronting Ghanaians between 1900 and 1955; to examine the medical and socio-economic forces which affected the distribution, prevalence, and severity of particular diseases; and to assess the demographic impact of these diseases. Doctors, hospitals, indigenous healing practices, and African responses to western medical technology are considered, but a systematic study of the colonial medical service or substantial discussion of the issues which concern medical anthropologists and sociologists is not attempted in this work. These and many other topics, which certainly deserve full treatment in their own right, are considered here as background material for understanding disease conditions. Obviously, then, this book is an initial exploration of the relationships between European colonial rule and African health, not a complete synthesis.

The study is restricted to Ghana in the first fifty-five years of this century. The temporal limits coincide with the assertion of British rule over the entire Gold Coast (except for mandated Togo), and the eve of independence. Ghana is a significant country, but its medical and demographic history was not representative of other African territories during the colonial period. A relatively rich colony without a settler population or a particularly harsh administration, Ghana fared better than most other areas. I did not choose to study Ghana because it was a "typical" case from which to generalize about health and colonialism; selection of a country on such a criterion would be impossible in any case. Ghana was selected partly because it is large and diverse enough to be a meaningful area of research without being overwhelming. It has a good archival system, a relatively rich historiography, and a tradition of hospitality to visiting scholars. Earlier research for articles on onchocerciasis and influenza suggested that a broader study was feasible and desirable. And, not surprisingly, I found Ghana a fascinating country and a congenial place to work.

This book is primarily addressed to historians, although I hope that it will also be of interest to professionals in health-related fields. I have included brief accounts of the etiology, transmission, and pathology of specific diseases, assuming that these passages, which inevitably over-simplify what are often complex or controversial issues, will assist non-medical readers without offending others. As an historian venturing beyond the normal limits of my discipline, I have relied heavily on a few basic works for medical and biological material. These books, not necessarily prominent in the footnotes, have helped me to understand modern knowledge of diseases of historical and contemporary interest in Ghana. *Manson's Tropical Diseases* has been the most important single reference; other key works, fully cited in the bibliography, include Dubos, *Man Adapting*; Burnet and White, *Natural History of Infectious Disease*; Faust, Russell, and Jung, *Craig and Faust's Clinical Parasitology*; Myrvik, Pearsall, and Weiser, *Fundamentals of Medical Bacteriology and Mycology*; Cruickshank, Standard, and Russell, *Epidemiology and Community Health in Warm Climate Countries*; Mausner and Bahn, *Epidemiology, An Introductory Text*, and *Dorland's Pocket Medical Dictionary*.

The major sources for this work are published documents, archival materials, and the medical literature, both contemporary and modern. The Medical Department's *Annual Reports* provide invaluable data on staff, budgets, hospitals and clinics, diseases treated, preventive measures, and research, and they often contain perceptive discussions of major health problems. They also reflect the weaknesses of the medical service which compiled them. Colonial physicians were few in number, mostly confined to fixed centers, extremely busy, and usually lacked laboratory facilities for diagnosis and research. Personal interests, the state of contemporary medical knowledge, and fears of certain epidemics affected both strategies against particular diseases and knowledge of their prevalence and distribution. Inevitably, the department was ignorant of the scope or even of the existence of some significant health problems, especially in remote areas and among rural people and children. The *Annual Reports* are especially rich and useful from about 1920 to 1938. Prior to that time, poor understanding of many diseases and limited contact between the medical system and the African population restrict their value. The extensive, informative reports of the 1920s and 1930s degenerate into scanty, almost pathetic pamphlets between 1939 and 1952, with a drastic curtailment in the number of diseases tabulated. The Ministry of Health issued substantial reports from 1953 to 1955, but, except for 1967, none since then. Unfortunately, internal files of the medical department are not available, but the archives contain some very helpful correspondence between the department and other branches of the administration. Members of the medical staff generally lacked the time or resources for extensive research, but their publications are often extremely informative, especially for the 1920s and 1950s. In general, although we can not be precise about morbidity and mortality from specific endemic and epidemic diseases, the data base is sensitive enough to detect major trends, at least in outline form.

As I have indicated at several points, there are numerous topics for future research in Ghana as well as in other regions of the continent. Gerald W. Hartwig and I have presented a discussion of medical and health issues confronting historians of Africa in another volume;[1] here it is sufficient to suggest that specific endemic and epidemic diseases, medical services, indigenous healing systems, local responses to scientific medicine, urban and rural public health, demography, living standards, and nutrition should be high on the agenda. I have already considered two specific diseases, urban public health, and veterinary medicine in Ghana in greater detail elsewhere.[2] A weakness of much of the data used in this book is that it is aggregated for the entire country, thus tending to obscure differing health conditions in, for example, the impoverished northeast, prosperous cocoa districts, or major towns. Detailed work on small local areas could be extremely informative, particularly if records of individual hospitals and clinics could be used. Needless to say, research on the medical history of other countries is urgently needed; Marc Dawson's forthcoming study of Kenya and Rita Headrick's work on former French

Equatorial Africa promise to be of great interest,[3] as does Gerald Hartwig's research on Sudan. The material presented here will, I hope, facilitate comparative work.

It is a pleasant task to thank those institutions and individuals who have assisted my research and writing. This study could never have been undertaken without grants LM 02517-01, LM 02517-02, and LM 02984 from the National Library of Medicine, which enabled me to conduct research in Ghana during the summers of 1975 and 1976, and in England and Ghana in the fall of 1977. The purchase of microfilm copies of Gold Coast Departmental Reports, made possible by a grant from the American Philosophical Society, permitted continuing accesss to these bulky and very important sources and enabled me to devote precious time abroad to other materials. The Interlibrary Loan Service of the library of the University of North Carolina at Charlottte, especially Barbara Lisenby, performed heroically. The staffs of the libraries and archives I visited were uniformly helpful; special thanks are owed to Miss Bernice Adu of the National Archives of Ghana, Accra, for her patient and capable assistance in tracking down documents. Roger Thomas of the University of Ghana has been a generous source of professional and personal support. I am also grateful to James W. Brown of the University of South Carolina at Spartanburg and Gerald W. Hartwig of Duke University for general encouragement and for helpful comments on earlier drafts of this work. The Secretaries of U.N.C.C.'s History Department, especially Mary Bottomly, Ann Cormier, and LeAnne May transformed an often difficult manuscript into legible typed pages with speed, competence, and good cheer. A final, obvious debt is to my family, who would very much have liked to have accompanied me to Ghana, but could not.

ABBREVIATIONS

Unless otherwise indicated, all archival citations are to materials in the National Archives of Ghana, Accra, and all public documents were produced in Accra by the Government of the Gold Coast.

A.R.	*Annual Report*
A.R.G.C.	*Annual Report on the Gold Coast*
A.R.N.T.	*Annual Report on the Northern Territories*
Af. Hist. St.	*African Historical Studies*
Ag.	Acting
Am. J. T. M. H.	*American Journal of Tropical Medicine and Hygiene*
Ann. Trop. Med. Parasit.	*Annals of Tropical Medicine and Parasitology*
Brit. Med. J.	*British Medical Journal*
Bull. Ent. Res.	*Bulletin of Entomological Research*
Bull. W.H.O.	*Bulletin of the World Health Organization*
CBR	Crude Birth Rate
CCA	Chief Commissioner, Ashanti
CCNT	Chief Commissioner, Northern Territories
CCP	Commissioner, Central Province
CDR	Crude Death Rate
CEP	Commissioner, Eastern Province
CNP	Commissioner, Northern Province
CS	Colonial Secretary
CSP	Commissioner, Southern Province
Can. J. Af. St.	*Canadian Journal of African Studies*
Comp. St. Soc. Hist.	*Comparative Studies on Society and History*
DC	District Commissioner
DDHS	Deputy Director, Health Services
DDMS	Deputy Director, Medical Services
DMS	Director of Medical Services
DMSS	Director of Medical and Sanitary Services
I.J.A.H.S.	*International Journal of African Historical Studies*
IMR	Infant Mortality Rate
J.	*Journal*
J.A.H.	*Journal of African History*
J.T.M.H.	*Journal of Tropical Medicine and Hygiene*
M.D.A.R.	*Medical Department Annual Report*
MFU	Medical Field Units
MO	Medical Officer

MOH	Medical Officer of Health
MRI	Medical Research Institute
NAG	National Archives of Ghana
PC	Provincial Commissioner
PCNEP	Provincial Commissioner, North-East Province
PMR	Principal Medical Officer
Prov.	Provincial
R.M.H.	*Report of the Ministry of Health*
R.R.B.D.	*Report of the Registrar of Births and Deaths*
SNA	Secretary for Native Affairs
SO	Sanitary Officer
S.P.	Sessional Paper, Legislative Council
Sr.	Senior
TNA	National Archives of Ghana, Tamale Branch
T.R.S.T.M.H.	*Transactions of the Royal Society of Tropical Medicine and Hygiene*
Trans. Hist. Soc. Ghana	*Transactions of the Historical Society of Ghana*
V.D.A.R.	*Veterinary Department Annual Report*
W.A.M.J.	*West African Medical Journal*
W.A.M.S.	West African Medical Staff (Service)
WMO	Woman Medical Officer

Gold Coast Medical Facilities, in 1937

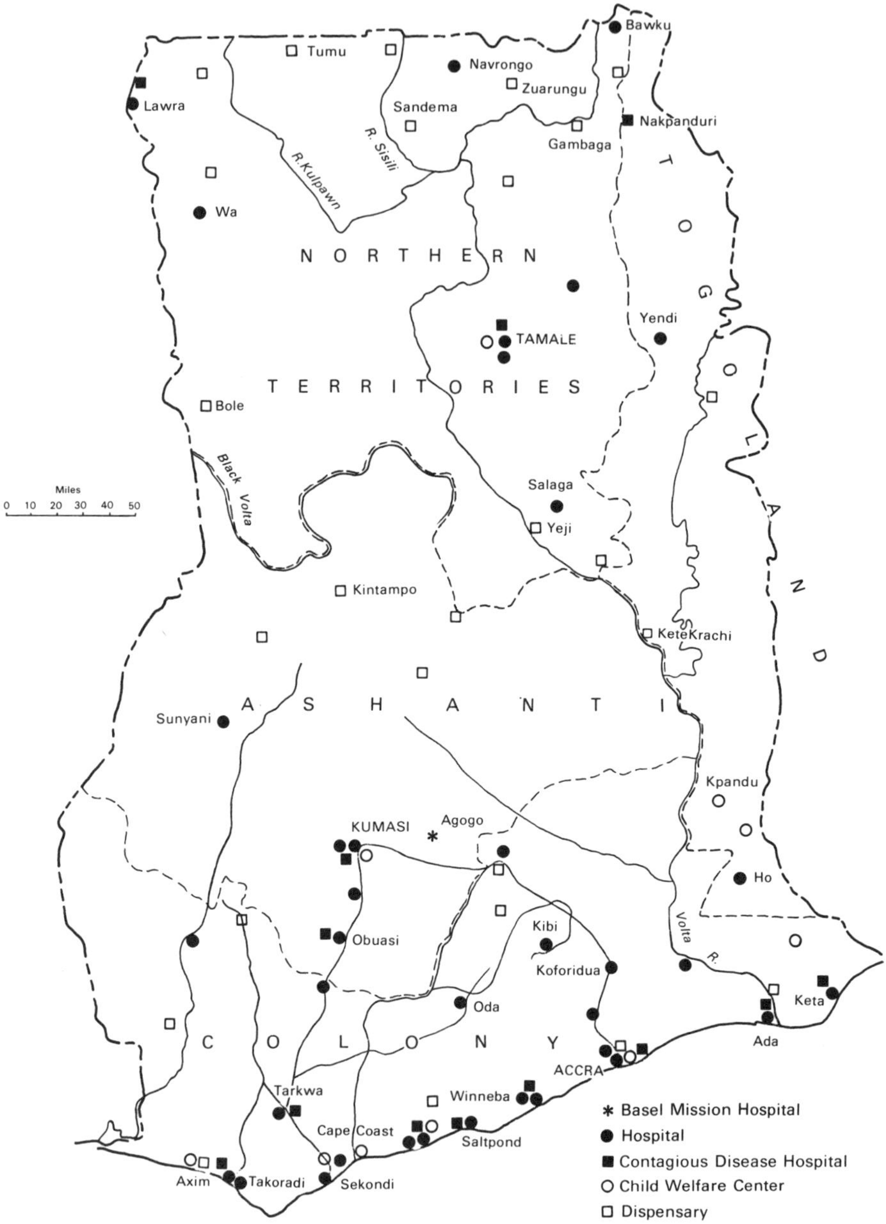

1

THE CHANGING HUMAN ENVIRONMENT: AN OVERVIEW

The purpose of this chapter is to outline some of the major socioeconomic changes in Ghana during the first fifty-five years of the twentieth century and to suggest some of the ways in which these changes influenced the disease environment confronting Ghanaians. Mobility, urbanization, and economic development have all had profound consequences for human health, as have the natural environment and modern preventive and curative medicine. The relationships between these factors and specific diseases will be discussed in detail in later chapters.

The environment exerts a continuing influence on health conditions in all human societies. The physical, biological, and socio-cultural milieu effects the physiological condition and behavior of man, his parasites, and the animal vectors which transmit many infectious diseases. Infectious disease occurs when the host-parasite relationship is disturbed by factors which reduce the host's resistance, increase the infectivity and/or virulence of the pathogen, or facilitate the transmission of pathogenic organisms to new victims. The biological resistance of a human host varies with age, heredity, diet, climate, previous disease exposure, and concommittant infections. Socio-economic factors, including clothing, food, housing, belief patterns, occupation, economic status, and travel can influence both resistance to infection and contacts with potential pathogens. Hence, major socio-economic changes almost always alter a society's disease patterns. In addition, pathogenic agents, the specific parasites which cause particular diseases, may become more or less virulent by mutation and natural selection. Generally, a long host-parasite association results in a less virulent disease. Natural selection tends to produce milder infections, because the evolutionarily successful parasite cannot kill off too many potential hosts or stimulate extremely strong immunological reactions.

Infectious diseases have accompanied human movement throughout history. Explorers, merchants, soldiers, pilgrims, refugees, and migrants have carried plague, measles, smallpox, typhus, tuberculosis, syphilis, malaria, yellow fever, cholera, and a host of other deadly afflictions around the world. Technological, economic, and political changes have encouraged contacts between pathogens, their vectors, and susceptible populations for centuries. Since newly introduced diseases encounter little biological or cultural resistance, they often have catastrophic effects, as in the familiar case of Mexico at the time of the Spanish conquest. Conversely, long-established diseases tend to be less deadly, as natural selection acts to produce milder strains of the pathogen, immunological and/or genetic resistance increases, and as societies learn techniques to treat the disease or to avoid contracting it.[1]

Ghana is a West African nation of about 92,000 square miles and a population (1970) of about 8.6 million. Its southern border lies along the Gulf of Guinea at about 5°N.; its northern frontier is in the savanna zone at about 11°N. A wide variety of diseases can florish in a tropical country like Ghana. In the forests of the central and southern regions, warm, humid conditions enable a large array of micro-organisms and multicellular parasites to survive outside their normal hosts and allow mosquitoes and other vectors to breed freely. The drier conditions which prevail for much of the year in the savannas of the north and in the coastal plains around Accra help produce a somewhat different, but still largely overlapping spectrum of diseases.

Ghana, the former Gold Coast, was administered in three major units during the period of British colonial rule: the Gold Coast Colony on the coast, Ashanti in the center, and further inland, the remote Protectorate of the Northern Territories. The governor at Accra was responsible for the entire country; Chief Commissioners for Ashanti and the Northern Territories, resident in Kumasi and Tamale respectively, reported directly to him. Only the Colony proper was represented in the Legislative Council. The three major regions were divided into provinces and districts. After World War I, the Gold Coast gained a strip of former German Togo as a League of Nations Mandate. The southern portion of Togo was ruled as part of the Colony; the northern section was assigned to the Northern Territories. Except for the purpose of annual reports to the League, Togo was not a distinct administrative entity, but portions of it were added to various Gold Coast districts along the old Anglo-German frontier. In most cases, geographical references will be to the colonial subdivisions, but the current regions, shown on page 00, will sometimes be used.

The area of present-day Ghana has been inhabited by village agriculturalists for at least a millenium, and probably much longer. These settled farmers were in daily contact with scores or hundreds or other people, and could readily exchange diseases which are spread by aerial droplets or by direct contact. They were also vulnerable to diseases transmitted by soil or water contaminated with human wastes. Settlements, clearings for farms, and domesticated animals provided habitats for other diseases and their vectors. Tropical Africa has borne at least as heavy a disease burden as any region of the earth, and we can assume that early Ghanaian societies were afflicted with a host of microbial and multicellular parasites. Ascaris, filaria, hookworms, tapeworms, guinea worm, schistosomiasis, yaws, leprosy, yellow fever, dengue, pneumonia, tropical ulcer, amebic and bacillary dysentery were all common in the early twentieth century and were certainly present in much earlier times as well.[2] Malaria was holoendemic throughout Ghana; in many areas, clearing forest lands for agriculture further facilitated the breeding of *Anopheles gambiae*, the mosquito which is the major vector of falciparum malaria. A genetic defense was evolving in the form of sickle-cell trait, but partial protection was achieved only at the cost of a high level of infant and child mortality from sickle-cell anemia.[3] Trypanosomiasis and onchocerciasis were endemic in some areas, especially in the north. Disease took a heavy toll in life and energy, but most afflictions were chronic and endemic. Severe local epidemics must have broken out from time to time, but major epidemics covering a wide area were probably rare because of sparse, scattered populations, absence of major changes in ways of life, and immunities developed over the centuries. The list of indigenous maladies is long, but many major diseases did not exist in the region until they were introduced from the outside world.

The peoples inhabiting the area that was to become modern Ghana were not isolated from the rest of the world before the present century. Indeed, by c. 1200 A.D. Mande gold traders from the states of the Western Sudan had begun to penetrate the country and to establish small commercial colonies. Relations with Hausa merchants from the northeast began as early as the mid-1400s with the rise of the kola trade. Sea-borne traffic may have linked coastal communities with places as far east as the Niger Delta. These early contacts almost certainly introduced some of the major infections of the Eurasian land mass, such as smallpox, measles, and perhaps gonorrhea and others, in pre-European times. Such introductions doubtlessly caused serious epidemics, but low population densities and limited mobility probably made most outbreaks local and sporadic.

The arrival of Europeans on the coast in the late fifteenth century greatly enhanced the opportunities for new disease introductions. Portuguese and later Dutch, British, Danish, and other Western European groups competed for a growing trade along what they called the Gold Coast, and, as the Hausa and Mande were doing in the market towns of the interior, they established permanently-manned trading centers in close contact with local host populations. The European ships and castles were foci for the diffusion of diseases like smallpox and syphilis, as accounts by contemporary observers make clear.[4] The steady growth of long-distance trade in gold, kola, slaves, salt, and other commodities, together with an increase in local commerce, facilitated the movement of microbes along with people and their goods in the centuries after 1500. Wars and political upheavals, often linked with commercial rivalries, also helped spread diseases. The rise and expansion of the Asante Empire is one obvious example.

Thus, in contrast to much of Eastern and Central Africa, most of modern Ghana had already experienced decades or centuries of exposure to Eurasian diseases by the mid-1800s. Repeated outbreaks of acute diseases like smallpox and measles had produced a large number of people with acquired immunities. Frequently introduced, they gradually became endemic in populous areas, such as the relatively densely inhabited coastal strip, and, as had happened in the past in Europe and Asia, were becoming diseases of childhood in at least some parts of Ghana. Similarly, although data are scarce, it is probable that other diseases which stimulate long-lasting immunities in people who recover from them, such as mumps, chickenpox, diphtheria, and whooping cough, were also becoming so common that they could only find significant numbers of victims in new generations of children. By the twentieth century these diseases had become, like smallpox in sixteenth century Europe, largely restricted to the only important pool of susceptibles, the young, and could only rarely cause destructive epidemics embracing all age groups. This long history of biological adjustment between hosts and parasites, plus perhaps cultural responses like variolization against smallpox, helped insure that Ghana, like the rest of West Africa, would be spared many of the epidemiological disasters which have afflicted more isolated regions of the continent in the last century or so. West Africans had paid most of the disease costs of increased intercommunications in earlier times, and unfortunately for our understanding of the process, largely beyond the knowledge of literate observers.[5]

Exposure to diseases and the development of defenses was, of course, a matter of degree. Despite increasing mobility in the nineteenth century, exemplified by such factors as the growth of commerce, the disorders resulting from the fluctuating fortunes of Asante and other states, the encroachment of the British and their French and German rivals, and the predatory activities of Samori and Babatu, many

Ghanaian peoples remained isolated. Relatively few people engaged in long-distance trade, lived along major trade routes, or took part in military campaigns or migrations. For most, life centered around a village or extended family compound. Travel was limited to short trips to nearby settlements to buy and sell or for social visits. Except for porters, slaves, and an economic and political elite, few people had the opportunity or the inclination to travel widely. Even in 1900, whole regions and ethnic groups remained largely or entirely unaffected by the rising mobility of people, goods, and diseases.

It is clear that the growing intensity of intercommunication in the colonial period must be viewed as part of a continuous process unfolding for centuries, and not as an abrupt break with the past. Change accellerated but remained uneven; some groups maintained relative isolation well into the century. For most Ghanaians, however, mobility and interaction with strangers became more and more frequent. With British rule came new motivations to travel, a breakdown in previous political obstacles to freedom of movement, and tremendous improvements in transportation. Despite the comparatively high degree of mobility and foreign contact in previous centuries, the revolution in transportation had a significant impact on human health.

Colonial officials had long realized that better communications were essential for economic progress in the Gold Coast, and by the 1890s they were beginning to improve the infrastructure. Road building received a major impetus in 1901 when Governor Mathew Nathan, impressed with the potential importance of motor vehicles, outlined an extensive construction program.[6] The highway network grew rapidly. In 1900, except for a third-class road extending from Cape Coast through Kumasi to Kintampo, and a few short stretches near Accra, Saltpond, and other ports, hardly any motorable roads existed. Hundreds of miles of road were built during the next decade. By 1910, the Kumasi-Kintampo road reached Lawra in the remote northwestern corner of the country, and other roads connected administrative centers in the north with the new capital of the Northern Territories, Tamale. Within a few years, Tamale had a good road link with Kumasi. In the south, the expansion of cocoa farming provided a powerful stimulus for opening roads. In many areas, villagers could not wait for the Public Works Department and built their own feeder routes. By the mid-1920s, the basic network was finished with the completions of connections between Accra, Kumasi, and Sunyani. Important new construction, both trunk routes and local feeder networks, continued throughout the thirties and forties, but greater emphasis was placed on improving existing roads for vehicular traffic.

Cars and trucks rapidly took over the new roads. Trypanosomiasis and other problems had caused experiments with animal transport to fail; head-loading and barrel rolling were expensive and inefficient. The first motor car was imported in 1902 for Governor Matthew Nathan, and lorries soon came into use. About 1914 the light Ford truck, which caused less damage to the roads than earlier heavier models, introduced the motor age to Ghana,. By the 1920s, modified lorries, the familiar "mammy wagons," were conveying passengers and their goods inexpensively, if not always in comfort, from town to town and deep into the countryside. Journeys which had taken days could now be made in a few hours. The public response was enormous and a new industry was born.[7]

The early twentieth century was also a period of railroad building, and, as with the roads, the task was undertaken by the colonial government.[8] Just as cocoa production was a major stimulus for road building, so the needs of another export industry, gold mining, strongly influenced the decision to build a railroad and the initial routes chosen. A line was started from the port of Sekondi in 1898. It reached the mining centers of Tarkwa in 1901 and Obuasi in 1902, and was continued to Kumasi for strategic as well as commercial reasons in 1903. Branches from this line reached Prestea in 1911 and Kade in 1927. Meanwhile, another line from Accra was completed to Koforidua in 1915 and to Kumasi in 1923. Governor F. G. Guggisberg had surveys made for an extension of the rail system from Kumasi to the Northern Territories, but the line was never built. Only a few roads linked the north to the more populous and prosperous southern half of the country.

Railroads carried large numbers of passengers as well as freight. Thirty-two thousand passenger journeys of varying distances were made in 1903; the number tripled within three years. There were well over one million journeys in 1919, over two million in 1927, three and a half million in 1936, and more than six million a year by the mid-1940s.[9] In addition to this heavy patronage, thousands of people who could not or would not pay the fares found that the railroad bed made an excellent footpath.[10]

Maritime trade also showed major growth, with hundreds of ships clearing the country's ports annually.[11] In most places, lighters were used to off-load freighters in open and sometimes dangerous surf ports. By 1914, protective breakwaters had been built at Sekondi and Accra, but the situation remained very unsatisfactory until 1928, when a deep-water artificial harbor was completed at Takoradi. Ships' crews and rats were responsible for the introduction of serious epidemics in 1907, 1918, and 1924, and visiting sailors helped distribute venereal diseases and other ailments in the port towns. After 1928, a growing percentage of ships called at Takoradi or Accra; ports like Cape Coast, Saltpond, and Winneba experienced some economic distress, but perhaps also better public health.

Thus, the basic elements of a modern transportation system existed by the 1920s. The expanding road network provided opportunities for flexible, low-cost lorry travel and vastly improved routes for pedestrian and bicycle traffic. The roads, supplemented in the south by the railroad, stimulated mobility. People moved about to trade, seek work, fish, attend school, get medical aid, visit friends and relatives, and to see more of the world. With an increasingly mobile population came enhanced risks of disease transmission. People entered unfamiliar disease environments, where they encountered new pathogens or new strains of familiar ones. They carried pathogens and vectors to potential new hosts and habitats, thus helping to break down previous isolation and make the country into a more and more homogenous epidemiological unit.

Urban growth has been another important phenomenon of the first half of the twentieth century. While Kumasi, Salaga, Elmina, and other substantial towns predate the colonial era, the pace and scale of recent urbanization was unprecedented. Accra grew from about 18,000 in 1901 to over 135,000 in 1948. Kumasi, the second largest city, increased from less than 19,000 in 1921 to almost 60,000 twenty-seven years later. Tamale, which became the capital of the Northern Territories in 1907, had 3,900 people in 1921 and 12,900 a decade later. In 1921, there were fourteen towns with over 5,000 inhabitants; there were twenty-seven in 1931, and thirty-nine by 1948. Only three cities had more than 10,000 people in 1921; eleven exceeded that figure in 1948. The urban population outpaced the growth rate of the country as a whole. In 1931, 295,492 people (9.35 percent) were living in urban areas; the 1948 census counted 528,909 urban dwellers, about 12.9 percent of the total population.[12] The rate of urbanization increased dramatically after World War II.

Cities attracted people from virtually all regions and ethnic groups. Accra and Kumasi in particular had residents from almost all linguistic groups in Ghana as well as sizeable contingents from other parts of West Africa. The towns were magnets for the young and for persons seeking employment as construction workers, stevedores, laborers, and in other unskilled jobs. Many traveled long distances to find very menial work; for example, in the early decades of the twentieth century, most of the latrine cleaners and garbage collectors in the coastal cities were Kru from eastern Liberia. Most government jobs were also located in towns. Thousands of Africans were employed by the colonial administration as clerks, teachers, policemen, soldiers, and in other subordinate positions. Government employees were frequently transferred and hence were, like most other wage earners, highly mobile.

Many urban dwellers were forced by lack of income and a continuing housing shortage to live in squalid, overcrowded conditions. Decrepit, poorly ventilated houses with several persons per room, inadequate latrines, non-existent drainage, and contaminated water were common. Despite sporadic efforts to ameliorate conditions, slums housed a substantial proportion of townspeople and were fertile centers for the propagation of a host of diseases, especially those spread by the respiratory and fecal-oral routes. The concentration of hospitals, water supply systems, and immunization efforts in urban areas helped to reduce the health menace of the cities, but, in Ghana as elsewhere in other historical periods, early urban growth exacted a high toll in human life and well-being.

Zongos and shantytowns were not only hazardous to their inhabitants, but also to the vast majority of the population which resided in rural areas. Diseases maintained in the crowded slums could easily be transmitted to the countryside. Towns were the foci of the transportation system. Rural people came to town for marketing; urbanites went back to home villages for visits. More importantly, most people in towns had no intention of residing there permanently, but returned home sooner or later. The towns and their crowd diseases were linked to their hinterlands by a constant flow of immigrants and returnees. This rural-urban circulation ensured that far more people experienced the rigors of the urban disease environment than the census figures suggest and that temporary urbanites could carry infectious diseases to almost every village in Ghana.

Other economic changes also had serious disease consequences. Most Ghanaians continued to depend on agriculture for their livelihood, but more and more people sought temporary or permanent jobs in the modernizing sectors of the economy. The growth of wage labor had major consequences for health and disease. Since most development was limited to particular places in the southern portion of the country, large-scale labor migration was inevitable.[13] A steady flow of job seekers trudged the roads or jammed into lorries and railroad cars heading to or from the towns, cocoa arms, mines, and lumber camps. Many reached their destinations exhausted, sick, and destitute. Northerners coming to Ashanti in 1930/1931 to find work in the cocoa harvest were described as "dirty, lousy, and of very poor physique. They are veritable museums of helminths of all descriptions, yaws, and guinea-worms."[14] Such migrants, often suffering from chronic infections acquired at home, worn out by long journeys, and sometimes unable to find work, swelled the hospital rolls and death statistics of the towns, despite some ameliorative measures in the form of rest houses and refuges in some cities and along major roads from the north. While labor migration apparently did not cause drastic declines in northern food production like those described in labor reservoir areas in southern Africa, uneven economic growth greatly enhanced the exchange of diseases between town and village and between north and south.[15]

The spectacular growth of the cocoa industry was one of the most crucial changes of the first half of the twentieth century. Cocoa brought prosperity to thousands of farmers in the forest zone and export duties on cocoa became an essential source of revenue for the colonial government. The expansion of cocoa cultivation from its early center in the Akwapim region into other areas of the Colony and Ashanti was caused in part by the migration of farmers seeking new lands for cocoa trees. The westward dispersal of this cash crop encouraged population movements as settlers entered alien districts and as they journeyed to and from their home villages. In addition, the cocoa frontier was closely linked to the construction of new roads, and traders were quick to follow the farmers.[16]

Clearing the forest, planting and maintaining the trees, and harvesting the crop required a steady flow of agricultural laborers. The farmer's family and the local population could not meet the need, so the cocoa regions depended on migrant workers. Every year tens of thousands of men came from the impoverished Northern Territories and from Upper Volta and other French colonies, seeking cash for taxes, consumer goods, and even food.

Migrants were also attracted to other zones of economic activity, especially in southwestern Ghana. Some found employment in the lumber industry, but the mines provided more jobs. Manganese, diamonds, and bauxite were produced at various times during the colonial era, but gold was by far the most important mineral. The mining work force, largely composed of northerners and other migrants seeking temporary jobs, ranged from 12,600 in 1905 to some 16,000 in 1933; it then grew to over 30,000 in the next few years and remained at or above that level during the 1940s and early 1950s.[17]

Miners were one of the very few groups exposed to industrial health hazards. Deaths from cave-ins, explosions, fires, falls, and other mishaps averaged 19 a year in the 1920s, 46 a year in the 1930s, and 34 a year in the 1940s, with the highest total for a single year being 77 fatalities in 1934.[18] Roughly one-third worked underground, where poor sanitation exposed them to hookworm infection, and quartz dust caused lung damage which sometimes resulted in silicosis or respiratory tuberculosis. Living conditions also posed health problems. Miners were not confined to compounds, but had to make their own arrangements for food and lodging. Many companies did provide housing and some of it was quite good, but many workers had to (or preferred to) rent rooms or houses in nearby villages. Local landlords made good profits, but often allowed slum conditions to develop.[19] Low wages and high food prices led to poor nutrition. Little food was grown in the immediate vicinity of most mines and transportation problems contributed to high prices, especially for meat. Equally important was price-fixing by a "close and powerful ring" of market women.[20] Some specific problems of miners will be discussed in later chapters.

Census figures provide a crude but useful measure of overall mobility. Substantial numbers of aliens entered the country. The number of persons of European descent rose from 716 in 1901 to 1,883 in 1921, 2,385 in 1931, and 5,026 in 1948. Syrians increased from 116 in 1921 to 570 in 1931 and 1,370 in 1946.[21] Far more significant in terms of numbers was the influx of Africans, attracted from other territories by Ghana's prosperity and relatively mild form of colonial rule.[22] In the 1931 census, when foreign-born Africans were enumerated for the first time, they constituted 6.3 percent of the population (199,438). The absolute number was about the same in 1948, when aliens comprised 4.4 percent of the total; in 1960, almost 10 percent of the population was foreign-born.[23] The extent of immigration and of internal migration is suggested by table 1 (page 109), which is based on 1931 census data. These figures greatly underestimate actual mobility because the geographical units are so large that moves of a hundred miles or more might still be intra-regional and hence not counted. In the 1960 census, roughly one Ghanaian in eight was enumerated in a region other than his region of birth.[24]

Since there was little industrialization during the colonial period, Ghanaians were spared some of the health hazards associated with the early industrial revolution in Europe and America. There were no factories to expose men, women, and children to dangerous machinery, poisonous substances, or twelve-hour days in dingy buildings. The air and water were not fouled by coal dust or industrial pollutants. In contrast to workers in colder climates, Ghanaians were able to spend much of their working and leisure time outdoors in fresh air and sunshine. On the other hand, lack of industrialization retarded economic growth, precluding a rapid rise in living standards which would have produced better health conditions. Delayed industrial development has, however, meant threats posed to human health by new methods of production are better known and more likely to be controlled by voluntary or state action.

Except for deforestation, there was relatively little environmental change in the pre-1955 period which effected human health. Destruction of forests has been going on for centuries and, indeed, much of the open country in the north and along the eastern coast was once wooded. Commercial lumbering began in the 1880s and has been an important industry ever since. The needs of households and mines for timber and fuel have encouraged further cutting. Roads, railroads, and cocoa farms have been carved out of the forest and population growth has necessitated the clearing of large tracts for food production.[25] Deforestation allows sunlight to reach pools of water, creating favorable breeding conditions for *Anopheles gambiae*, the major vector of falciparium malaria.

Water provides essential habitats for many species of pathogenic microbes, helminths, and arthropod and mollusc vectors of serious diseases. As Hughes and Hunter have pointed out in an important review, water development projects such as dams, fish farms, and irrigation schemes always have the potential to alter local disease environments.[26] However, little work of this nature was done prior to 1955, except for a few small dams. More recently, the completion of the Akosombo Dam and the filling of Lake Volta have had important ecological effects.

Economic changes did have several positive implications for human health. As will be described in the next chapter, rising government revenues allowed slow but significant progress in the provision of therapeutic and preventive medicine. The colony's relative prosperity, at least in comparison with other territories in Africa, also permitted a steady expansion of western education, although schools and teachers were provided much too slowly to please many Ghanaians. There were pronounced regional imbalances in education, as with health care and other services, with the coast and urban areas being highly favored. The north, as usual, lagged far behind.[27] However, despite serious problems with the number, quality, and distribution of schools, Ghana probably had as good an educational system as existed in colonial Africa.[28] Although most Ghanaians remained unschooled even in the last years of British rule, education exposed hundreds of thousands of people, however briefly and incompletely, to Western ideas. Health education was part of the curriculum[29] and literates were able to read Medical Department posters and other publications. More important perhaps was the role of eductation in changing old beliefs and making people more receptive to western medical ideas.

The single most important consequence of socio-economic change for public health in twentieth century Ghana was a gradual improvement in the standard of living. Small farmers, migrant laborers, cocoa growers, traders, clerks, and the small but growing numbers of skilled workers and professionals had cash incomes. Slowly and unevenly, more and more people acquired money to spend on such goods as clothing, food, and housing. As will be discussed in a later chapter, rising living standards helped improve health conditions. Better clothes kept people warmer; additional garments meant that a person was more likely to be able to wear something clean and dry. Metal roofs that replaced thatch and concrete blocks that substituted for mud and wattle provided warmer and drier homes with reduced habitats for domestic insect and rodent pests. Higher incomes could be used to buy more meat, fish, fruits, vegetables, and other nutritious foods. On the other hand, consumers could also choose white bread, sugar, tea, tinned milk for infants, and other foodstuffs of dubious value.

Thus, it is clear that major changes took place in the socio-economic environment in which man and pathogen interacted during the first half of the twentieth century. Tens of thousands of villagers moved to the crowded towns; many farmers became, at least from time to time, wage earners. Economic stratification certainly existed prior to 1900, but increased as the economy began to change. Some lived in wretched poverty, many enjoyed modest increases in income, and a very few achiveved substantial prosperity. Rising incomes were used, in part, for better clothing, food, and housing. Educational growth facilitated sanitary and health reforms. Finally, increasing intercommunication was breaking down local isolation and making the country into a single epidemiological unit; a unit with growing ties to wider African and world disease pools. Some of these changes encouraged the propagation of disease, while others helped to raise health standards. The next chapter deals with the development of modern medical services and subsequent chapters will describe the behavior of particular diseases and the significance of changing living conditions. Two key factors, however, were and are unchanged. Ghana is a tropical country and, despite some economic progress, it is still a very poor country. These facts ensure that, despite the ebb and flow of individual diseases and some real gains in preventive and curative medicine, the burden of disease will remain heavy.

2

THE DEVELOPMENT AND RECEPTION OF MODERN MEDICAL SERVICES

Curative and preventive medicine introduced by the British colonial administration has had a significant impact on Ghanaian health during the twentieth century, especially since the early 1920s. By that time, improvements in the medical department, advances in scientific knowledge and awareness of local health conditions, a growing sense of responsibility toward the African population, and increasing public acceptance of an alien medical system made slow but real progress possible. The purpose of this chapter is to describe the evolution of medical services in the former Gold Coast and African responses to them. Measures against major diseases and the demographic consequences of medical work will be discussed in later sections.

The rudiments of a colonial medical service date back well into the nineteenth century and a Gold Coast Medical Department was created in the 1880s. It was administered by a physician whose title was Principal Medical Officer (P.M.O.) until 1923. Director of Medical and Sanitary Services (D.M.S.S.) from 1923 until 1934, and later, Director of Medical Services (D.M.S.). Like other departmental heads, he reported to the Governor through the Colonial Secretary. After the creation of the Sanitary (Health) Branch in 1909 and the Medical Research Institute (Laboratory) Branch in 1919, a deputy presided over each of these organizations while a third was in charge of the Medical Branch. As the titles suggest, the Health Branch was responsible for sanitation, vaccinations, and other preventive measures; the Laboratory Branch conducted scientific investigations as well as routine clinical and pathological tests and post-mortem examinations; while the Medical Branch encompassed all hospitals and clinics. The Medical Department also gathered meterological data and was responsible for animal health until the creation of a separate Veterinary Department in 1920. The Medical Department became the Ministry of Health in 1953 with a Ghanaian, Imoru Egala, as Minister.[1]

Most government physicians were members of the West African Medical Staff, an organization established in 1902 to provide a common pay and promotion roll for Britain's West African colonies. The W.A.M.S. was an extremely conservative body whose members, vigorously supported by the British Medical Association, were articulate and effective defenders of their own salaries, status, and perquisites.[2] Their high pay irked other officials and drained colonial treasuries, but the W.A.M.S. was usually able to get its way because doctors were so essential and so difficult to recruit.[3] Indeed, service in West Africa had little attraction for the vast majority of graduates of Britain's medical schools, who were in rising demand at home as well as in more congenial parts of the Empire. Consequently, there frequently were high vacancy rates in the Gold Coast Medical Department, despite liberal attitudes toward private practice as an additional source of income.[4] Furthermore, as will be described later, officials bowed to the demands of white doctors that potential African competitors be excluded from the medical service, especially prior to 1920. As a European unofficial member of the Legislative Council complained in 1914, "Medical Officers are not renowned for being broad-minded," their high salaries and political clout being due to the fact that the "medical service of West Africa is a sort of trade union."[5]

The department was chronically understaffed. Recruitment was always difficult, and there were generally a number of authorized positions which could not be filled for lack of suitable candidates. Staff shortages were especially acute during the wars and in the early 1930s, when the economic crisis forced the government to cut back the number of medical officers. In the first two decades, Medical Officers (M.O.) often had to fill vacancies in the political service.[6] Equally serious was a shortage of specialists. The Gold Coast was the first West African colony to appoint a specialist medical officer, Dr. J. W. S. Macfie, a very able pathologist, in 1914.[7] Surgeons, ophthalmologists, pathologists, radiologists, and other specialists were retained, but leaves, resignations, and recruitment problems[8] reduced their availability. Table 2 (page 000) shows the total staff performing medical duties, including M.O.s, Medical Officers of Health (M.O.H.), Senior M.O.s, and specialists, but excluding full-time administrators. The figures are somewhat higher than the number of doctors actually in the field because leaves, resignations, and new appointments meant that some on the list served only for part of a year.

The relative stability of the size of the medical staff between the late 1920s and the late 1940s, except for a decline during the depression, is striking. Demographic growth and increasing African acceptance of colonial medicine created high population/physician and patient/physician ratios. Certainly, as the data in table 1 indicate, a conscientious M.O. did much more work in 1930 than in 1910, and had a huge patient load in 1940 or 1950. As early as 1926, Governor Guggisberg complained that "we have become compelled by lack of staff to shut our eyes deliberately in the case of several diseases."[9] By 1930/1931 case loads per physician far exceeded the maximum of 2,500 permitted general practitioners in Britain under National Health Insurance.[10] Several stations had to be closed during the depression for lack of staff.[11] Similar cutbacks were made during World War II and the years immediately after,[12] partly because doctors were transferred to military duty and partly because low pay encouraged early retirements and hampered recruitment.[13]

The competence of colonial physicians and their willingness and ability to provide sympathetic treatment for African patients varied widely. The primary missions of the medical services during the early years of colonial rule were to protect the health of European officials, other Europeans, and African soldiers and civil servants.[14] Little attention was given to the general population, partly because of lack of resources and public response, but also because of the priorities of most physicians. However, a sense of responsibility for African welfare was not entirely lacking. As early as 1908 a committee charged with re-organizing the W.A.M.S. stated that:

> The idea that the officers of the West African Medical Service are appointed solely to look after Government officers should be discouraged. It is a part of the duty of a medical officer to increase the progress of sanitation amongst natives dwelling

> in his district, and he should be encouraged to devote himself to medical work amongst the natives and to research.[15]

Governor Hugh Clifford was appalled by the conservatism, racism, and complacency of much of his medical staff and was anxious "to afford to the native population of their Colony a larger share in the benefits of European medical science than they enjoy at the present time," but could do little because of wartime pressures.[16] By the end of World War I, European mortality rates had been greatly reduced[17] and there was a growing awareness of the "trusteeship" role of colonial governments.[18] During the 1920s the medical department, encouraged by Governor F. G. Guggisberg, developed a much broader perception of its duties and, as the clinical returns in table 6 (page 115) show, began to treat larger numbers of Africans.

Many doctors were extremely capable, dedicated, and popular, and a few were able to conduct useful research. A number of outstanding men and women will be mentioned elsewhere in various contexts. Of course, there were many who simply did their jobs without special achievement or failure, and a few really unsuitable persons. Some of the latter were weeded out after one or two tours. Physicians were encouraged to take special courses at government expense while on leave, and many doctors used this opportunity to brush up their skills or develop new areas of competence. The government also tried to ensure that physicians, even in isolated posts, had proper equipment and access to medical literature. Despite some early grumbling about the "considerable expense" of microscopes,[19] they were soon made available to all. A major abstracting journal, the *Tropical Diseases Bulletin*, was supplied from 1912,[20] and later the *Bulletin of Hygiene* was also sent to all M.O.s.[21] A library at the Medical Research Institute in Accra sent data and articles to doctors around the country. In 1923/1924, it held 418 volumes and subscribed to thirty-two journals; by 1957 it received 108 journals.[22]

Africans had been employed in the colony's medical service in the nineteenth century; indeed, from 1892 to 1897 the department was headed by a Sierra Leonean, Dr. J. F. Easmon. However, by the end of the century rising racism and a desire by Europeans to monopolize higher posts in the empire blocked the careers of educated Africans in all branches of the colonial service. An earlier, albeit sometimes grudging, willingness to appoint qualified Africans to important positions in West Africa gave way to an increasingly rigid color bar. Dr. Easmon was removed in 1897 and an able Gold Coast physician, Dr. B. W. Quartey-Papafio, was passed over in favor of a white candidate. In 1902 applications for the newly-created W.A.M.S. were formally restricted to persons of European parentage, and the medical service became, despite strong protests from Africans and the objections of Governors John Rodger and Hugh Clifford, a white preserve. Proposals for changing the policy or allowing exceptions were met with violent opposition from the W.A.M.S.[23]

Systematic racial discrimination did not enhance the Medical Department's public image. Educated Africans repeatedly criticized racial barriers in the press, complaining of the basic unfairness of the policy, its assumption of African ineptitude, and the great need for more doctors, regardless of color.[24] Protesting the barring of Dr. Easmon's son from a vacant post, the *Gold Coast Leader* denounced most of the white physicians for being more interested in making money in private practice than serving the public, and for not having the inclination or ability to conduct research. Could African doctors possibly be worse?[25] Similar complaints were made by traditional leaders, with equal lack of results.[26]

In 1919 Dr. C. E. Reindorf, an African who had been associated with the Basel Mission, was appointed a part-time M.O. for Akwapim. Reindorf left for England shortly thereafter and, at his own initiative and expense, took a special course on venereal diseases. He was given a full-time but "temporary" appointment as head of the newly-opened venereal diseases clinic in Accra upon his return in 1920.[27] Governor Guggisberg was, like Clifford, anxious to increase the number of doctors and to employ indigenous physicians. He made several other African appointments, but at the special rank of "African Medical Officer," on a separate list and with a lower salary scale. While genuinely concerned with public health and the advancement of Africans in government service, Guggisberg refused to appoint African doctors to a common list with Europeans. In a speech in Britain he argued that half of the Africans with M.D. degrees were incompetent,[28] which drew a long and angry rejoinder from a prominent African physician in private practice, Dr. F. V. Nanka-Bruce.[29] The Governor held his ground and explained his policies in a confidential letter to the Colonial Office. He sympathized with African aspirations but argued, with characteristic paternalism, that "character-training in the Gold Coast, as elsewhere in West Africa, is generally deficient" and that education in Europe was likely to have "serious effects" on character. Furthermore, he claimed that training was not as rigorous because of "a certain amount of laxity in the grant of medical degrees in Europe to Africans," and erroneously stated that African medical students in Europe did not get clinical training. Africans in the Medical Service, he argued, had "on the whole not been too successful, although there are conspicuous examples to the contrary." For all these reasons, Guggisberg insisted that Africans be placed in a special rank and be required to take a year of clinical training in the Gold Coast.[30] Needless to say, Guggisberg's policy was roundly criticized[31] and he was able to find very few among the handful of Gold Coast physicians who would accept appointment under terms inferior to those offered to Europeans. However, the Governor did resist some acts of racism, as in his vigorous defense of Dr. Tagoe, whose posting to a mining area was viciously assailed by local whites.[32] Guggisberg secured the admission of Africans into the medical service but, because of his own paternalism as well as lingering opposition within the medical establishment, only in inferior positions.

The number of African Medical Officers grew very slowly. There were only two in 1922, three in 1927, six in 1929, three or four in the depression years, and ten in 1938. Reindorf, the pioneer, was released on grounds of economy, in 1930, and, as his appointment was still "temporary" after a decade of service, he did not receive a pension.[33] In 1939 the D.M.S. agreed to fill two European vacancies with Africans. This would reduce the number of Europeans to thirty-eight and raise the Africans to twelve, but the "ratio" would not be too high.[34] African and European doctors were placed on a common list in 1946.

One of Governor Guggisberg's innovations was the hiring of female physicians, variously titled Woman Medical Officer (W.M.O.) or Lady Medical Officer (L.M.O.). Like their African counterparts, females had an inferior status and were not members of the W.A.M.S. Concern over infant and maternal health had been evident since the early years of Clifford's administration and Guggisberg was eager to engage women doctors to staff infant welfare centers and his new children's hospital and maternity hospital. Dr. Mary Magill was working with Accra school children in 1920; four women were employed by 1926, and their numbers reached a high of eleven in 1930. Most were engaged in some aspect of child or maternal health, but Dr. Helen Hendrie served as M.O. at Yendi and did good work with lepers, while Dr.

Helen Russell was a pathologist. An African woman, Dr. A. Y. Savage, was appointed in 1935, with leave conditions equal to those of Europeans.[35]

Women, like Africans, resented their exclusion from the full privileges of membership in the W.A.M.S. M.O.s had rights to private practice and M.O.H.s had an extra stipend of £150 in lieu of private practice, but W.M.O.s had neither. In 1930, all but one signed a petition protesting this inequity.[36] The D.M.S.S. was initially unmoved by this "somewhat ill-considered and premature movement made by our local feminists,"[37] but as various Governors and Secretaries of State had already been debating for three years over whether to pay women the stipend or allow them private practice,[38] he was pleased when the £150 stipend was approved.[39] However, money could not be found during the depression, and in 1932 Dr. Cecily D. Williams submitted a petition protesting the continuing injustice and reminding her superiors that "medical training for a woman costs as much as for a man."[40] The right to private practice was promptly granted, to be replaced in 1935 by the stipend.[41]

The colonial physician was often a puzzling figure for Africans. He was usually a white male, a stranger who had to use an interpreter. He often asked impolite questions; demanded, for unknown reasons, samples of blood, urine, and feces; and sometimes cut open the bodies of the dead. On the other hand, he frequently had great power over sickness and injury. Some were so disagreeable that people avoided them,[42] but others, such as C. V. Le Fanu, were highly popular. Le Fanu learned Twi and there were petitions for his return when he was transferred from Cape Coast. He respected Africans, and a number of children were named after him.[43] The retirement party for Dr. A. N. Dyce-Sharpe attracted six hundred African and European guests in Cape Coast. Dyce-Sharpe was honored for devoted services over many years, for helping to secure a new hospital for the city, and for founding the Cape Coast Historical Society.[44] Dr. P. S. Selwyn-Clarke, an able and energetic M.O.H., was criticized early in his career as "the terror of ignorant people in his mosquito raids," and his vigorous public health work made him so unpopular that there was strong opposition to naming a new market he designed in Accra "Selwyn Market" after him.[45] Several years later, when he was transferred to Malaya, the same paper acknowledged that:

> The improved health conditions of Accra and Kumasi are testimonies to the excellent work he has done. At one time we did not see eye to eye with Dr. Selwyn-Clarke but eventually what was considered by an ultraconservative people to be a ruthless and inconsiderate overthrow of their accepted order of things was nothing but an over-zealousness on his part for the work for which he came out. If anybody earned his pay in the Government service, Dr. Selwyn-Clarke did. His transfer is a great loss to this colony which we genuinely regret.[47]

Many other examples could be given, for in Navrongo and elsewhere, an empathetic physician like Stanley Batchelor could always attract patients.[47]

Most physicians in colonial Ghana were employed by the government, but some were engaged by mining companies or missions, or were in private practice. Several mining firms retained doctors to treat their employees; there were eight mine doctors in 1936.[48] In contrast to the extensive medical work of missionaries in Nigeria, mission health work in Ghana was almost entirely limited to a few dispensaries and infant clinics. The government provided subsidies for drugs and supplies, but aid for medical activities was miniscule compared to the sums budgeted to assist mission schools. The Basel Mission employed a few doctors in the Aburi and Akwapim areas prior to World War I, and from 1931 to 1940, and again after 1945, operated a highly-regarded hospital at Agogo in Ashanti.[49] An English medical missionary was stationed at Mampong, Ashanti, in the 1930s.[50] In 1919, there were three African doctors in private practice. Their ranks grew slowly, partly because discrimination in the medical service discouraged young men from entering the profession. There were twenty-five by 1934; eight in Accra, twelve elsewhere in the Colony, five in Ashanti, and none in the Northern Territories.[51] Eighty-nine doctors were self-employed or retained by firms in 1953.[52] These physicians congregated in a few urban centers and, except for some charity work, served the small minority of the population who could afford their fees.[53]

There were, and still are, far too few doctors to give primary care to all potential patients. The authorities realized that it would be impossible to recruit, or pay for, enough white doctors to provide mass health care. Extensive employment of African nurses, dispensers, midwives, vaccinators, and other auxilliary personnel was essential, and indeed, African subordinate staff had been used since the nineteenth century. Governor Clifford, drawing on his experience in Ceylon, proposed a dispensary scheme in 1917. Paramedical personnel would be trained to run these centers under the general supervision of an M.O. Dr. T. E. Rice, the relatively liberal P.M.O., endorsed the scheme, but raised the argument which would continue to plague attempts to expand health care; African staff required close supervision from European doctors if standards were to be maintained.[54] Later plans, including those of Governor Guggisberg, repeatedly ran into the same objections. The training of African health workers lagged far behind French West Africa.[55]

When Clifford left Ghana in 1919, there were twenty-three dispensers and twenty-eight nurses in training at major hospitals. Guggisberg thought the program was below standard and terminated it,[56] although he supported training dispensers as well as doctors at his proposed medical school.[57] The heads of the Medical Departments in the four British West African colonies had, by the early 1920s, fully accepted responsibility for all residents of their territories, not just the whites, and they acknowledged the necessity of engaging Africans at all levels if the region's crucial health needs were to be met. They supported Guggisberg's plan for a combined school for doctors and medical auxilliaries,[58] but a special committee chaired by Dr. W. J. D. Inness, D.M.S.S. for the Gold Coast, while endorsing the proposal for an inter-colonial medical school in Accra, recommended that each colony develop its own separate school for assistants.[59] The Colonial Office considered a medical school premature and squashed the idea, substituting a scholarship program which enabled a small number of West Africans to study medicine in the United Kingdom.[60] Dr. Innes, who regarded trained medical assistants as more vital to progress in public health than more hospitals or M.O.s, then proposed a scheme for a rigorous four-year school for dispensers. This was approved by Governor A. R. Slater and implemented in 1931.[61]

The training program for dispensers survived the collapse of the proposed medical school, but systematic training of paramedical staff to serve the rural areas was not begun until the fourth decade of the twentieth century. The program was slowed by the depression,[62] but by 1941, thirty-three dispensers were running rural stations with only sporadic supervision from touring M.O.s. The number of trainees rose after 1945, especially with the opening of a school for Native Authority health staff at Kintampo. Problems of staff quality and absence of regular inspection were evident by the early 1950s.[63]

The training of Africans as nurses and midwives also developed very slowly. A handful of nurses were trained in hospitals, especially Korle Bu after 1927, in a three-year apprentice system. A full course of study for the degree of Registered Nurse was not available in the Gold Coast until 1944, when a Nurses Training College was opened in Kumasi. The College was moved to its present location at Korle Bu in 1948, the same year that it graduated its first four R.N.s. Although the majority of practicing nurses were African men, only female students were admitted to the College. Over 350 nurses with various qualifications were at work by 1953, but the demand far exceeded the supply.[64] A midwifery school was opened in 1928 at the new Maternity Hospital at Korle Bu. An ordinance to regulate midwives was promulgated in 1931. By 1937, there were twenty-six trained and licensed midwives; nine in government service and seventeen in private practice. A subsidy of £3 per month was paid to private practitioners who worked in small towns or in rural areas with inadequate maternity services.[65] There were almost four hundred trained midwives practicing by 1953.[66]

The basic health care unit in colonial Ghana was the hospital, with one or more resident M.O.s. People went to out-patient clinics for most complaints; those who had serious conditions and would agree to hospitalization were admitted to the wards. Table 5 (page 114) shows the numbers of hospitals and beds for various years. The basic hospital network was established by the late 1920s, when Guggisberg completed Clifford's dream of the Gold Coast Hospital at Korle Bu, Accra. Later, larger buildings permitted a gradual increase in the number of beds and modest improvements in the population per hospital bed ratio. The apparent decline in the number of hospitals after 1944 is partly due to the merger of previously separate institutions for Europeans and Africans. In addition to government hospitals, several mining companies operated small hospitals for their employees. The only mission hospital was the excellent institution run by the Basel Mission at Agogo, Ashanti.[67]

Dispensaries were usually located in rural areas and were supervised by African dispensers who were periodically visited by a medical officer. They were geared toward out-patient care; bed space was limited and serious cases were referred to hospitals. There were only four dispensaries in 1927/1928, all in the Colony. The total rose to 28 in 1939, 38 in 1945, and increased dramatically to 124 in 1952. Most were run by the Medical Department or, after 1945, Native Authority governments, but a few were operated by missions, such as the White Fathers in the far north.

Another approach to rural health care was the Health Centre plan. This was formally proposed by Dr. J. Balfour Kirk in 1943, who had been interested in the concept since 1927. Kirk wanted to establish a network of several health centres in small communities around every major hospital. Each centre was to have a sanitary inspector, nurse, dispenser, and, if possible, a midwife. Centres would provide care for local people and for persons referred to them from surrounding village dispensaries. In turn, the health centres would act as screening bodies, treating common or minor conditions and sending patients requiring complex treatment to the district hospital. The centres would also attempt to educate the public on the causes and prevention of common diseases, with the sanitary inspector and other personnel lecturing, talking with patients, and touring nearby villages to speak or, if necessary, issue summonses. An M.O.H. from the district hospital would visit centres weekly.[68] In regions of the north with non-nucleated settlement patterns, community health nurses scattered in a hospital's zone of attendance could take the place of complete centres.[69]

Unfortunately, little was done to implement the scheme. Successive Directors supported the concept, but lack of staff and funds, combined with heavy expenditures on large hospitals, retarded progress. Only two were functioning in early 1952. A special commission recommended a network of forty-three centres be established by 1957,[70] but the goal was never reached.

Hospitals, as shown on map 1 (page xii), were located in large towns. An urban bias was perhaps natural, but the problem was compounded by two factors; the failure to develop an adequate system of rural dispensaries or health centers, and gross regional maldistribution of hospitals. For example, in 1927/1928, twenty-eight out of the thirty-nine hospitals were in the Colony, which had about 54 percent of the total population; six were in Ashanti (18 percent), and five, with a total of thirty-eight beds, were in the Northern Territories (28 percent of the Gold Coast population). In 1953, over 70 percent of hospital beds were in the Colony, with about 15 percent in each of the two other regions. Estimates of population/bed ratios in 1954 ranged from 478:1 in the Accra Region to 35,000:1 in Trans-Volta Togoland.[71] The uneven distribution of hospitals, and of doctors, since virtually all colonial physicians were assigned to a hospital, was a serious problem throughout the colonial era and remained so two decades after independence. The North, Brong-Ahafo, and indeed most areas outside of the Accra-Kumasi-Takoradi triangle, have been neglected.[72] Today, as in the past, physicians detest bush stations and the remote north. One D.M.S.S. ordered his staff "to eradicate from their minds" the notion that such postings were inferior.[73] However, when B. B. Waddy requested re-assignment to the north in 1946, he was the first doctor to volunteer for a second tour there.[74]

Even in the most favored areas, few Ghanaians had ready access to a hospital or dispensary unless they lived in a large town or along a road with lorry service. People were willing to travel longer or shorter distances depending on their perceptions of how sick they were and how effective therapy was likely to be, but attendances varied inversely with distances, especially if patients had to walk more than a few miles.[75] Except for major hospitals with wide drawing powers like those in Accra and Kumasi, most medical facilities drew the bulk of their patients from within a radius of several miles or so. A glance at the map shows that only a small portion of Ghana and its people were within five or even ten miles of a hospital or clinic. The post-war expansion of medical services helped, but as late as 1973 it was estimated that the number and distribution of hospitals and clinics was such that "they cannot offer any kind of service to more than, at most, 20 percent of the population."[76]

Educated Africans consistently demanded that the colonial government improve hospitals and increase their number.[77] They protested cuts both during the depression and World War II,[78] when acute staff shortages necessitated the closing of several hospitals, or their downgrading to dispensaries.[79] The quality of care was also sometimes criticized, as at the African hospital in Sekondi in 1923, which was crowded, noisy, exposed patients to contagious diseases, and deprived them of familiar foods.[80] The elite did not generally oppose the existence of separate European hospitals, but instead sought admission to these superior institutions, where per-patient expenditure averaged almost ten times greater than for "native" hospitals.[81] In Sekondi and elsewhere, "better class Africans" resented being relegated to the Native Hospital, which they considered "a place unsuitable for people of our type."[82]

Officials as well as the public were often critical of hospital facilities and management. In Accra, doctors complained bitterly about "primitive and disgusting" conditions in the old African hospital prior to the completion of the Gold Coast Hospital at Korle Bu. Indeed, African complaints about over-crowded and antiquated hospitals were often justified.[83]

Some of the worst conditions were in the north, where hospitals were usually small swish structures with corrugated iron roofs until well into the 1930s. The Salaga hospital was reportedly adequate in 1927, except that there were bats in the roof of the operating theater and no latrines for patients. There were no beds at the Zuarungu hospital.[84] The "ramshackle building" there was replaced by 1932, and new structures erected at Lawra, Wa, and Navrongo, after Governor Slater's complaint that the lack of adequate hospitals in the north was "nothing short of a scandal."[85] Still, Governor Arnold Hodson was horrified by the conditions he found in northern hospitals during his 1937 tour, finding several dirty and describing at least one M.O. as "indolent and lack[ing] all interest in his work and the people." The D.M.S. queried his staff and sent a nursing supervisor, M. G. Le Bas, to inspect Bawku and Navrongo.[86] The M.O.s defended their establishments as being not too bad, considering the staff shortage, the poor quality of African subordinates, and the habits of the patients. "It should be realized," wrote Dr. J. D. Reid of Navrongo, "that the natives of this region are naturally dirty and it is with the greatest difficulty that one can have them washed." If rules were rigidly enforced, the patients ran away.[87] At Lawra, it was impossible to keep the wards clean because the patients chewed tobacco and spat all over the floor and walls. The people oiled their bodies and thus ruined sheets, so no sheets were issued.[88] The Governor "was not satisfied" by such explanations, but dropped the matter.[89]

Dr. J. Balfour Kirk, an energetic but acerbic D.M.S. in the early 1940s, was highly critical of hospitals at Sekondi, Koforidua, Nsawam,[90] and other towns. He thought that the distribution of hospitals was not bad in the Colony, but that accessibility was very poor in Ashanti and the north. The total number of beds was, he wrote, "quite inadequate even when judged by standards which are admittedly low."[91] Smaller hospitals continued to require a patient's family or friends to supply his meals, despite obvious nutritional and sanitary problems.[92] Crowding remained common during and after the war, as demand for services rose much more rapidly than improvements could be made.[93] There was a burst of hospital construction in the post-war years, but heavy costs and shortages of staff, especially nurses, limited the building of new hospitals and the expansion of existing ones. Fortunately, some of the scarce funds available for health were allocated to dispensaries and staff development, rather than expensive large hospitals.[94]

The data in table 6 (page 115) show the growing popularity of western medical care. Case loads rose steadily and, as table 7 (page 117) demonstrates, they rose faster than the rate of population increase. Several trends deserve comment. One is the out-patient to in-patient ratio; only 6 to 10 percent of all patients were hospitalized. People avoided hospitalization when they could, and in any case, the hospitals were often too crowded to accommodate any but the most serious cases. Males consistently outnumbered females, both for persons hospitalized and for those treated in out-patient clinics, even though women had the extra health hazards associated with pregnancy and childbirth. A small part of the difference is due to the fact that the colonial government provided free medical care for several almost exclusively male groups; its police, soldiers, clerks, and prisoners. Males had greater exposure to some diseases because of occupations and mobility. More importantly, women were less likely to be educated or to have direct contacts with the British, hence they probably had greater fears about western medicine. Women may have been more culturally conservative in general, and hence more suspicious of medical and other innovations. As females, they were probably more reluctant to submit to examinations by male doctors, particularly alien ones. Finally, only a small fraction of the total population received modern medical attention, despite what was, at least by western standards, an enormous disease burden. Most Ghanaians, particularly the females, suffered in silence, clung to traditional remedies, or resorted to quacks.

The Medical Department also provided limited dental services. M.O.s did some extractions and other emergency work. In the 1920s, a dental surgeon was based in Accra; in some years, a second dentist worked in Kumasi. The second appointment was retrenched in 1931 and was not restored until the late 1940s. There were seven government dentists in 1951. Dentists toured major towns from time to time and during the course of the year examined several hundred school children. They provided treatment for several thousands of Africans and Europeans, with special attention to employees of the government.[95] There were also a handful of expatriate dentists in private practice, including J. M. Hyatt, an American who established himself in Accra in 1915 after ten years of itinerating from Bathurst to Calabar,[96] and Oliver C. Arthur, a graduate of Howard University.[97] However, despite African complaints and official recognition of the acute need for more dentists,[98] the Medical Department refused to sanction the practice of private dentists who had not been registered in the U.K.[99]

The hospitals and physicians of the Medical Branch gained some popularity for their curative work, but the preventive medicine practiced by the Health Branch resulted in more resentment than esteem. The Health Branch was established in 1909 as a direct result of the bubonic plague epidemic of the preceding year.[100] The Gold Coast took a greater interest in public health work than Britain's other West African colonies; by 1930, it had fourteen Medical Officers of Health, while Nigeria had only seven and Gambia and Sierra Leone none.[101] The Health Branch was responsible for a number of unglamorous tasks, such as nuisance abatement; cleaning of drains, latrines, and dustbins; inspecting housing, markets, slaughterhouses, and restaurants; vaccinations; and, most vexatious of all, mosquito control. In short, an M.O.H. practiced "social medicine" and was intimately concerned with the living conditions and values of the population. The M.O.H. and his African inspectors did not erect impressive hospitals or provide injections to heal the sick; instead, they poked around people's compounds, looking for mosquito larvae, unauthorized buildings, excess lodgers, or the sick; they issued a steady stream of summonses and fines for those who relieved themselves in a place other than the filthy public latrines, sold food on the streets without an expensive cover, or dumped garbage in a handy gutter rather than a distant and already overflowing dustbin. In short, the M.O.H. and his men badgered people in many ways, without any obvious benefit to anyone except those who collected the fines or got jobs as inspectors.

Sanitary inspection could produce collisions between rulers and ruled, as at Awungawa, near Keta, in 1939. The District Commissioner (D.C.) toured the town and, finding it dirty, told the African sanitary inspector to have the place cleaned up. The inspector asked for a police escort because the people were "very obstructive and threatened him." No police were available, so the D.C. accompanied the inspector to search compounds for larvae of *Aedes aegypti*, the mosquito vector of yellow fever. All the houses were locked and a large crowd looked on, refusing to identify the owners of premises to be searched. The D.C. spotted people in one house and, when they refused to open to his repeated knocks, he broke down the door. A modicum of cooperation was achieved only after he had forced several other doors. Larvae were discovered in only two houses.[102]

Political officials were not always so eager to provide physical support for health officials. Indeed, as an angry exchange of letters showed in 1932, Europeans as well as Africans often resented the activities of the M.O.H.s and their staffs. Dr. P. S. Selwyn-Clarke criticized the inadequacy of the health laws and the unwillingness of chiefs or political officers to enforce them or to levy substantial fines on those found guilty of violations. He argued that because indirect rule should not be allowed to endanger lives, health should be under the direct control of the government, and concluded by asking that all D.C.s be sent a circular telling them to cooperate with their M.O.H.[103] The circular was sent and the response was vociferous. The Ag. C.C.P. wrote that he and his D.C.s resented the circular and argued that although the average villager did not understand the disease-mosquito link, heavy fines were not the best means of education.[104] The C.C.N.T. denounced the insinuation that sanitary laws were ignored as a "slur on the reputation of the Political Administration," and presented figures to show that slack enforcement of mosquito or cleanliness laws had nothing to do with the outbreak of yellow fever in Tamale the previous year. He noted with understanding that the people of Tamale referred to the M.O.H. and his staff as "Summa Summa"–summons, summons–and concluded by claiming that Selwyn-Clarke's attack on indirect rule was typical of the short-sighted views of the technical departments, as Lugard had foreseen, and perhaps they needed a circular on indirect rule.[105] The reply of the C.C.A. was even sharper. In nine vitriolic pages he denounced the "insatiable demands of Dr. P. S. Selwyn-Clarke," who sought "carte blanche" to meddle in relations with the chiefs and to influence magistrates' sentences. Selwyn-Clarke and his colleagues were allegedly possessed of "a narrow-minded belief that the world is largely peopled with persons who are wrong in everything and that the righteous minority consists exclusively of Health Officers."[106] Like nineteenth century Londoners in the face of cholera, both Ghanaians and their rulers resented being "bullied into health."[107]

Still, the value of preventive medicine was widely appreciated in both medical and administrative circles, as is shown by the fairly high percentage of the total medical budget usually awarded to the Health Branch. As the necessity for reduced expenditure became obvious in 1931 and 1932, a major intra-departmental struggle developed over funds. The D.D.H.S., arguing that the Health Branch must be able to prevent epidemics, fought any cuts; while the D.M.S. wanted to cut back all "specialized services," including those of the Health Branch. The Branch did lose some funds and several M.O.H. positions, but retained most of its pre-depression percentage of the total medical budget.[108] Curative services were much less severely cut. A decade later, a D.M.S. blasted retrenchment in preventive and research staffs as shortsighted. Hospitals and M.O.s should have been pruned instead, if "the welfare of the population rather than the popularity of the administration had been the guiding motive."[109] This judgment may be harsh, but both administrators and the public were much more impressed with the visible and immediate results of clinical medicine than the humdrum and almost imperceptible work of the public health officer.

As the distribution, etiology, and means of transmission of the country's major diseases became better understood, the necessity for prevention became more and more obvious. Repeatedly, as discussions of individual diseases in subsequent chapters will show, medical authorities became aware that therapy was ineffective in reducing disease burdens as long as conditions which permitted continuing re-infection remained unchanged. Broad improvements in water supply, sewage disposal, housing, vector control, diet, and specific immunization were essential. However, large hospitals, expensive doctors, and advanced drugs were, and still are, more familiar and more satisfying to the public and the government than incremental progress in more mundane spheres. Hence, a suggestion that new dispensaries only be opened in areas where the chiefs and people had already maintained simple sanitary measures for several years won the approval of M.O.s,[110] but was politically impossible. Preventive medicine continued to lay behind its more visible curative counterpart, but not hopelessly so.

The Medical Research Institute or Laboratory Branch was, as its various titles suggest, responsible for both routine clinical and pathological work and for basic scientific and medical research. A distinct laboratory service was created in 1908 to deal with a plague epidemic. It carried on routine work and for a few years produced smallpox vaccine, which unfortunately turned out to be ineffective. Research commenced in 1914 with the engagement of Dr. J. W. S. Macfie as a full-time pathologist. A medical entomologist, Dr. A. Ingram, was appointed in 1916. In 1920, the erstwhile Accra Laboratory became the Medical Research Institute, a separate branch of the Medical Department, and was given an increase in personnel.[111] The staff, notably Macfie, Ingram, and J. F. Corson, conducted an active research program, with special emphasis on insect vectors, parasitology, and malaria. By 1932, staff members had produced over 120 scientific papers. A mobile laboratory was created in 1925 to investigate trypanosomiasis and other epidemic diseases,[112] and branch laboratories were opened at the Kumasi and Sekondi hospitals in 1926. Two years later, a field laboratory for the study of trypanosomiasis was opened at Yeji. However, except for routine tests, most clinical and pathological work had to be done in Accra throughout the colonial period.[113]

The decline of the Medical Research Institute began in mid-1928, when two researchers, including the Director, died of yellow fever acquired while studying the disease. A growing volume of clinical work, coupled with severe staff reductions in 1931, virtually ended original research until after 1945.[114] Indeed, compared with the French West African colonies, little scientific work was conducted in Ghana or elsewhere in British West Africa.[115] Dr. F. M. Purcell, who had conducted a two-year investigation of nutritional problems, resigned in 1944, partly because of lack of interest in and support for research.[116] The same D.M.S. whose demand for tighter administration apparently rankled Purcell agreed that the intellectual atmosphere in the department was not very stimulating.[117] Dr. M. H. Hughes, whose research on onchocerciasis was interrupted when he was shifted to clinical work because of acute staff shortages, resigned in frustration in 1949.[118] Research in the post-war years was hampered by continuing difficulties in filling departmental vacancies, which made it impossible to relieve physicians from routine diagnostic and curative work,[119] but, beyond that, the climate for research was not good. Those medical officers who found time and resources for original investigations were given little encouragement, and, in fact, were sometimes denied permission to publish.[120] Nonetheless, the quality and quantity of research improved greatly after 1950.[121] Examples of research conducted by the staff of the M.R.I. and other members of the department will be discussed in connection with specific health problems in the following chapters.

Among the most popular services of the Medical Department were the Infant Welfare and Maternity Clinics administered by the Health Branch. High infant mortality rates had long concerned colonial officials, and during World War I a committee appointed by Governor Clifford investigated the problem in Accra.[122] Clifford advocated a maternity hospital and a school for midwives,[123] but these did not materialize until almost a decade after he left office in 1919. A second study in 1920 reiterated the need for action.[124] The Registrar of Births and Deaths reported high infant mortality rates and argued that "the importance of maternity and infant welfare work is thus more than ever apparent as perhaps the greatest need of Accra and other Gold Coast towns."[125] Examination and treatment of school children began in Accra in 1920 and was expanded with the appointment of additional women medical officers.[126] In 1924, Governor Guggisberg approved a plan advanced by Dr. G. J. Pirie for midwife training at the projected maternity hospital, infant welfare centers to demonstrate proper care to mothers, and a league of African women volunteers, "with a few Europeans as guides," to conduct home visits and educational work.[127] That same year, the Government took over an infant welfare clinic in Christiansborg that had been started in 1923 by Dr. Jesse Beveridge of the Scottish Mission and established another center in the James Town section of Accra. Construction was begun on the Princess Marie Louise Hospital, an institution for infants and children, also in central Accra.[128] Governor Guggisberg's plan was for the government to open a few clinics, involve local volunteers to assist in educational work, and stimulate local chiefs and educated Africans to establish centers in their own communities.[129] For many years, committees of women did useful work in Accra and elsewhere under the banner of the Gold Coast League for Maternity and Child Welfare,[130] but local groups proved unable to found their own centers.

Infant Welfare Centres run by government W.M.O.s were opened in Sekondi in 1925, Shama in 1926, Kumasi in 1927, Cape Coast in 1928, and Koforidua in 1929. The M.O. at Ho began touring his area in 1924, lecturing, demonstrating, and treating sick infants. Missionaries opened infant clinics at Amedjope and Kpandu, and a government W.M.O. was posted to a Centre in Ho in 1930.[131] In the north, a centre was approved for Tamale in 1932,[132] but it soon ceased operation. Cadbury Bros. Ltd., the great chocolate firm, contributed £600 over three years for infant welfare work in Kumasi and the Colony.[133] The centres were, as table 8 (page 118) indicates, extremely popular. Pregnant women, new mothers, and infants were examined and treated free until 1930, when a small fee was established. Indeed, case-loads became so great that the original plan, patterned on the U.K., that the W.M.O.s act primarily as educators, giving periodic examinations, minor treatment, and advice, was lost. The press of curative work made preventive and educational efforts almost impossible. By 1932, the D.M.S.S. was complaining that the Centres had become hospitals and, in view of the budgetary crisis, it was unfair to have two hospitals in some towns when others had none. He agreed that the W.M.O.s were, with one or two exceptions, clinicians who were not especially interested in or good at preventive work.[134] The D.D.M.S. wanted them transferred to the Medical Branch; but the leaders of the Health Branch were hotly opposed,[135] arguing that if clinical work was stopped nobody would come to a centre or heed its advice and that the solution should be to add Health Visitors to augment the preventive effort. It was impossible to turn away the sick; cures were a better means of public education than fines for violating sanitary ordinances. Despite the burden of clinical work, Health Branch officials argued that every effort was made to talk to mothers about how to keep themselves and their children healthy.[136] The centres remained part of the Health Branch, but, despite efforts to emphasize educational and preventive measures, remained primarily clinics.[137] The overwhelming demand for treatment and the long journeys some patients undertook to get help made this inevitable. Despite continuing bureaucratic complaints, there was little choice but to allow the infant welfare centres to function as hospitals.[138]

Like other aspects of medical care, welfare centres were hard hit by the depression. Several W.M.O.s were terminated, requests for new centres were rejected, and, to the great consternation of urban Africans, the government threatened to close several centres.[139] In Cape Coast, sixty-three citizens petitioned that their centre and W.M.O. not be taken away. Infant mortality was said to have been reduced by 50 percent, and even those who had once been skeptical were now enthusiastic.[140] Women in Sekondi protested that the retrenchment of their Nurse-Midwife "would spell untold misery to expectant mothers and break the hearts of mothers and babies who have learnt to love the service she has given and in whose homes her very presence has dispelled sadness and gloom at critical periods."[141] The petition bore thirty-two signatures and 248 marks; it had been read in Fanti to those who were illiterate.[142]

Some W.M.O.s were lost but, thanks to private funding, all of the centres were kept open. Dr. P. S. Selwyn-Clarke had long been interested in the League for Maternal and Child Welfare's efforts in home visiting, encouraging attendance at clinics, and "breaking down the racial barriers which are a bar to progress by the association of European and African women in social service." When the depression threatened the closing of the centres, he took the suggestion of another doctor and, in April 1932, transformed the League into the Gold Coast Branch of the Red Cross. The Governor agreed to be the Patron, the C.S. served as President, the D.M.S.S. became Chairman of the Central Committee, and distinguished Africans held majorities on all committees. The Red Cross raised sufficient funds from private donations and civic organizations to hire European nurses to keep the Sekondi and Cape Coast Infant Welfare Centres open, and also contributed to new buildings at the Maternity Hospital, an X-ray machine for Kumasi, supplies for four leper colonies, an asylum for derelicts near Tamale, and a car for midwives and health visitors at the Princess Marie Louise Hospital in Accra.[143] It was a remarkable performance and Selwyn-Clarke was justly praised.[144] The Red Cross soon assumed responsibility for the Koforidua Infant Welfare Centre and continued over the years to contribute to the welfare of the sick, notably lepers, the insane, and the disabled.[145]

In summary, the Infant Welfare centres did much good work, treating hundreds of thousands of women and children for worms, malaria, yaws, wounds, anemia, and other major and minor problems. Although designed as clinics, they also functioned as hospitals. Mothers were usually allowed to stay in wards with their sick children.[146] In Kumasi, the clinic became a maternity hospital, because nothing else was available.[147] However, the system was never expanded beyond a few towns and only reached a tiny percentage of the population. The huge demand for care made it impossible to carry out much educational or preventive work; anxious mothers wanted their children cured and perhaps were not often receptive to comments in a foreign language from a busy woman doctor. The overall impact of the program will be discussed in a later chapter.

The Gold Coast Medical Service was not entirely wedded to fixed medical centers and, in fact, tried a number of schemes to bring medical services to the people. M.O.s in bush stations were expected to travel in their districts as much as possible. Some were quite conscientious about this, but most could do little touring because they were in charge of hospital patients and had to handle out-patients as well as care for government employees and prisoners at the district headquarters.

Traveling dispensaries were tried in the 1920s. In Togo, an M.O. with a lorry tried to maintain a regular circuit in the Ho and Kpandu areas. The response was good, but bad roads and mechanical problems made it impossible to keep to the announced schedules, so the sick often assembled when the doctor was unable to come, and when he did arrive his patients might be miles away.[148] Two traveling dispensaries served the Ho area and a leprosy survey team until 1931.[149] A third was assigned to the remote northwestern corner of the country in early 1927. Dr. G. F. T. Saunders treated over 11,000 patients in Lawra-Tumu District in his first year, including more than 7,000 cases of yaws.[150] The program looked very promising, especially in Lawra, which had a dense population but a non-nucleated settlement pattern. Dr. D. W. Seth-Smith, Saunders' successor, aided by a very capable dispenser named Forson, treated thousands for yaws and other diseases and used his mobile service to popularize the newly-constructed hospital in the town of Lawra. However, vehicle maintenance was a continuing problem and the rains made roads virtually impassable from July to September.[151] The depression ended the mobile dispensary experiment; all three had been grounded for lack of funds by 1932.[152]

Campaigns against specific diseases also produced attempts to bring health care directly to the people instead of waiting for them to report to fixed centers. The trypanosomiasis epidemic which developed in the north after 1930 was too serious and widespread to be contained by the meager medical facilities in the region. The government, following the example set by the French under Dr. Eugène Jamot,[153] established mobile teams to search for foci of infection, treat victims, and supervise the clearing of bush which harbored the tsetse fly vectors of the disease. Dr. Saunders, who had pioneered the traveling dispensary in the northwest, headed the campaign against trypanosomiasis. A similar approach was taken against a much more common disease in the north, yaws. A mobile survey and treatment campaign began in Eastern Dagomba in 1943 and was later extended to other areas. The yaws and trypanosomiasis campaigns were amalgamated in early 1947; by this time the government was greatly impressed with the possibilities of mobile health care teams and was eager to expand them.[154] A proposal for a "flying doctor" service was, quite properly, rejected as impractical and unnecessary,[155] but an important innovation was on the horizon.

In early 1951, Dr. B. B. Waddy was appointed director of the Trypanosomiasis Campaign, with authorization to transform it into an organization with a broad mandate to seek out and combat the major endemic diseases of rural Ghana. This organization, the Medical Field Units, was in many respects the most important initiative ever undertaken by the Gold Coast Medical Department. The roots of the M.F.U. concept were diverse: the anti-trypanosomiasis work begun under Jamot in French Equatorial Africa during World War I, later French and Belgian experiments with field medicine, the experience and local knowledge built up in Ghana by the Trypanosomiasis Campaign conducted by Saunders, the mixed results of mobile anti-yaws teams, and a growing recognition by many health officials that fixed health centers could not control, or in some cases even identify, the health problems of rural areas.[156] The idea of M.F.U.s was not universally popular in the medical service; many high departmental officials in Accra were unenthusiastic and some of the anti-trypanosomiasis workers would have preferred to concentrate their efforts on their own disease.[157] Waddy himself played a vital role in establishing the M.F.U. system.[158] Experience in the north had convinced him that traditional clinics were of limited value and could not give an accurate picture of the local disease environment. In particular, Waddy and the rest of the medical service had been entirely unaware of major foci of hyperendemic onchocerciasis and mass blindness until the 1940s. The full extent of this crucial problem was not appreciated until Waddy's surveys of 1948 and 1949.[159] Waddy now believed that active searches must be made to determine an area's health problems. As he later wrote, people

> who come and ask for treatment [at hospitals and clinics] are those who believe that they can be treated. A gap is left in which mass plagues can flourish for years, they very existence unsuspected by medical authorities because their victims did not know that treatment is possible and do not report to hospitals.[160]

The structure and functions of the M.F.U.s marked a major change in departmental policies. Fixed centers, while still essential, were of lesser importance. Great reliance was placed on indigenous supporting personnel and the focus was clearly on mass rural medicine. None of these concepts were, of course, entirely new, but the M.F.U. scheme did reflect a shift in emphasis. Drawing on past experience in the Gold Coast and elsewhere, notably the French colonies,[161] it embodied many ideas now widely advocated by experts on health care in poor countries.[162] The key to the M.F.U. system was a corps of well-trained, highly motivated Africans who were willing to make their careers in rural areas. They were to be closely supervised by physicians with an equally strong commitment to rural health care. Applicants for positions weere screened for basic literacy and a high score on the Progressive Matrix test, used as a non-verbal measure of innate reasoning powers. Recruits were given a month of basic instruction in microscopy and other skills and then sent off with a survey team for six months of practical work in the field. Those who stayed on for the full term and did well were given further training in such skills as elementary clinical and laboratory diagnosis, dispensing, intravenous therapy, record keeping, mapping, or administration of stores. Close supervision in the field provided further education and an assurance of proper standards. A career ladder with well-defined responsibilities and rewards encouraged continued excellence. The training program was designed to produce health workers with relevant skills who would be trained in rural conditions, and, if they survived their first "bush" experience, would be likely to remain with the M.F.U.s and not drift off to the towns. Doctors set general strategy for survey and treatment and spent much time visiting and supervising the African teams who did the routine work. They had to know their men, keep up their morale, and take a personal interest in their welfare.[163]

Villages were informed in advance when a survey team was beginning work in their area. After setting up camp, the team listed the inhabitants and requested them to appear on a given day at a central, open-air site. People were examined between 6 a.m. and 8 a.m. for symptoms of major diseases, a blood sample was taken and, depending on the circumstances, skin snips or cervical gland juice might be obtained or penicillin injections given for yaws. Villagers finished early enough to get in a full day's work and the survey team had time to examine blood slides and other specimens and to prepare a list of people to be seen the next day. When work in a village was finished, the team moved on to the next point on its itinerary. By the end of the tour, the survey team leader prepared a report on disease prevalence for planning a treatment campaign. Treatment was carried out by a second traveling team and, especially for trypanosomiasis work, which involved lumbar puncture and drugs with potentially dangerous side effects, was conducted by highly skilled and responsible staff.[164]

The Medical Field Units showed that good quality mass health care could be given for several major diseases over large rural areas with only a few physicians.[165] Intelligent, motivated, carefully trained workers, even those with only elementary education, or in a few cases none at all, supervised by only a few scarce and expensive physicians, provided tremendous benefits at minimal cost. The major difficulty was recruiting doctors, few of whom were willing to exchange urban clinical practice for a semi-nomadic, largely supervisory career in the bush. Unfortunately, the system did not survive long after Dr. Waddy, who resigned in 1955, and his successor, Dr. David Scott, left their posts. Despite the support of Imoru Egala, Ghana's first minister of health, familiar patterns and career preferences soon reasserted themselves and the M.F.U.s were moribund within a few years after independence.[166]

Health expenditures were summarized in table 3 (page 111) and table 4 (page 112). Spending rose steadily, except for a marked decline during the depression. Per capita expenditure was always low, but it too showed a generally upward trend. The Medical Department was allocated roughly 8-12 percent of the total colonial budget, a percentage it maintained with considerable constancy until major developmental spending skewed the picture after 1946. The Gold Coast's budgeting for health, both as a percentage of total expenditure and per capita, was somewhat more generous than that of Nyasaland or Britain's East African possessions.[167] In comparison, independent Ghana's health expenditure ranged from 6.4 percent to 8.2 percent of total government spending between 1965 and 1969.[168] Table 4 (page 112) shows the allocation of funds within the functional branches of the department. The Medical Branch, which operated the hospitals and curative services, consistently got the largest share, although the Health Branch, which was responsible for preventive measures and, after the mid-1920s, infant welfare centres, had gained a substantial percentage by 1914. Except for a short period in the late 1920s and early 1930s, relatively little was spent on the Laboratory Branch.

Ghanaian responses to modern medicine were cautious and pragmatic. Indigenous concepts of "sickness" differed from European ideas. The "sick" person was one whose health interfered with the ability to work or to fulfill social roles; obvious disease symptoms might be ignored as long as the sufferer could function.[169] Hence, persons "sick" by European standards might not bother to seek aid until they were disabled, or (to the annoyance of doctors) the case was quite advanced and difficult to treat. Western physicians were often viewed as powerful figures and their skills in surgery and anesthesia won quick respect, but many Africans preferred their own medicines to the pills and potions administered by aliens.[170] Most Ghanaians wanted quick results, such as they obtained from yaws injections. Yaws treatment often increased the popularity of modern therapy for other diseases[171] and has certainly contributed to the widespread belief in the value of injections for almost any condition.[172] Receptivity to western medicine varied directly with education and exposure to European ideas. For example, educated coastal Africans living in the north were quick to seek medical care, while Dagomba villagers were reticent for decades.[173] People in the Ho area of Togo, long accustomed to European rule, walked for miles to see the M.O. and chiefs promptly reported epidemics, but there was an almost total lack of response in the remote northeastern corner of the Mandate.[174] Ghanaians were also pragmatic about the conditions for which they sought care. British doctors were obviously good for yaws or broken limbs, but lepers or people going blind had little reason to see them. Out-patient care was much more popular than hospitalization. Hospitals were unfamiliar and widely feared, especially since so many people went to the hospital only after everything else had failed that many reached them only when moribund, and consequently, death rates were very high.[175]

Western medicine had to compete with indigenous health care systems that, while tightly bound up with religious beliefs and other aspects of culture, were by no means inflexible.[176] Since most illnesses are self-limiting and even terminal conditions sometimes have temporary relapses, there was ample pragmatic evidence that "traditional" remedies worked. People used them and, sometimes at least, felt better. Faith in remedies and the psychological benefits derived from contact with concerned professional healers were, and are, medically valuable. Some traditional remedies doubtlessly provided symptomatic relief for fever, nausea, diarrhea, constipation, or pain, even though the high incidence of disease and the low life-expectancy show the general weakness of local pharmacopoeias and practitioners. Still, familiar ways were useful and were often preferable to the alien customs of the British. There were, of course, real limits to the effectiveness of scientific therapy. Certainly there was little reason for a Ghanaian suffering from cancer in 1910 or psychosis in 1950 to prefer the services of a western-trained doctor.

Many people took an eclectic approach, seeking the best elements of various medical systems. Advised or directed by family or friends, they might consult a colonial physician and a local practitioner simultaneously or, more likely, go to the clinic after the village healer had failed. Western medicines might be used in "traditional" ways, such as wearing pills around the neck as charms.[177] There was an extensive traffic in drugs stolen from hospitals and clinics, sometimes with harmless or even useful results,[178] but frequently with tragic consequences. In Ashanti, for instance, fourteen deaths resulted from illegal injections over a thirty-two-month period in the early 1940s; several illicit practitioners were convicted of manslaughter by negligence.[179] European patent medicines were also widely sold. For example, in 1922 one issue of a newspaper carried advertisements for the following: Burgess' Lion Pills and Ointment, Dr. Guillie's Elixir, DeWitt's Kidney and Bladder Pills, Sloan's Liniment, Calabar Ointment, Halls's Wine, and Dr. Morse's Indian Root Pills.[180] These and other nostrums were readily available in stores and markets.

Another approach was to attempt to modernize traditional remedies, validate them by scientific procedures, and persuade the government to license "qualified" indigenous healers.[181] The Society of African Herbalists, formed at Sekondi on 12 December 1931 by J. A. Kwesi Aaba, a photographer, sought "to raise the local practice of medical herbalism up to a high and refined standard, and to seek for free or unhindered practice for its members."[182] The government, while agreeing that there might be much virtue in *bona fide* "native doctors,"[183] denied this and other requests for official recognition, but made no attempt to suppress herbalists or any other indigenous healers.[184] The Society tried again in 1934, informing the D.M.S.S. that they were endeavoring to "stabilize" herbal medicine and were "securing it from charlatanry, fraud, and supersition." Members were instructed to report all contagious diseases to government doctors.[185] P. S. Selwyn-Clarke, then acting D.M.S.S., responded courteously, wishing the society "a long and useful career" and asking them to inform him of any discoveries. He agreed that "a number of native drugs have definite utility in the treatment of disease," but these exceptions were "swamped beneath a veritable heap of quack remedies."[186] A subsequent plea by Aaba that the depression was bringing forth a host of charlatans who could only be eliminated by the licensing of reputable practitioners was rebuffed on the grounds that recognition was impossible "at the present stage of development of your society."[187]

This statement, implying that official recognition might eventually be possible, may have encouraged Aaba to publish a 38-page booklet explaining his methods and goals. This work, *African Herbalism: A Mine of Health, Part I*,[188] was dedicated to the Aborigines Rights Protection Society and contained a forward by the leader of that organization, Kobina Seyki. Aaba denounced the habit of some Ghanaians of "decrying everything African" and predicted that future African chemists would find useful medicines in local herbs. The Society of African Herbalists sought to preserve the wisdom of the past, and the members, as educated men, had a duty to improve on it. Present methods were merely empirical; a rational basis for herbal medicine must be found.[189] The bulk of the book was made up of lists of medicinal plants and instructions on preparing them for various diseases. One interesting suggestion was a ground-up potion of herbs and salamander heads which was innoculated on the wrists as a temporary vaccine against syphilis.[190] Some of Aaba's ideas on malaria etiology and therapy echoed earlier European beliefs; he thought that malaria could be caused by "atmospheric influences" such as swamp vapors, eating too many mangoes, excessive drinking, or by mosquitoes carrying a "malarial germ or poison" from marshy areas. Useful remedies would probably be found in swampy places, Aaba wrote, citing the old European doctrine that remedies for diseases were found near their causes.[191]

Aaba, in a later plea for support from traditional chiefs, indicated his acquaintance with such western pseudo-scientific doctrines as naturopathy, hydropathy, theosophy, and electrotherapy. He wanted to teach these subjects, as well as African dietetics, materia medica, diagnosis, modern hygiene and sanitation, "African herbal massage or manipulative therapy," "astro-herbalism," and organic chemistry in a proposed school for herbalists.[192] He later tried to reinforce his case by producing a description of a school with a faculty of twenty-six practitioners, nineteen of whom were in the Western Province. These persons, with titles such as M.S.A.M.H. (Member, Society of African Medical Herbalists) or M.B.H.S.L. (Member of the Bronze Health and Strength League-London) were listed, together with their specialties. Examinations , both theoretical and practical, were held at several locations and those who passed were given Certificates of Efficiency.[193]

The Society of African Herbalists, like a later group, the Ga Medical Association,[194] represented an ambitious attempt to legitimize, regulate, improve, and supplement traditional medical practices, as well as, no doubt, ensure an adequate living for its members. It appealed to many, including those chiefs who were "irresistably drawn to the conclusion that there is substance in the claims of African Herbalism and that it will be ruthlessly unreasonable to regard it with contempt because it is African."[195] Perhaps because it challenged the assumption that there was no African "science," Aaba's group won the support of such notables as J. B. Danquah, Nana Sir Ofori Atta, and G. L. Christian, Legislative Council member for the Western Province.[196] Official recognition was, of course, out of the question, and the Society's petitions, like similar appeals by individual practitioners, were routinely rejected.[197] Administrators were reluctant to write official letters of rejection to petitioners, for fear that they would be presented as government licenses to illiterate prospective patients.[198] Customary rulers, such as the Ashanti Confederation Council, were, however, free to license traditional practitioners they determined to be honest and capable.[199]

The Medical Department never did carry out the scientific screening program advocated by Aaba and his associates. A Colonial Office circular dispatch, citing a suggestion made by Lord Hailey in *An African Survey*, raised the question of studying native medicines, but the Medical Department lacked the resources to do so, especially since substantial local cooperation was apparently not forthcoming. The Society of African Herbalists was "regarded with sympathy" by the department, but it had failed to respond to requests for materials for analysis. Nana Sir Ofori Atta had broached the issue in the Legislative Council, but his questions ended when he was asked to provide specimens of medicinal plants. Individual M.O.s had sent samples to Britain for analysis, but not in enough quantity for active ingredients to be found. Any screening program would be expensive and would have to be done in Britain because there were no local laboratories with the necessary facilities. The D.M.S. doubted that anything useful enough to enter the pharmacopeia would be found.[200]

As the clinical returns show, western therapy won increasing acceptance, but its triumph was never complete. Traditional beliefs and practices, sometimes influenced by scientific and/or pseudoscientific European concepts, continued to flourish throughout the colonial era. The Medical Department, while skeptical, was not entirely intolerant. Dr. F. V. Nanka-Bruce, a prominent African physician, expressed the consensus of orthodox practitioners when he denounced most traditional healers as dangerous frauds, but conceded that a minority, primarily among the herbalists, were honest and were able to help some patients.[201]

Present-day observers might take an even more sympathetic view. The continued popularity of various types of "traditional" practitioners, even among literate people in Accra, shows that they still meet real social, psychological, and even medical needs.[202] Indeed, indigenous healers may have much to offer modern medicine in psychiatric services[203] and in bringing preventive medicine to ordinary citizens.[204] African reactions to modern medicine require much more historical study. We know little about changes in concepts of sickness and disease causation, the adaptations of "traditional" systems to European competition, or factors which led ill persons and/or their families to elect particular methods of treatment for specific complaints. In any case, for the foreseeable future, medical care in Ghana, as in all countries, will be based on traditional and neo-traditional beliefs and self-treatment, as well as on orthodox scientific medicine.

The effectiveness of modern medical services increased markedly between 1900 and 1955, especially after 1920. Despite world wars, the depression, and the slow growth of knowledge concerning the etiology, mode of transmission, and methods of prevention and cure of major diseases, the basis had been laid for a modern medical system and a good start ahad been made for an organized attack on rural health problems by the early 1940s.[205] The Medical Department might, as its wartime director claimed, have lacked an effective organization or an overall strategy, and there was an overemphasis on clinical work at fixed centers, but the quality of medical personnel was good.[206] A sound base, enhanced concern for mass rural health care, and technological advances such as antibiotics and persistent insecticides, made substantial progress possible after 1945. Ghanaians played a larger role after the war, thanks to better educational opportunities and the belated collapse of the W.A.M.S. color bar.

It is difficult to compare the growth, strategies, and effectiveness of the Gold Coast Medical Service with medical services in other colonies because relatively little research has been done yet. Certainly colonial medical work deserves more than the casual praise or condemnation given by most historians. By 1920, the British administration had accepted responsibility for improving the level of health of the Ghanaian population. This was partly done out of self-interest, partly because it seemed to be the duty of any reasonable government, and partly, I am convinced, because many administrators and physicians were sincerely interested in alleviating human suffering. The Medical Department was, of course, grossly understaffed and underfunded, especially during the depression and World War II, but it did get a respectable share of a chronically inadequate colonial budget. The staff was generally competent and hard-working, especially after the first two decades of the century, and many doctors displayed real insights into social and health problems and a willingness to innovate, despite what were often difficult and isolated working conditions. Compared to the French in West Africa, and to some extent the Belgians in the Congo, the Gold Coast relied too heavily on large hospitals and was slow to develop techniques to meet rural needs. It was inexcusably slow to use African doctors and to train paramedical staff. There was, however, considerable attention to preventive work, and both the density of health care facilities and the proportion of the population receiving treatment were probably quite high by the standards of the time. Medical work in the Gold Coast, while terribly inadequate by modern standards, was more effective than in most colonies.

3

DISEASES TRANSMITTED BY INSECT VECTORS

Some of the most important diseases afflicting mankind are caused by microorganisms or worms transmitted by insect or other invertebrate vectors. Malaria, yellow fever, dengue fever, and bancroftian filariasis are transmitted to man by mosquitoes; trypanosomiasis by tsetse flies; bubonic plague is spread by fleas, while lice transmit a form of relapsing fever. Diseases which reach humans via aquatic invertebrate intermediaries, such as guinea worm and schistosomiasis, will be discussed in a later chapter.

In recent decades, infectious diseases transmitted by insect vectors have been largely restricted to underdeveloped countries in the tropics, but many have only recently become "tropical" diseases. Bubonic plague epidemics have afflicted Europe and Asia for many centuries; typhus was common in European slums and armies from at least the sixteenth century, and malaria was found in much of Europe and the United States well after 1900. Socio-economic development and advances in medicine and public health have virtually eliminated the dangers of most insect-vectored diseases in the richer countries, but they remain critical problems in Ghana and other warm-climate countries.

Malaria is, and has been for centuries, Ghana's most devastating disease. The "fevers" which struck down so many European traders were often malarial; but they exacted a much heavier, if less conspicuous, toll on the lives and energies of the indigenous people. Malaria is caused by any of four species of protozoa, all of which are found in Ghana. *Plasmodium vivax* and *P. ovale* cause benign tertian malaria, while *P. malariae* causes quartan malaria. *P. falciparum* produces by far the most dangerous form; falciparum, malignant, or aestivoautumnal malaria. Simultaneous infections with two or three species can occur. *P. ovale* was first described in Ghana,[1] but seems to have been rare. Indeed, the discovery of two cases of ovale malaria in Kumasi in 1933 was considered worthy of special notice.[2] *P. vivax* and *P. malariae* are more common and cause more serious disease; one study suggests that *P. malariae* infection is especially common in children.[3] An increasing incidence of vivax malaria was noted during the 1940s, perhaps as a result of war-time population movements.[4] Falciparum malaria is the most abundant as well as the most deadly type. Since treatment was similar for all forms of malaria, colonial physicians usually did not bother to establish which particular form their patients had, so the majority of cases in any given year were reported as "unclassified."

Malaria is transmitted to man by the bite of female mosquitoes of the genus *Anopheles*. *A. gambiae*, which breeds in sunlit pools and ponds, is the major vector, with *A. funestus* playing a strong secondary role. Other species, such as *A. melas* (which breeds in salt water), may be locally important.[5]

Plasmodium species go through extremely complex life cycles in their human and anopheline hosts. Man is infected when a feeding mosquito injects sporozoite forms into the bloodstream. Sporozoites multiply inside liver cells for a week or more, producing merozoites, which enter red blood cells. There they undergo asexual reproduction, producing more merozoites, which are released when the red blood cell bursts. These in turn attack other red blood cells, multiply, and destroy them. Cycles of reproduction and cell destruction produce periodic fever and chills; regular attacks may occur every third or fourth day, depending on the species of parasite. Eventually, some of the merozoites produce male and female gametocytes, which cannot develop in man, but if ingested by mosquitoes feeding on the victim's blood, they produce zygotes which develop through further stages in the gut of the insect host. Two or three weeks later sporozoites are formed, which make their way to the mosquitoes' salivary glands, where they await transmission to a human host.[6]

Malaria produces a wide variety of clinical manifestations. Chills and fever are characteristic, while destruction of red blood cells frequently causes severe anemia. Fatal cerebal malaria may result if parasites affect the blood vessels of the brain. Damage to the spleen, kidneys, and liver is common, as are severe vomiting and diarrhea and adrenal failure. Fever and anemia in pregnant women can cause miscarriages, premature births, and smaller infants.[7] Relapses may occur years after the initial infection, especially in vivax and malariae malaria. Indeed, malaria is a complex disease which can take a variety of clinical forms, often mimicking other diseases and complicating diagnosis.

Blackwater fever is a very serious complication of falciparum malaria. It mostly affects expatriates and is almost always associated with quinine therapy. The exact etiology is unclear, but hypersensitivity to quinine is apparently involved. Massive destruction of red blood cells gives the urine a dark color and kidney failure is the most dangerous feature of the disease. Management of victims is difficult. There are no specific cures; rest and good nursing are essential. Several deaths from blackwater fever were reported every year, mostly among Europeans. This disease was second only to yellow fever as a source of anxiety about the health of whites and, as was done for yellow fever, detailed clinical case reports were submitted to the Colonial Office. During World War II, mepacrine was substituted for quinine in malaria prophylaxis and therapy, and blackwater fever almost disappeared. It was never a significant factor in African mortality.

Immunities against malaria may be inherited or acquired as the result of infection. Sickle-cell trait, and perhaps some other genetically-determined abnormal hemoglobins, conveys partial resistance to falciparum malaria, but at the cost of sickle-cell anemia deaths of persons homozygous for the gene. Absence of a particular red blood cell antigen, Duffy, may be involved in resistance to *P. vivax*. About 90 percent of West Africans are Duffy negative. *In vitro* experiments show that the parasite cannot penetrate red blood cells lacking this antigen, so persons without it are not susceptible to vivax malaria.[8]

Survivors of malaria infections acquire antibodies which provide partial protection against later attacks by the same species of parasite. Infants get temporary passive immunity from their mothers by the passage of maternal antibodies across the placenta. This immunity wears off after a few months and the child is then very vulnerable to infection. Each infection, assuming that the child survives, leads to the development of antibodies and, hence, greater resistance. Heavy injections of sporozoites, especially in poorly nourished children or those weakened by diarrhea, dysentery, intestinal worms, or other concomittant diseases, may result in death. Malaria is hyperendemic throughout Ghana. It attacks almost every infant before it is two or three years old and is a leading cause of child mortality. However, those who survive do gradually gain resistance and subsequent attacks tend to be milder and less frequent. Microscopic examination of blood films show progressively lower rates of parasitemia with increasing age, and enlarged spleens, a common diagnostic sign in children, become less common. In adults who have grown up in malarious areas, the disease can cause occasional periods of sickness, but rarely results in death unless the victim is in poor general health.[9]

Malaria has been Ghana's most serious disease throughout the twentieth century. Hospital cases, shown in table 9 (page 119), indicate only a small fraction of the real incidence, as most Africans suffered (and allowed their children to suffer) without treatment, even though effective therapy was available. Periodic bouts of "fever" were simply part of life. The Medical Department was well aware of underreporting of malaria. Every Annual Report notes the severity and ubiquity of the disease; most contain surveys showing high incidences of enlarged spleens and/or parasitemia in school children in Accra, Kumasi, Sekondi, Cape Coast, Koforidua, or other cities.[10] The problem was clear, but there was no obvious solution.

Anti-malaria measures took several forms. The earliest official concern was, not unnaturally, for the health of Europeans. Mortality was high among colonial officials and the government was eager to keep its personnel alive and well. Ronald Ross discovered in 1898 that malaria was transmitted by the bites of infected mosquitoes, not by poisons in the air as had been previously supposed. This knowledge was put to immediate use; officials were encouraged to screen their houses and to sleep under mosquito nets.[11] Malaria was one of the very few diseases for which both an effective preventive and a curative drug was known at the turn of the century. Quinine, produced from the bark of a South American tree, had been employed against "fever" for centuries; by the mid-nineteenth century, it was commonly used by Europeans in West Africa.[12] Thus, many Europeans and a few educated Africans used quinine even before 1900. Further protection for Europeans was attempted by enforcing residential segregation so that whites would live in special areas, away from infected Africans and beyond the presumed flight range of the vectors.[13]

Measures designed to safeguard the expatriate community satisfied many officials, but others, including Ross, argued for broader measures to protect the entire population.[14] Fortunately, colonial rulers did increasingly recognize that they had responsibilities to protect their subjects' lives as well as their own. Four approaches to malaria control were tried: treatment, prophylaxis, control of mosquito larvae, and control of adult anophelines. In theory, malaria could be eradicated by killing all of the Plasmodium parasites in human liver and blood cells. Massive treatment could greatly reduce the number of parasites and extinction would occur if therapy continued long enough to allow all infected mosquitoes to die, assuming that relapses and imported cases were controlled. However, mass chemotherapy was not practical medically or administratively and was never contemplated. Thousands of cases were successfully treated ever year and, at least in a few towns, this probably did produce some reduction in the transmission of the disease.

Another approach was distribution of quinine as a preventive. Experiments began as early as 1910, when Accra school children were given regular doses in chocolate candy.[15] The government spent £500 over the next several years, but the program was not a success. Proper spleen index records were not kept and the chocolate could not conceal the bitter taste of quinine. The children considered it "a penal measure with the result that attendance on 'quinine day' is perceptably smaller, while the majority of those who receive it from the schoolmaster throw it out the window."[16] Despite this failure, the idea was not dropped. In 1919, examination of single blood smears of 143 Accra schoolboys showed that over half harbored malaria parasites; over three-quarters of the five-eight year-olds were infected. Sixty-two boys were treated with two doses of quinine; all became free of parasites. However, as they lived at home and were exposed to mosquito bites, the majority were re-infected within seven weeks. Clearly, regular prophylaxis was required to prevent weakened health, reduced growth, lethargy, and "early arrest of intellectual development."[17] Partly as a result of this study, a school medical officer, Dr. Mary Magill, was appointed for Accra. Dr. Magill tried weekly doses, but with little success.[18]

An experiment in quinine distribution to the general population began in August 1935. Four-grain quinine tablets in tubes of sixteen were sold at cost (6d) in 270 post offices around the country. Tablets were grooved so that they could be broken into two child-sized doses.[19] Sales began at a rate of 36,000 tubes annually and doubled in two years.[20] In May 1937, distribution began in the Northern Territories through the Native Authorities at 1d per tube. Forty-five thousand were sold in the first year.[21] The Lobi and Dagarti of Lawra District were reportedly "very keen" on quinine;[22] in Kusasi, the drug was considered a cure-all, and people complained when it arrived late.[23] During World War II, prices had to be raised, and distribution of anti-malarial drugs was switched to dispensaries.[24] The program doubtlessly helped many to avoid malaria or to treat cases themselves, but quinine reached only a small fraction of the population and many no doubt did not take it according to directions. Individuals benefitted, especially those with some cash, education, and access to distribution centers, but except for a relatively few elite Africans, the immediate impact on the public was small, and the long-term results negligible.

Larval control was attempted in the larger towns and near administrative stations. *A. gambiae* prefers to breed in standing water with vegetation on the edges and some exposure to sunlight. Knowledge of these habits led to a variety of antilarval measures. Holes, puddles, borrow pits, and ponds were filled, oiled, or treated with arsenicals like Paris Green; vegetation was trimmed; larvaceous fish were introduced into coastal lagoons; and elaborate drainage systems were constructed.[25] Despite much effort and expenditure, however, success was limited, even in major towns. Results were modest even in Accra, where the Korle Bu Lagoon produced myriads of mosquitoes despite the best efforts of a series of health officers and engineers. During the Second World War, there was an influx of highly susceptible British and American troops into Accra and Takoradi. Malaria was a serious problem, but the military authorities managed to protect their men by extensive draining and oiling operations and by the use of newly-developed insecticides. Military leaders were contemptuous of previous anti-malaria measures, claiming that "malaria control in any sense of the word simply did not exist at either Takoradi or Accra" when they arrived.[26] After the war, civilian officials were unable to maintain the hundreds of miles of military drainage ditches; the costs did not seem to be worth the benefits.[27]

Killing adult mosquitoes was impractical until the introduction of DDT and other insecticides during the war. House to house spraying was begun in Takoradi, where pyrethrum was used with some success. *A. gambiae* rests in houses after feeding, so spraying rooms with pyrethrum did provide some protection to the public and the troops.[28] DDT was tried in Takoradi in 1944; the results were better and lasted longer, the chemical killing anophelines which landed on sprayed walls or ceilings for weeks after its application.[29] DDT and related agents have played a major role in mosquito control in many countries, but were not extensively used in Ghana during the period under consideration.

Two factors may have worsened the malaria burden during the colonial period. The major vectors, *A. gambiae* and *A. funestus*, were common everywhere except in dense forest. However, when the forest was cleared, these insects, especially *A. gambiae*, soon established themselves.[30] Logging, food production, the extension of cocoa farms, and road and railroad construction all created clearings where vectors could breed. Borrow pits, where earth was removed for road, railroad, or housing construction, also provided breeding sites.[31] In addition, human mobility probably contributed to the greater severity of the disease. Authorities do not agree on the importance of strain differences within *Plasmodium* species, but immunity does seem to vary from strain to strain.[32] It seems probably that different strains are found in various regions of Ghana and that immigrants to an area might suffer from unfamiliar varieties of parasites against which they had little resistance. Conversely, immigrants might bring in a strain against which they had acquired some tolerance but which was dangerous for the indigenous people. Immigrants could also be more vulnerable to malaria attack because they entered a more malarious area and hence got larger doses of sporozoites with each infested bite, or because they tended to be in poor general health.

Whatever the balance sheet, the medical authorities were aware that little progress had been made. Malaria, wrote a frustrated Director of Medical Services in 1943, "occurs everywhere and yet there is little evidence that any sustained work has been undertaken to give even centers of population adequate protection." For all the impact of the measures taken, they "might never have been undertaken at all."[33] Although the central districts of Accra, Kumasi, and some other towns had reduced transmission, at least partially because of control measures, children continued to have very high infection rates because they were frequently taken on visits to the countryside. Quinine was routinely administered to any child appearing at a hospital or clinic with even the slightest hint of malaria.[34]

Studies done in the fifties and sixties show little change, except that more people sought and received therapy. Infection rates were very low in Central Accra, higher in older suburbs like Adabraka, and very high in peripheral suburbs.[35] In Bomfa, a cocoa village in the forest zone, investigators found that 85 percent of the one-to-three year-olds were infected; overall rates were as high as in the hyperendemic outer suburbs of Accra.[36] At Yorugu, a northern village near Bolgatanga, 82 percent of the three-to-five month-old infants had malaria parasites in their blood; 98 percent of the six-month-to-one-year group were infected.[37] In most of the country, infection was almost universal by age two; exposure was less intense in central Accra, but most children had been attacked by age four. Colbourne and Wright suggested that about 5 percent of all infants died in their first attacks and that something like 4,000 children died of malaria annually in the mid-1950s.[38] Ten years later, Colbourne saw little change in the situation.[39] Control measures were reducing *A. gambiae* in Accra, but little had been accomplished elsewhere.[40] The continuing death toll of malaria in urban areas is shown in table 40 (page 152).

Thus, little progress was made against malaria during the years 1900-1955. The impact of malaria on adult health and productivity was not known, although many people suffered periodic attacks and at least a few died. Clearly, adult immunities were acquired at the cost of very heavy infant and child mortality. Preventive drugs, larva control, and spraying to kill adult anophelines benefited relatively few. Therapy was more important. Persons with access to medical care and the inclination to use it could almost always be cured and, as table 9 (page 119) shows, growing numbers were treated every year. To what degree migration and the inadvertent creation of vector breeding sites affected control and curative measures is problematical; at best, the impact of malaria on the health of Ghanaians was only slightly alleviated during the colonial period.

Yellow fever is the most significant member of the group of diseases caused by arthropod-borne viruses (arboviruses). The pathogen, like all viruses an obligate intracellular parasite, is transmitted by the bite of female mosquitoes, primarily members of the genus *Aedes*. The primary vector in Ghana is *Aedes aegypti*, a "domestic" mosquito whose habits are quite unlike those of the vectors of malaria. It thrives in towns and villages, breeding in stored water, gutters, puddles, and in discarded cans, bottles, and tires. The growth of towns and their rubbish has favored the spread of this insect. However, the *Ae. aegypti*-man-*Ae. aegypti* cycle of urban yellow fever is not the only problem because yellow fever also exists in monkeys, creating a virus reservoir which is spread among these animals by other species of mosquitoes. Hunters and woodsmen may contract yellow fever from the bites of these forest-dwelling *Aedes* species and may in turn infect the *Ae. aegypti* populations in their villages, thus setting off an urban outbreak. The discovery of the sylvan reservoir in the mid-1930s[41] eliminated hopes of totally eradicating yellow fever, but vector control in town has reduced its impact.

The symptoms of yellow fever are dramatic and frightening. High fever, internal bleeding resulting in dark-colored vomit, liver damage producing a jaundiced, yellowish color, and neurological symptoms are common. Little can be done for the patient except to provide good nursing and symptomatic relief as, with other viral diseases, there is no specific therapy. Case mortality varies greatly; it may run as high as 80 percent. Survivors produce antibodies which convey long-lasting, generally lifetime immunity against further attack.

Yellow fever has caused terrifying epidemics among susceptible populations. Spread to the New World by the slave trade, "yellow jack" periodically decimated European populations in the Caribbean and in ports along the Atlantic coast of North America. Philadelphia suffered a severe outbreak in 1795; New Orleans experienced a major epidemic in 1853.[42] Yellow fever occasionally appeared in Europe and was a dreaded scourge among whites residing in or trading with Africa well into the twentieth century. Spanish and American forces suffered severely in Cuba in the 1890s; military needs led to the work of an American army team in Havana under Dr. Walter Reed which in 1901 proved that yellow fever was transmitted by *Aedes*.

The small, scattered European community in Ghana in the early twentieth century had good reason to fear deadly and apparently capricious outbreaks of yellow fever. The disease was a major preoccupation of the medical department and, after the discovery of the role of *Ae. aegypti*, draconian measures were taken to control it. Clinical details of individual cases, whether of Europeans, Lebanese, or Africans, were regularly reported to London.[43] However, as the figures in table 10 (page 120) show, yellow fever was not as serious a public health problem as the attention given it would suggest. Indeed, even allowing for substantial under-reporting, it was not a major cause of sickness or death for the population as a whole. Had it not caused a disproportionate mortality among expatriates, the Medical Department would have hardly noticed the disease.

Yellow fever can, of course, attack susceptible Africans, as the major epidemics in the Nuba Hills of Sudan in the early 1940s and in southwestern Ethiopia in 1960-1962 illustrate,[44] but, except for the Asamankese outbreak of 1926 and for seventy-six African cases in 1937-38, there were few yellow fever cases among Ghanaians between 1900 and 1955. A large percentage of the population acquired lasting immunity from mild or inapparent infections in childhood. Serological surveys in the 1930s showed that immunity was widespread in Ghana and other West African countries.[45] Perhaps yellow fever did cause some childhood deaths, and adult cases were certainly more common than official records indicate, but mild or subclinical childhood infections of yellow fever (related arboviruses may also give some cross immunity)[46] assured that Ghanaians were much less vulnerable than expatriates.

The colonial authorities, because of their special concern with the health of Europeans, regarded yellow fever as a major menace. Worried officials sought to reduce fear and economic dislocation by suppressing information on yellow fever until the 1910-11 outbreak in Sekondi and Accra.[47] This epidemic, with twenty-four reported cases, together with cases in other colonies, caused such alarm that the Colonial Office dispatched a team of experts under the leadership of Sir Rupert Boyce to West Africa. The commission established rigid quarantines, evacuated Europeans from threatened areas, waged a vigorous campaign against *Ae. aegypti* larvae, and fumigated downtown buildings and European bungalows with sulphur. Seventeen of the twenty-four cases were among Europeans; sixteen Europeans and three Africans died.[48] The response to the 1910-11 epidemic illustrates the primary methods used to combat the disease for the next twenty years and more: segregation of Europeans, larva eradication, and vigorous quarantines and anti-mosquito drives when cases were reported. Another factor was also evident; African skepticism of the dangers of yellow fever and opposition to the measures taken to control it.[49]

Medical authorities advocated residential segregation to protect Europeans from yellow fever and other local diseases as soon as the role of mosquito vectors was known.[50] This policy was officially adopted in all four colonies of British West Africa, despite the opposition of many governors. A four-hundred yard "neutral zone" was to be created and maintained between European and African housing areas and Europeans were not to live in African parts of town, even if their businesses were there.[51] Segregation did not work. Purchase of land, removal of Africans and their houses, and the construction of European bungalows in designated areas, such as the Ridge in Accra, were all very expensive. Most governors wanted to spend their sparse funds on other projects. Many Europeans refused to move; traders wanted to be near their stores and missionaries near their congregations. Those who did reside in the proper areas often accomodated African servants and mistresses on their premises, to the continuing dismay of the medical department. African bitterly resented the policy of prophylactic segregation, partly because they viewed it as yet another manifestation of racial arrogance, and partly because it implied a lack of interest and resources for the health of the entire community. The whites abdicated their responsibilities and retired to privileged enclaves, leaving the

Africans "to stew in their own juices, instead of improving the town so as to make it fit for any class of human beings to live in."[52]

In practice, residential segreation did little good for the Europeans since mosquito flight ranges exceed the width of the "neutral belts" and the Europeans did not always remain in their reservations or keep Africans out. Governors J. P. Rodger, J. J. Thorburn, Hugh Clifford, and F. G. Guggisberg opposed segregation as needlessly expensive, offensive to Africans, and ineffectual. Nonetheless, leading medical figures continued to urge rigid residential segregation, albeit with diminishing success, well into the 1930s.[53] The increasing use of vaccines in the 1930s ended the yellow fever menace for expatriates, and with it, the medical justification for residential segregation.[54]

Larval control measures were also unpopular with Africans. The basic method was to inspect dwellings for larval breeding and fine householders on whose premises larvae were discovered, an approach pioneered by Col. William Gorgas of the U.S. Army in Havana before 1903, and later applied with brilliant results to the Panama Canal Zone. Towns were divided into sanitary districts under the control of special inspectors. These inspectors or their subordinates entered and searched every home at least once every two weeks, without warrants or prior notice. Rainwater in discarded containers, hollows of trees, and puddles, as well as water stored for household use were checked; offenders might escape with a caution, but were usually taken to a magistrate and fined. Complaints over the policy and the conduct of the inspectors were frequent. It was "monstrous," wrote one editorialist in Cape Coast, to dump out stored water when people had no public water supply.[55] Fines were arbitrary and excessive.[56] Women were disturbed in their baths by zealous inspectors.[57] The whole policy seemed useless and self-serving to many, as the *Cape Coast Observer* editorialized. The "yellow fever bogey"[58]

> has proven a fairy godmother to white doctors and to the class of men from whom the white Sanitary Inspectors are drawn; and so fast is the appointment of white sanitary officers increasing and so completely do they monopolize these appointments and jealously guard them against the admission of black doctors that people are led to believe that Sanitation is but a device for the white man to find jobs for himself, to humbug the natives by sanitary prosecutions and fines to levy irregular taxes on the people for the maintenance and upkeep of the sanitary show.[59]

Opposition did not abate over the years. In 1926, an Accra editorialist noted that most people were skeptical about the alleged role of mosquitoes in spreading diseases and regarded larva inspection and fines as "white man's humbug." Education of the public was needed, not continued coercion.[60] Indeed, some welcomed the presence of larvae in their water, because this proved that it was not poisoned.[61] Education may have been lacking, but coercion was not; thousands of householders were fined every year.[62]

Inspection caused resentment, but it did reduce the breeding of *Ae. aegypti* and other domestic mosquitoes. Larval indexes (the percentages of houses with larvae) were kept below 1 percent in most towns.[63] It was true that the M.O.H. might find more larvae than his African staff when he made personal checks on their work,[64] but independent observers testified to the relative efficiency of this type of control measure.[65] Indeed, there were sometimes fewer vectors of yellow fever breeding in the African towns than in the segregated residential areas designed to protect Europeans. In 1930, a public health officer complained that the larval index in the European section of Accra was 7.0 percent, fourteen times that for the rest of the city.

Europeans were not liable to prosecution under the existing larva ordinance and many refused to cooperate with the health department; the law had to be changed to force the residents of the segregated areas to protect themselves.[66]

The Medical Department reacted vigorously to all reports of yellow fever. Victims and contacts were isolated, larval and adult mosquitoes assailed with various chemicals and fumigants, and quarantines were frequently enforced. These measures, and particularly the latter, did little to encourage Africans to report the disease, as was shown by an outbreak in Asamankese, a town about fifty miles northwest of Accra. Yellow fever was discovered in July 1926, but it had been unreported since deaths began in May. The chief had brought in an expensive fetisher from Togo to combat the epidemic, but this specialist lost credibility when his son, his assistant, and the chief's sister died. Doctors from the government and experts from the Rockefeller Foundation were regarded with hostility and suspicion; they gained some cooperation by treating other diseases, notably by the successful use of injections to cure the large number of yaws victims.[67] The epidemic ended by September, after 100 or more deaths.[68] The Medical Department was embarrassed that yellow fever on this scale had gone undetected for so long so close to Accra. It was now clear that Africans could be vulnerable to yellow fever. People did fear the government enough to conceal cases, but the gloomy conclusion of the Director of the Medical Research Institute that the Asamankese epidemic and a smaller outbreak at Sunhum "appear unique, but the uniqueness probably exists in their being discovered and studied,"[69] is probably exaggerated.

Yellow fever was a dramatic enough disease to attract international attention. The Rockefeller Foundation sent a team on a short visit to West Africa in 1920, and five years later, a larger group was sent out. Their main base was at Yaba, Nigeria, but much work was done in Accra in collaboration with the staff of the Gold Coast Medical Research Institute. The Commission was able to study the 1926-27 outbreak. The vector role of *Ae. aegypti* was clearly proven and, after a series of failures, an experimental animal, the rhesus monkey, was infected in the laboratory with blood from a laborer named Asibi. It was established that the agent, still unknown, must be a virus. The Asibi strain of yellow fever virus was sent to laboratories in other countries and was later used to develop the modern vaccine. However, the research proved dangerous. A scientist died of a laboratory infection in Nigeria in 1927; in 1928, the eminent Japanese-American investigator Hideyo Noguchi died of yellow fever in Accra, almost certainly the result of an infection acquired in the course of his experiments. To compound the tragedy, Dr. W. A. Young of the M.R.I. died of yellow fever a few days later; apparently becoming infected while performing the post-mortem of his colleague. The head of the medical department stopped the work, disinfected the laboratory, and destroyed its contents.[70]

A vaccine to protect researchers was developed a few years later, and by the late 1930s, mass vaccination was feasible. Many Europeans and a few Africans were protected, but, with one exception, large scale prophylaxis was not attempted in Ghana. In 1951, over 330,000 people were vaccinated in the endemic area between Winneba and Akwapim, but the campaign was halted because similar vaccines produced a few encephalitis cases in eastern Nigeria and because of difficulties in supervising the program.[71]

It is probable that medical efforts did prevent some African yellow fever deaths as well as reduce European mortality. However, even if several epidemics of the Asamankese scale were never detected, yellow fever was never a major threat to

African life and well-being. Moreover, with a few exceptions, the disease was restricted to the southern part of the country, especially the region between Accra, Kibi, Oda, and Akuse. The campaign against yellow fever cost the medical department a great deal in terms of African goodwill, and the heavy effort and expenditure could only be justified on the grounds of protecting expatriates.

Dengue fever is, like yellow fever, caused by an arbovirus and the primary vector in Ghana is the same mosquito, *Ae. aegypti.* Victims are often prostrated and frequently suffer from severe pains in bones and joints, hence the popular name "break-bone fever." Uncomplicated dengue is rarely fatal. The disease was first reported in Ghana in 1913 and 1918, and scattered cases were noted in subsequent medical returns.[72] The highest reported incidence was in 1955, when 375 cases were treated, with no deaths. Dengue was "not a disease of any importance,"[73] and, except for an occasional outbreak in a school or institution, such as one in 1933 which affected forty girls at a school in Odumase,[74] it attracted little attention. Measures against *Ae. aegypti* provided town dwellers with incidental protection against dengue, as well as yellow fever. An apparent increase in the 1950s is due to more people seeking treatment, not to a real increase in incidence.

There were no reportssof other arbovirus diseases. Several are now known to exist in West Africa, but their public health importance is still unclear. In the 1930s, some doctors strongly suspected that a "dengue-like" fever was being transmitted in forest areas by midges (*Culicoides*), but this was never confirmed.[75]

Insects also serve as vectors for several species of filarial worms in Ghana. *Wuchereria bancrofti* produces a variety of pathological conditions, sometimes including elephantiasis, but many infections are mild or sub-clinical. Microfilarial stages of the worms are commonly transmitted by bites of mosquitoes of the *Culex pipiens* group, which have, like *Ae. aegypti*, become adapted to urban conditions. These mosquitoes are very common in Accra and other towns.[76] The anopheline vectors of malaria can also transmit bancroftian filariasis.

Unfortunately, there is little data on the incidence of this disease in medical reports. It was said to be common in Navrongo,[77] but the official opinion that it was "not a disease of great importance"[78] is probably correct. Although bancroftian filariasis was frequently lumped under the rubric of "other helminthic infections," elephantiasis, which was regularly listed in the disease returns, was uncommon. Even this condition was under-reported; physicians complained that patients tolerated elephantiasis, waiting until it got very bad before seeking treatment. Table 10a (page 121) shows cases of this disease and other filarial infections treated from 1953-55. The impact of this parasite on public health is unclear, but mosquito control measures doubtlessly reduced its prevalence, at least in major towns.

The most important filarial parasite in Ghana is *Onchocerca volvulus*, a worm transmitted by the bite of the black fly *Simulium damnosum*. Chronic infection produces damage to the skin and eyes and can lead to blindness. Onchocerciasis, or "river blindness," occurs in areas where turbulent streams create proper breeding conditions for the vector. The disease is most prevalent in the north, especially in the valleys of rivers such as the Kulpawn, Sissili, Red Volta, and White Volta, but there are also significant foci in southern Ghana along the lower Volta River. Hyperendemic onchocerciasis has disastrous effects on rural communities; high blindness rates reduce agricultural productivity and force people to abandon valuable farmland near rivers where *S. damnosum* breeds. The economic and social costs of the disease are enormous.[79]

The most remarkable fact about onchocerciasis is that medical officials had no inkling of its significance until well into the 1940s. *O. volvulus* infection was known; indeed, the parasite was first discovered in 1875 in a Ghanaian. However, despite research in Guatemala, the Belgian Congo, and neighboring Upper Volta, doctors in Ghana did not associate the disease with blindness until well into the 1940s. Even as late as the 1930s, knowledge of health conditions in the northern districts was so scanty that the existence of mass blindness was only vaguely suspected. "It is fantastic," wrote the medical officer primarily responsible for the eventual recognition of the significance of the disease, "that blindness on the scale of up to ten per cent of the population in some villages should go unnoticed, or if noticed, disregarded until the 1940's, but that is the plain unvarnished truth."[80] Dr. B. B. Waddy's epidemiological survey of 1949 showed the magnitude of the problem for the first time. Obviously, the medical department did nothing to combat a condition that it did not know existed. Durg therapy had some success after 1950, but vector control has proven difficult. Human mobility in the colonial era probably allowed *O. volvulus* to spread to new areas. On a small scale, new breeding sites for the vector were inadvertently created by construction of dams and bridges.[81]

Little can be said about other forms of filariasis which occur in Ghana *Loa loa* infection was occasionally noted. In 1931, the medical officer at Ho found the parasite in 23 percent of the 515 inmates of the leper colony and in 17 of 100 townspeople examined.[82] Large biting flies of the genus *Chrysops* are vectors. In most cases, the worms seem to do little damage to their hosts, although they can cause eye problems and skin irritations. *Dipetalonema perstans* and *D. streptocerca* are both spread by midges of the genus *Culicoides*. Neither species seems to cause much illness in its victims; the host and parasite are apparently well adapted to each other. *D. streptocerca* was discovered by two members of the Gold Coast Medical Department.[83] A survey of a forest village in 1950 showed that almost 21 percent of the population harbored this parasite. The medical reports are almost silent on *Dipetalonema*, although a 1909 survey did show that 44 out of 94 (47 percent) of people surveyed in an Ashanti village harbored *D. perstans*.[84] Nothing was done to combat these or the more serious filarial infections except for the treatment of a few victims, and the incidental benefits of mosquito control.

Trypanosomiasis was a major medical and veterinary problem. The human pathogen in Ghana is *Trypanosoma brucei gambiense*, a flagellate protozoan closely related to a major cause of bovine disease. Another very similar organism, *T. br. rhodesiense*, causes an acute human disease in eastern and central Africa. The West African or Gambian type of sleeping sickness is a slower-acting disease, but it commonly kills untreated patients within several months to a few years. Flagellates are injected into the bloodstream by the bite of tsetse flies, producing fever and a common diagnostic sign, enlarged cervical glands. Sleeping sickness develops when the parasites and/or their toxins enter the central nervous system, causing gradual decay in mental functions and body coordination, which culminates in extreme listlessness, coma, and death. Diagnosis may be on clinical grounds or by discovery of flagellates during microscopic examinations of blood, gland juice, or of cerebrospinal fluid obtained by lumbar puncture.

The epidemiology of trypanosomiasis is extremely complex, with many local variations. The primary vector of human trypanosomiasis in Ghana is the tsetse fly *Glossina palpalis*; *G. tachinoides* is important in a few places and other species can be involved. In contrast to mosquitoes, both male and female tsetse feed on vertebrate blood and thus both sexes can transmit trypanosomes. *G. palpalis* requires a warm, moist habitat. It is widely distributed in the forests of the south, but in the savanna zone it is mostly restricted to wooded strips along rivers, especially during the long dry season. Humans as well as tsetses congregate near water sources, so man and fly are in much closer contact in the north than in the wetter south, ensuring more efficient transmission of parasites and a higher prevalence of the disease. Outbreaks may be caused by changes in man-fly relationships or by the advent of a new strain of pathogen in an area, whether by genetic mutation or by migration of infected people or flies.[86] Domestic animals, notably cattle and swine, apparently can harbor the flagellate, but the importance, if any, of this possible reservoir of Gambian sleeping sickness is unclear.[87] However, in contrast to the Rhodesian form of the disease, wild animals are not a source of human infection.

Trypanosomiasis is an ancient disease in Ghana. Oral evidence suggests that in the nineteenth century its basic behavior was the same as in the twentieth century, with sporadic cases in the forest zone and sharp but irregular outbreaks in the savanna.[88] There was a major epidemic along the Kamba and Black Volta Rivers in the Lawra area in the 1880s.[89]

The devastating Uganda outbreak of the early 1900s naturally caused alarm in other colonies. By 1903, the cause and vector were known and, despite the belief of the Principal Medical Officer that the disease did not exist in the Gold Coast,[90] the first case was recorded that year and scattered cases detected thereafter.[91] Clinical reports and small scale surveys turned up enough sleeping sickness to warrant a special investigation. Beginning in 1909, Dr. Alan Kinghorn spent a year surveying central Ashanti and portions of Brong-Ahafo. He found only 106 cases out of 18,000 people examined.[92] More disquieting was the finding that people in Gonja were very familiar with the disease and blamed it for the destruction of villages. However, very few infected people could be found there.[93] Three years later, Dr. W. M. Wade completed a thorough survey of Western Ashanti. People were aware of sleeping sickness and attempted to treat it by scarifying or removing enlarged cervical glands, but the disease was rare. Of 39,742 people examined in 196 villages, only 110 (0.2 percent) were infected; many of the victims were migrants from the Northern Territories.[94] Vegetation which sheltered the fly was cleared near some villages, fords, and ferries,[95] but the low incidence of the disease gave little cause for alarm. Further investigations in the north[96] and in the Oda District of the Colony[97] in the mid-1920s revealed very little sleeping sickness. In contrast to Nigeria, human trypanosomiasis was not a serious problem in Ghana in the 1920s.[98]

However, as table 10 (page 120) shows, trypanosomiasis notifications shot up around 1930. At first the increase was attributed to better reporting; the medical department did not see a serious threat.[99] During the next few years, however, it became apparent that there was a major epidemic in the Northern Territories. Although some of the new cases were believed to be attracted by better treatment, clinical measures and clearing operations were stepped up.[100] A number of cases were found in Gonja, although it was not apparent whether the disease was increasing there or not. Oral evidence suggested that there had been an important outbreak in Gonja in 1912-13.[101] By 1932, numerous cases were turning up in South Mamprussi, where surveys showed villages with infection rates as high as 7 percent, 12 percent, and 18 percent. A special field hospital was established at

Nakpanduri in 1933; it treated over 1,000 cases in its first year. In 1934, a new focus was discovered in Tumu District.[102]

Official concern grew. French authorities, troubled by outbreaks in their own colonies, initiated contacts with the Gold Coast and medical experts of the two empires, contrary to general practice, began to exchange epidemiological information.[103] However, the epidemic did not come in time to save the jobs of the government entomologist, A. W. J. Pomeroy,[104] or his assistant, K. R. S. Morris. Both were victims of the depression; despite good records, they were released for reasons of economy in 1931. For four years, until the re-appointment of Morris,[105] the Gold Coast combated the worst sleeping sickness epidemic in its recorded history without an entomologist.

Dr. David Scott, an epidemiologist with extensive experience with trypanosomiasis in Ghana, believes that the country was hit by a great western African epidemic which began in the Congo about 1912. It was well established in Cameroun by the mid-1920s, reached northern Nigeria a couple of years later, and entered Ghana about 1930. The spread of a new strain of trypanosome was probably responsible for the change from a scattered, endemic disease to a major epidemic.[106] The evidence seems to support Scott's hypothesis, although the epidemic in northwestern Ghana had at least partially independent origins. Trypanosomiasis spread in the Lawra-Tumu-Wa area from an old focus in the Black Volta region. K. R. S. Morris, using oral evidence, examinations of ruined villages, and data obtained from French colleagues, has shown that there was a major epidemic late in the nineteenth century along the Black Volta, north of Ghana and in territory adjacent to its western border. Serious depopulation had developed by 1907 in the Cercle de Gaoua, across the river from Lawra District. British territory was also affected, and by 1920-25, trypanosomiasis was advancing up the tributaries of the Black Volta on both sides of the frontier.[107] A number of cases were discovered in Lawra in 1924.[108] Thus, northern Ghana probably suffered from the spread of sleeping sickness from two directions. Two distinct strains of parasite may have been involved. In any case, enhanced mobility certainly facilitated the advance of this disease.

By 1934, the Gold Coast government had become concerned enough to appoint a special committee of medical officials and administrators to study the problem and make recommendations. The committee reported that the situation should not "give rise to undue concern" and was "no cause for panic." Cautious endorsement was given to the medical department's view that much of the apparent rise in incidence was due to better diagnosis and reporting and greater confidence in European medicine.[109] However, there was a growing problem. In 1933, the D.D.M.S., Dr. Selwyn-Clarke, had argued that trypanosomiasis was not a sufficient cause of morbidity and mortality "to justify the diversion of large sums of money in the attempt to eradicate it at the expense of the neglect of other medical services needed by the inhabitants of the Colony and its dependencies as a whole."[110] Both medical and political authorities were more alarmed in 1934.[111] The situation in the Gambaga area of South Mamprussi and in Tumu was menacing, and further survey work was essential. The committee rejected as impractical the French policy of mass prophylaxis of susceptible populations with periodic pentamide injections in favor of searching out and treating victims and the removal of vegetation which provided shelter for tsetse around villages, fords, ferries, and watering places.[112]

A special organization, the Trypanosomiasis Campaign, was created in 1937. The tactics of the director, Dr. G. F. T. Saunders, were basically those recommended in

1935 by the committee. Mobile teams surveyed villages in affected areas, searching for flagellates in blood, gland juice, and, after sufficient staff had been trained for lumbar puncture, more advanced cases were detected by microscopic examination of cerebrospinal fluid. Infected persons were treated with a series of antrypol (suramin) shots; tryparsamide was employed for late cases discovered by lumbar puncture.[113] Serious cases were handled at the special camp at Nakpanduri or in district hospitals.

There were two major tragedies in the course of the anti-trypanosomiasis campaign. In November 1936, 11 out of a group of 14 died shortly after receiving intravenous tryparsamide injections in Bawku.[114] An extensive investigation failed to explain the deaths; the drug may have been prepared erroneously with hot water; or sobita, used to treat yaws, may have been injected by mistake.[115] This disaster did not stop other patients from continuing treatment at the Bawku clinic. In August 1937, eight people died in Navrongo in a similarly unexplained incident.[116]

By late 1937, the epidemic in South Mamprussi was sufficiently under control to allow more systematic attention to the northwestern districts, where hospital returns suggested that the disease was spreading rapidly. K. R. S. Morris, the reinstated medical entomologist, found that the vector was almost entirely restricted to wooded areas along the rivers, except for small populations in sacred groves. These groves were a problem because they were near the villages, often surrounding the only water supply, and had too much religious significance to be summarily destroyed. However, Morris argued that control would be much easier than in Mamprussi. Riverine clearing would be effective, as the absence of tsetse in well-farmed areas showed. Hand catching and digging up pupae could reduce fly populations in the sacred groves. Morris advocated a major campaign in Lawra District.[117]

By 1939, considerable progress was reported in both major foci. In Lawra, a suspicious public had been partially won over by curative work against malaria, yaws, and other endemic diseases. Almost 13,000 people in Lawra and Tumu had been surveyed, and although some villages had infection rates as high as 16 percent, a start had been made. The disease was declining in South Mamprussi, primarily because of extensive clearing of vegetation. Incidence remained low in Kusasi, Zuarungu, and Navrongo Districts.[118] The government was pleased with the progress achieved and approved the emphasis on the travelling survey and treatment teams directed by Saunders. Morris's plan for an experimental selective clearing campaign in Lawra was endorsed and both men were praised for their good attitude toward the population and their ability to work with local Native Authorities.[119] By 1940, the tide had turned, and trypanosomiasis declined over the next fifteen years. Survey, treatment, and clearing were effective, although the virulence of the epidemic was waning as well, so it is impossible to quantify the benefits of control measures.[120]

Morris's selective clearing campaigns, begun on the Kamba River in Lawra District in 1939 and later extended in Lawra and Wa Districts, proved very successful. His basic strategy was to start at the headwaters of a stream and selectively remove plant associations which provided dry season shelter for *G. palpalis*. The plan was cheap, effective, did not destroy forests or clear so much vegetation that soil erosion followed, and was easy to maintain by periodic re-clearing. An integral part of permanent tsetse control was re-colonization of abandoned lands. Settlers were to be taught to keep cattle and became modern mixed farmers by agricultural officers.[121] Tsetse control was designed to improve local conditions, not only by increasing the amount of arable land, but as part of a broader effort to develop animal husbandry and agriculture. Considerable success was achieved in tsetse control and some in agricultural colonization, but the latter was hampered by shortages of agricultural officers and, at least in some areas, by the continuing presence of hyperendemic onchocerciasis.[122]

The anti-trypanosomiasis team was promoted to the status of Department of Tsetse Control in 1949,[123] showing that control of the disease continued to be a major objective. The re-organization was designed to improve coordination between health workers and officials in the Veterinary, Agriculture, and Forestry Departments. The Department, later absorbed into the Medical Field Units, pursued a vigorous policy of clearing, surveys, and mass treatment. As shown in table 10 (page 0000), cases continued to decline. Trypanosomiasis was virtually eliminated in Lawra, Wa, and Tumu Districts,[124] and, despite a small outbreak in the late 1950s, was largely confined to a few small foci in South Mamprussi and other scattered locations in the north.[125] Control of the northern epidemic reduced incidence in Ashanti because fewer of the laborers going south harbored trypanosomes which could infect local tsetse.[126]

The increased mobility which has characterized twentieth century Ghana helped spread trypanosomes and thus introduced the disease into new areas. As was discussed above, trypanosomiasis was no respecter of colonial frontiers. Within the north, the disease spread between socially-linked villages as much as one hundred miles apart.[127] In districts like Navrongo, which had very little sleeping sickness, many cases were imported from Ashanti by returning migrant workers.[128] Conversely, while the disease was associated with rivers in the north because of the habits of the vector, its distribution in Ashanti was linked to the road network. Tsetse were abundant everywhere, but along the roads northerners brought trypanosomes in their blood which could infect the local flies.[129] However, the disease was not nearly so prevalent in central and southern Ghana as it was in parts of the north because there was much less contact between man and fly.[130]

It is obviously impossible to estimate how much improved communications contributed to the trypanosomiasis death toll, or how the disease would have behaved without countermeasures. Trypanosomiasis had long been endemic and could produce devastating epidemics in pre-colonial times, as the nineteenth century Kamba outbreak shows. On the other hand, virtually all of the victims treated by the colonial medical service would have died without modern therapy. Vector control by clearing vegetation (insecticides were not employed during the period under consideration) doubtlessly saved many lives, most notably in the northwest. It is probably safe to say that colonial health measures saved more lives than were lost as an indirect result of changing socio-economic conditions.

Bubonic plague epidemics occurred in Ghana in 1908 and 1924 and, given the significance of plague in European history, caused great alarm. Plague is caused by a bacterium, *Yersinia* (formerly *Pasteurella*) *pestis*, which normally infects wild rodents. The disease is transmitted from rats to humans by the bite of rat fleas. Once established in man, the parasite may be transmitted by flea bites, causing the bubonic form of the disease. Bacteria may also be passed by droplet infection from the lungs of a victim to the lungs of a new host, causing pneumonic plague. Both forms of plague can spread very rapidly and both are extremely lethal. The vast majority of untreated cases are fatal.

Plague was introduced into Ghana on at least two separate occasions when the disease was present elsewhere in West Africa. In early January 1908, doctors in

Accra became aware of a mysterious new disease in the city. After several cases and post-mortem examinations, plague was conclusively diagnosed on January 9. A study of previous deaths showed that the disease had appeared in the city late in 1907.[131] It had doubtlessly been brought in by infected rats which landed in cargoes at the port of Accra.

Many Africans blamed the epidemic on poor sanitation. The *Gold Coast Leader*, a Cape Coast newspaper, noted that many in Accra believed that plague was a form of poisoning. Accra was filthy, and the water supply "execrable."[132] Later, a miasmatic theory was suggested. "As it is the air chiefly that carries this disease about, it is no wonder Accra has been the spot selected for its visit."[133]

However, plague soon spread from the capital. Travellers transmitted the disease along the coast in the pneumonic form; persons attending funerals of victims often became infected themselves. Winneba, Anomabu, and Cape Coast were attacked, and several towns near Accra suffered heavily.[134]

The colonial authorities appealed for expert assistance. Professor W. J. Simpson arrived from England on February 2 to coordinate anti-plague measures and to study the epidemic. He intensified the campaign against rats, with special attention to the slums of the James Town section of Accra.[135] A strong cordon was established around Accra to contain the epidemic. Although this was not entirely effective, it probably did do some good.[136] Patients were isolated and their contacts were kept under observation. Thousands were innoculated with Haffkine's plague vaccine, which probably provided some protection. The epidemic was checked by early April, although there were a number of deaths in May and June and two fatalities in Accra in October. In all, there were 344 reported cases with 300 deaths, more than half of them in Accra.[137] Fortunately, *Y. pestis* did not become established in local rodents, and infected rats were not found outside the capital.[138]

Plague was reported at Tunga, a village in the Northern Territories only a mile from the busy Yeji ferry in July 1913. The Medical Officer at Salaga, F. W. Fraser, isolated victims, burned their houses and clothes, and threw up a police cordon around the village. Between July 29 and August 7, eight out of the eleven victims died, but the disease did not spread beyond Tunga. The village of Kawlaw had supposedly been attacked by the same or a very similar disease about 1911 and had been abandoned.[139] In 1914, plague was suspected in Tunga and Makongo; a new M.O. at Salaga, Dr. Burgess, thought it was not plague but a "septic infection."[140] Indeed, the 1913 outbreak probably was not plague either; symptoms were not given, but Fraser could capture only one rat in Tunga.[141]

Except for scattered cases in Accra and environs and in Axim in 1917-19,[142] plague was absent until a major epidemic developed in 1924 when it was introduced, again by infected rats, at the port of Sekondi. Six cases were seen on March 12 and 13, and the disease spread in the town, especially in the poor districts inhabited by Kru laborers and northern migrants.[143] An anti-rat campaign was started and an unpopular quarantine was set up around the city. Enforcement caused at least one fatality; a woman seeking to cross the cordon was stopped by a guard, who shoved her into a gutter. The fall killed the baby she was carrying on her back. Quarantines were resented because they interfered with commercial and social travel and most Africans doubted their efficacy. Since "contaminated air is productive of disease," some felt that a better approach would be to do something about the stench from drains and latrines.[144] In all, Sekondi had 122 cases and 92 deaths.[145]

Rats conveyed plague up the railroad to Kumasi by the end of March. Dr. Selwyn Selwyn-Clarke, the able M.O.H., led an anti-rat drive, began a massive slum clearance and re-housing effort, and had over 100,000 injections of Haffkine's vaccine administered in Kumasi and nearby towns.[146] The disease was largely confined to the poor, overcrowded Zongo area and nearly all of the cases and deaths were among migrants from the north or from Nigeria.[147] The Kumasi epidemic was over by September, but sporadic cases were discovered for several months afterward. One hundred and sixty-five cases were reported in Kumasi, with 146 deaths.

Other scattered localities also suffered from plague, which was probably spread in pneumonic form by travellers. The worst hit was Tantum, near Winneba, which had twenty-five cases in August, all fatal. On the other hand, there were only two cases in Accra. During 1924 and early 1925, a total of 322 plague victims were recorded in Ghana; of these, 272 died, for a case mortality of over 84 percent.[148]

Plague has not appeared in Ghana since 1925. Rat control efforts continued in the major towns and a sample was routinely examined for *Y. pestis*, but the rat population remained free from infection. The disease reached West Africa, and Ghana, on modern ships and, especially in the case of Kumasi, was disseminated along lines of communication. However, for unknown reasons, the bacterium did not become established in rats or other local rodents. Although the completion of the artificial harbor at Takoradi in 1928 meant that rats could jump directly from ship to wharf instead of having to hide in cargoes transfered from ship to shore in lighters, bubonic plague was not re-introduced. Therapy was ineffective, as the high case mortalities in both epidemics demonstrate. While it is obviously impossible to say what might have happened if the disease had been allowed to run its course, preventive measures were effective and certainly prevented some deaths, and perhaps a catastrophic amount of suffering and death in 1908 and 1924.

Louse-borne relapsing fever was, like plague, introduced into Ghana as a result of modern communications, and was also effectively controlled by the medical service. The agent, a spirochete known as *Borrelia recurrentis*, is transmitted to man by body lice when an infected louse is crushed on the skin and the pathogen is able to penetrate through a cut or abrasion. Tick-borne relapsing fever, caused by a closely related organism, is a serious problem in East Africa,[149] but does not occur in Ghana.

Relapsing fever reached Ghana in 1923 as the result of a general West African epidemic. The disease appeared in Guinea in 1921, introduced by demobilized troops. It spread rapidly across the savanna zone and caused great loss of life, especially in Sudan, which was attacked in 1926.[150] There was an outbreak in Accra in March 1923, the first reported case being an Italian contractor. The epidemic was over in early July, after causing 158 cases and three deaths. Virtually all victims were poor laborers from the north, and 139 cases were in one ethnic group, the Zabarima, who came from French territory along the Niger River. These people lived in great poverty in Accra and were invariably infested with lice.[151] Louse transmission was suspected from the first, and the authorities inspected and disinfected houses, clothes, and people in the heavily affected Tudu and Zongo areas. Cases and their contacts were aggressively sought out. Treatment with intravenous injection of novarsenobillon (N.A.B.) was extremely effective, so the low case mortality rate in Accra was in stark contrast to the heavy death toll in Sudan and Mali. A milder strain of pathogen may well have been involved. Health authorities in Accra did an excellent job containing this new, unfamiliar disease.[152]

The Medical Research Institute conducted a series of experiments to determine the vector. The role of lice was positively established by the Director, Dr. A. Ingram, who contracted the disease in the course of his research.[153]

Accra was almost certainly infected by Zabarima migrants who had walked hundreds of miles to the city to seek work. It is highly likely that they introduced the disease in Kumasi and at other points along their route, but no other foci were detected. This is probably because victims did not seek medical aid and because Accra had the only laboratory where a positive diagnosis could be made, not because relapsing fever was entirely restricted to the capital.[154]

There were a few confirmed cases in Accra and in mining camps in 1926 and about 100 cases in Kumasi the next year, again mostly in Zabarima migrants. Treatment of victims plus disinfection of the residents of the Zongo and of unemployed laborers rounded up in police sweeps of the markets contained the outbreak.[155] As table 10 (page 120) shows, there was another epidemic in 1929-31, with migrants in Accra and Kumasi again the primary victims. Many cases must have gone undetected, as the disease afflicted a segment of the population which was unlikely to seek medical assistance. To prevent further outbreaks, a de-lousing station was created on the road just north of Kumasi in 1931; 18,345 migrants were bathed, shaved, and had their clothes disinfected before being allowed to procede south.[156] Another station was established at the junction of the Savelugu and Karaga roads in 1932.[157]

Relapsing fever has almost disappeared from the country since the early 1930s. One reason for this is the effectiveness of control measures, but cultural factors are much more important. The disease is restricted to lousy populations; in Ghana, it was almost entirely confined to the Zabarimas and other migrants from the interior. These people lived in crowded, filthy conditions in urban slums. More importantly, perhaps because they came from a region with limited water supplies, they did not keep themselves or their clothes clean. Indigenous peoples had high standards of personal cleanliness, adequate water, and, because of the humid climate, wore fewer clothes. They seldom had lice and, hence, relapsing fever was unable to progress beyond a small group of socially marginal and fairly easily controlled foreigners.[158]

The sudden appearance of relapsing fever naturally caused fears that louse-borne epidemic typhus would also be brought into Ghana by labor migrants,[159] but fortunately, this has not happened, at least not on any scale. Tick-borne typhus, a relatively mild disease, was first recorded in 1936,[160] and sporadic cases have been described since then,[161] but it does not seem to be of much importance in Ghana.

Insect-vectored diseases were, and continue to be, among the major public health problems in Ghana. Climatic conditions are favorable for an abundance of insects, including those which transmit pathogenic viruses, bacteria, and helminths. Faster transportation and greater mobility spread indigenous diseases, disseminated new strains to susceptible populations, and made it possible for two new diseases, plague and relapsing fever, to enter the country. However, due to medical measures and to natural and cultural factors, neither plague nor relapsing fever became established. Vector control was hampered by the lack of persistent insecticides until after 1945, but efforts to control the breeding of domestic mosquitoes reduced, at least in some of the large towns, three minor causes of morbidity and mortality: yellow fever, dengue fever, and bancroftian filariasis. Control of the vector of trypanosomiasis was achieved in parts of the north by clearing vegetation, without resort to the elaborate resettlement and game eradication programs tried against the *rhodesiense* form of the disease in Tanganyika and Rhodesia. The vector of onchocerciasis was ignored, because nobody in Ghana realized how serious the problem was until the late 1940s.

The impact of therapy was, like that of vector control, limited. By the early 1920s, effective treatment was available for relapsing fever and trypanosomiasis, and, of course, malaria. The Gold Coast authorities chose not to follow the mass chemical prophylaxis tactics developed by the French in Cameroun and Equatorial Africa, but treatment of victims did reduce the trypanosome population, thus reducing the transmission of trypanosomiasis to some extent as well as saving the lives of thousands of patients. Malaria was one of the most common reasons for people to seek medical treatment. Therapy saved thousands of lives and reduced suffering for hundreds of thousands, but had little impact on the prevalence of the disease. In 1955, malaria remained almost as serious a cause of sickness and death as it had been in 1900, a fact which greatly weakens the colonial government's otherwise fairly commendable record against insect-vectored diseases. This is hardly surprising, considering that malaria is still hyperendemic in tropical Africa, despite World Health Organization programs and far superior financial and technical resources. Indeed, it is unlikely that any colonial government had substantial success against malaria, except perhaps in small, specially targeted areas and in arid regions with limited surface water for mosquito breeding.

4

DISEASES SPREAD IN CONTAMINATED WATER, FOOD, AND SOIL

Poor sanitation and a warm, moist climate provide excellent conditions for the transmission of pathogenic organisms which are ingested or which penetrate the skin from soil or water. In almost every instance, the diseases described in this chapter result from contamination of the environment by the improper disposal of human wastes. As with the insect-vectored diseases, prevention conveys greater public health benefits than clinical medicine. Adequate sewage disposal and safe water were, and remain, prerequisites for relief from a host of epidemic and endemic conditions which endanger the health of Ghanaians.

Dysentery and diarrhea were common throughout Ghana. There is no hard and fast distinction between the two conditions. Dysentery involves inflammation of the lower bowel and sometimes the passage of blood, and diarrhea the frequent passage of loose stools; diagnosis was doubtlessly inconsistent in many cases. The hospital data in table 11 (page 122) grossly underestimate actual incidence, as relatively few people sought treatment. Both syndromes have multiple etiologies and, except for amebic dysentery, treatment was generally symptomatic rather than specific.

Several species of intestinal protozoa can cause dysentery, but most cases result from infection with an ameba, *Entamoeba histolytica*, or with bacteria of the genus *Shigella*. The severity of amebic dysentery varies from asymptomatic and apparently harmless infections to lethal damage to the bowel. Dangerous complications can occur if amebas gain access to other organs, notably abcesses of the liver. Persons harboring *E. histolytica* excrete cysts in their feces which are infective for new victims when ingested. Polluted water and uncooked foods, such as lettuce or tomatoes grown with nightsoil as fertilizer, may contain cysts. Cysts can also be transmitted by food handlers with poor personal hygiene, and flies and roaches may carry cysts from feces to food or water. All of these modes of transmission were common in Ghana.[1]

Amebic dysentery was a continuing problem throughout the period. As will be discussed later, sanitary improvements and piped water supplies reduced the chance of infection in some areas, notably in the larger towns, but such changes were less common in rural areas, and amebic dysentery was probably more common in the countryside than in the cities.[2] Effective therapy with emetine was employed from early in the twentieth century, so case-mortality for amebic dysentery was much lower than for the bacillary form.[3] Therapy, however, reached comparatively few people. Prevention and treatment had little overall effect, except for a few individuals and localities. Since strains of *E. histolytica* vary in infectivity and virulence,[4] increased intercommunication probably worsened the situation by dispersing local strains around the country, thus exposing populations to unfamiliar strains against which they had fewer immunological defenses.

Bacillary dysentery was less common but, at least until the availability of sulpha drugs in the later 1930s, more deadly. Modes of transmission, and hence appropriate preventive measures, are similar to those for amebic dysentery. Several species and strains of *Shigella* are found in Ghana.[5] Doubtlessly both international and local travel introduced new varieties to susceptible populations.

Diarrhea was a frequent complain at colonial hospitals and clinics. However, because such a tiny percentage of cases were reported and because the syndrome can be caused by so many types of infectious and non-infectious diseases, detailed analysis is pointless. As with dysentery, poor sewage disposal and contaminated food and water were responsible for much morbidity. The continuing high death toll from intestinal infections in cities is shown in table 40 (page 152). The special problem of infantile diarrhea will be discussed in chapter 7.

Typhoid fever and paratyphoid fever were lumped together under the rubric "enteric" until 1926. Table 11 (page 122) shows hospital returns for this diseases; again, relatively few cases were known to the medical department.[6] *Salmonella typhi*, the agent of typhoid, is generally spread by water contaminated with human wastes, either directly or by flies. Food is a less frequent source of infection, but asymptomatic human carriers can also disseminate the disease, especially when they work as food handlers. *S. paratyphi*, which causes paratyphoid fever, may be spread by water or by human carriers, but the organism is usually contracted in food. Case mortality was high until the advent of antibiotics after 1945. A reasonably effective vaccine was used by many Europeans by the late 1920s, but few Africans received it.[7]

Cholera did not occur in Ghana during the period under consideration. The introduction of the disease was feared, especially with the influx of Levantines and Indians and the poor sanitary conditions of the colony,[8] but it did not appear until November 1970, when the most recent pandemic reached the country.[9] Cholera was still present in late 1977. The previous absence of this dreaded disease was not due to anything done by the colonial authorities, but simply a matter of luck.

Poliomyelitis is caused by a virus which is usually acquired from fecally contaminated water, food, or objects. In underdeveloped countries, acute, paralytic cases are rare because most small children acquire mild or sub-clinical infections which convey immunity. Infection commonly is delayed until late childhood or adolescence in countries with high sanitary standards. Severe cases involving temporary or permanent paralysis are more likely to develop in older children. In Europe and North America, paralytic polio is a disease whose incidence was a function of technological change. It rose during the public health revolution of the nineteenth century, when improved water and sewer systems reduced the chances for early infection. Viruses were not, however, totally eliminated, so when infection came, it frequently affected older persons who developed diagnosable symptoms. The disease declined rapidly after the development of effective vaccines in the mid-1950s.[10] Only scattered cases of "acute poliomyelitis" (see table 12, page 000) were reported in Ghana during the period under consideration, and it probably was rare then, given the low level of sanitation and the presumed ubiquity of mild early infections. Notifications rose after 1948, perhaps reflecting a real increase in incidence and, indirectly, advances in sanitation. The vast majority of cases in 1953 and 1954 were in large towns with piped water supplies.[11] By the 1950s, the importance of poliomyelitis may have been much greater than generally suspected.[12] Prevention was impossible before the discovery of vaccines, and treatment was difficult, so little was (or could have been) done to combat the disease.

Dracontiasis, or infection with guinea worm (*Dracunculus medinensis*), is a serious cause of disability in many localities in Ghana. It is acquired by drinking water which contains infected minute crustaceans of the genus *Cyclops*, which are intermediate hosts in the parasites' complex life cycle. Larval worms are liberated when the crustacean is digested and migrate to the connective tissues, where they develop for several months or longer. Mature gravid females migrate to the body surface, usually on the foot, ankle, or lower leg, where they produce irritating lesions. When the victim bathes the affected area, or wades in water (as, for example, when getting household water supplies), the worm penetrates to the surface and releases larvae. The wound may be kept open for days, allowing repeated release of offspring. The adult female soon dies; the cycle is continued if the larvae are eaten by an appropriate crustacean. Thus, unlike most diseases discussed in this chapter, guinea worm transmission is not dependent on improper disposal of human wastes. The distribution of dracontiasis is spotty; there are infested water sources scattered all over Ghana. Incidence is especially high in parts of the north where people may have little choice about where they get their water during the dry season.

Guinea worm is not a killing disease, but dead or dying worms can cause severe local damage in the host's tissues. Toxins produced when the gravid worm erupts produce nausea, diarrhea, and other symptoms. More importantly, lesions may be infected with various bacteria, which frequently cause serious complications. The traditional African remedy, employed at least as early as the seventeenth century, was to try to remove adult worms by gradually winding them up on a stick.[13] Extraction took days and acute sepsis resulted if the worm was broken. Guinea worm is a common cause of disability and a sufferer may be crippled for months or even years. In 1955, it was estimated that in the Northern Territories, 10,000 adults were completely disabled during the farming season every year, and another 90,000 were partially disabled out of a population of some 800,000. In an area of the south, it was described as the "major preventable cause of agricultural work loss."[14]

The seriousness of dracontiasis and its mode of transmission were understood early in the century. Infection was common in Accra before the introduction of piped water, because people had to wade into contaminated ponds to fill vessels with water.[15] By 1911, it was recognized that guinea worm was most frequently contracted during the dry season, when water sources were scarcer.[16] It was described as "almost universal" in parts of the north;[17] policemen and soldiers, many of whom were northerners, were frequent victims.[18] High incidences were reported in parts of mandated Togo[19] and elsewhere throughout the entire colony. Official figures do not give an accurate indication of prevalence or the amount of invalidism produced because few Africans sought aid until large, ulcerated lesions developed.[20]

Attempts were made to stop transmission by improving water supplies and by killing the crustacean intermediate hosts. The best preventive was piped water, which eliminated the problem in Accra,[21] and, later, in other large towns. Improved wells protected some rural villages.[22] Efforts to eliminate *Cyclops* were less successful. Trials were made with chlorinated lime[23] and DDT,[24] but neither method proved practical.

Therapy is still unsatisfactory today. Experiments with intravenous injections of tartar emetic were conducted in the early 1920s in Accra,[25] Winneba, Keta,[26] and Yendi.[27] Initial results were encouraging, but it became obvious in a few years that the technique was not very helpful.[28] Medical aid was useful in treating external lesions and secondary infections, but only a small percentage of sufferers sought assistance.

Thus, little was or could be done to combat this disease in the absence of funds sufficient to provide adequate wells in rural areas so people would not have to immerse their legs in the drinking water supply. Indeed, greater travel opportunities helped spread the worm. Africans were well aware that some bodies of water were contaminated and tried to avoid them.[29] They often linked outbreaks to the arrival of an infected stranger.[30]

Studies done in the 1950s showed the continued importance of dracontiasis. In one forest village, over half of the 257 inhabitants had a history of the disease.[31] Surveys of northern and Ashanti villages showed average infection rates of slightly under 1 percent; many villages were totally unaffected; others had 10-20 percent prevalence rates.[32] In ten villages in the Mo area of Brong-Ahafo, almost one-fourth of the people had guinea worm.[33] The disease was still a major public health problem which deserved high priority attention.[34]

Numerous other helminths have weakened and killed Ghanaians during the twentieth century. The significance of some of these parasites has been vaguely understood for decades, but helminthic diseases have attracted relatively little attention from medical workers because symptoms are often ill-defined, because they usually cause chronic sickness rather than sudden death, and because they do not occur in spectacular epidemics. As with many other diseases, relatively few patients were treated, and hospital records shed little light on the actual prevalence of helminthic infections or the burden they imposed on human well-being. Another problem is that clinical returns from 1939 to 1952 list only schistosomiasis and ancylostomiasis separately; a residual category of "other helminthic diseases" lumps the rest. Clinical returns for helminthic diseases are given in table 13 (page 124) and table 14 (page 125).

Three species of worms transmitted in raw or poorly cooked meat should be noted. Trichinosis, acquired from pork, is caused by the roundworm *Trichinella spiralis*. The greatest number of cases, sixty-eight, was recorded in 1927-28; only a handful were reported in most years. Trichinosis was probably not very common in Ghana, but since it is difficult to diagnose, physicians doubtlessly missed many cases. The pork tapeworm, *Taenia solium*, and the beef tapeworm, *T. saginata*, were especially common in the north, notably in Tamale and in Lawra and Zuarungu Districts.[35] Transmission was encouraged by shortages of firewood, which prevented adequate cooking of meat.[36] Cattle and swine become infected by eating human feces which contain eggs; people acquire the worms when they ingest larval forms in the muscles of these animals. Thus, tapeworm transmission can be halted by sanitary disposal of excrement and by meat inspection in slaughterhouses. The inspection of municipal slaughterhouses and condemnation of diseased carcasses reduced the prevalence of taeniasis in major towns. Clinical records do not distinguish between the two species, but the beef tapeworm was reportedly much more common.[37]

Pinworm infection was not diagnosed very frequently, although 194 cases were treated in 1937. The parasite, *Enterobius vermicularis*, is acquired by ingesting eggs from fingers or other objects contaminated with feces or, especially in crowded conditions, from the air. *E. vermicularis* produces annoying perianal itching, but rarely causes serious disease. Laboratory analysis of 5,326 stool specimens obtained from hospital patients in 1911-1914 showed 174 (3.3 percent) infected with this parasite.[38]

Soil-transmitted helminths were very important in Ghana. Eggs of several pathogenic worms reach the soil in human feces and undergo developmental changes there which make them infectious for man. Two common species, *Trichuris trichiura* and *Ascaris lumbricoides* are acquired by swallowing embryonated eggs. Larvae of the hookworm, *Nector americanus*, and of *Strongyloides stercoralis* burrow into unprotected skin, especially the soles of the feet.

The whipworm, *T. trichiura*, is often found in children, who play in the dirt and transfer mature eggs to their mouths on their fingers and other objects. Heavy infestations can cause diarrhea, anemia, serious damage to the intestinal mucosa, and other pathological conditions. Prior to 1939, when the disease disappears from the condensed disease returns, only scattered cases were reported, and in some years, none at all. Whipworm infection was not uncommon; in 1911-14, 544 out of 5,326 persons surveyed (10.2 percent) were infected,[39] although in 1950 only 8 out of 240 people (3.3 percent) surveyed in a forest village harbored the parasite.[40]

Ascariasis was a much more serious problem. Ascaris infection was more widespread and caused more ill-health than any other helminth, including hookworm and schistosomiasis. Its effects were much less dramatic than those of onchocerciasis, but that disease is restricted by the requirements of its vector to a few specific areas, mostly in the far north. *Ascaris lumbricoides* was found everywhere; infection was common in adults and "almost universal" in children.[41] Worms are acquired by the accidental ingestion of embryonated eggs from soil contaminated with feces or from contaminated food, water, fingers, toys, or other objects. *A. lumbricoides* goes through a remarkable series of movements within the host's body. Larvae leave the eggs in the small intestine and burrow out into blood vessels which take them to the liver and thence to the heart. From there they go to the lungs, penetrate the alveolar sacs, ascend the bronchi and trachea to the mouth, where they are swallowed, return to the small intestine, develop into adults, and produce eggs. The whole process takes two to three months. Larvae cause tissue damage during their migrations, especially in the lungs, and may end up in the brain, kidney, spleen, or other organs. The adult worms compete with the host for food, produce toxins with a wide range of effects, and masses of worms may block the bowel. Cases range in severity from inapparent to lethal and a wide range of symptoms may be present.

Ascaris is especially serious in young children, who often get their first infections when they learn to crawl.[42] Most cases were only discovered when the patient sought help for some other condition;[43] some medical officers routinely treated all children admitted to hospitals for ascariasis.[44] Unlike hookworm, wrote one medical administrator,

> Ascaris causes very extensive morbidity in children and a very definite mortality. It is perhaps one of the largest factors in infant mortality as an associate of malaria and a precursor of respiratory disease. The figures given in this report give only a faint indication of its prevalence for it is rarely the sole condition for which treatment is sought.[45]

As the data in table 14 (page 125) show, treatment helped a few people and could have had no impact on the total community worm load. Ascaris remained a serious problem, and, despite its known importance, received little attention. In 1950, stool examinations showed that 88 out of 511 schoolchildren (17.2 percent) in southern Togo and 182 out of 240 people in a forest village (75.8 percent)[46] harbored egg-producing adult worms.

Hookworm disease, ancylostomiasis, received more study than most other helminthic infection in Ghana, but the medical department still knew little about its distribution or consequences for public health. Larval forms of the parasite, *Necator americanus*, develop in the soil from eggs deposited in feces. They enter a new host by penetrating the skin, generally on the foot, and are transported in the blood to the lungs, where, like ascaris, they break out into the air sacs, ascend the respiratory tree to the mouth, and are swallowed. They pass to the small intestine and attach to its wall, where they suck blood and develop into adults. Migrating larvae damage lung tissues, while adults cause mechanical damage to the intestine and may consume enough blood to cause severe anemia. Many infestations produce few or no clinical symptoms, but in some cases, depending on the number of worms and the general health and nutritional state of the host, severe disease results.

The hookworm campaigns of the Rockefeller Foundation in the southern United States from 1909-1914, later extended to several tropical countries, helped stimulate interest in the disease. Ancylostomiasis was first recorded in Ghana in 1905; three years later, a Basel mission doctor reported that it was common in Aburi.[47] Surveys of hundreds of prisoners and hospital patients in 1911, 1912, and 1913 revealed prevalence rates of 7.4 percent, 4 percent, and 13.3 percent respectively.[48] The Colonial Office requested further information on hookworm infection in the Gold Coast in 1913. In response, workers in the gold mines were surveyed, and the mine doctors and the head of the medical service agreed that the problem was not at all serious.[49] In addition, Dr. G. H. H. Le Fanu was sent to investigate reports from another Basel Mission doctor that hookworm was widespread in Akwapim.[50] Le Fanu discovered that obtaining specimens was "a matter of some delicacy," perhaps because of fears of sorcery, but seventy-seven people eventually contributed stool samples for examination. *N. americanus* eggs were found in twenty-eight (38.6 percent); *Ascaris* and *T. trichiura* were also detected. The only solution was improved sanitation; since feces were "deposited at random," re-infection would negate the value of therapy. Le Fanu also observed that none of the four Africans he examined who wore shoes were infected.[51]

In 1920, another circular dispatch from London promoted a new, if somewhat vague, report on ancylostomiasis in the Gold Coast. Local physicians believed that hookworm was common in some coastal areas such as Saltpond, Keta, Ada, and especially Axim, where the M.O. estimated that 80 percent of the population was infected. It was rare in Accra, Cape Coast, and Kumasi. Other than that, little could be said because accurate data was lacking and, except for Le Fanu's 1914 work, no special study had been made.[52] Not much was done after 1920 to clarify the picture. Annual reports generally noted that the parasite was common, especially at Axim, but that severe anemia seemed rare.[53] Hospital figures were low, but recognized to be "of little value" as routine exams showed high rates of infection.[54] It seemed most common in places with sandy soils favorable to larval development and was very widespread in Southern Mamprussi. Underground workers in mines with poor sanitary facilities were frequently infected. Like malaria, hookworm probably produced widespread debility. Simple sanitary pit latrines for all villages in the country were a high-priority need; "the general good resulting would be incalculable."[55] In 1945, the Director of Medical Services urged that a special study be made. Pointing out that 251 out of 701 (35.6 percent) stool specimens examined in Koforidua were positive, he asked, unsuccessfully, for special staff to conduct a general survey.[56] In 1950, 125 out of 240 people in a forest village (52 percent) had eggs in their feces; 130 of 511 schoolchildren in southern Togo (25.4 percent) were infected.[57]

Therapeutic measures had no impact on the incidence of ancylostomiasis; as with ascaris, few people were treated and conditions for re-infection remained excellent, except in large towns and some villages, where sanitary disposal of excrement was practiced. Increasing use of footwear was also helpful.

Strongyloides stercoralis, a worm whose mode of transmission is similar to that of the hookworm, is also found in Ghana. This organism can produce serious, sometimes fatal, disease, but it is apparently not very common. Seventy-eight cases were recorded in 1928-29; figures were much lower in most years.

Schistosomiasis (or bilharzia) is another helminthic disease which was known to be widespread and a potentially serious menace to health quite early in the century, but which received little clinical or investigative attention for most of the colonial period. However, in contrast to hookworm, several important studies of schistosomiasis were made in 1952-55 and in subsequent years. There are two distinct forms of schistosomiasis in Ghana. The most common is urinary schistosomiasis, caused by *Schistosoma haematobium*; *S. mansoni* is the agent of the intestinal variety of the disease. Both species have complex life cycles which require certain species of fresh water snails as intermediate hosts. People become infected when the free-living larval forms penetrate the skin while they wade, bathe, wash clothes, or play in contaminated waters. *S. haematobium* inhabits veins near the urinary bladder. Its spined eggs pass out through the wall of the bladder, causing cumulative damage to that structure, and are excreted in the urine. If the host urinates into water containing the proper species of snail (primarily *Bulinus globosus* in Ghana),[58] the life cycle can be completed. *S. mansoni* colonizes the veins of the large intestine. Its eggs penetrate the gut wall, causing tissue damage, and are voided with the feces. Defecation into water enables the larval schistosomes to reach the snail which serves as their intermediate host (*Biomphalaria pfeifferi gaudi* in Ghana).[59] Both parasites can produce infections which range in severity from inapparent to fatal, and a wide variety of symptoms. Long-standing *S. haematobium* infection may be a predisposing factor in cancer of the urinary tract.

S. haematobium disease was reported in Ghana as early as 1895; *S. mansoni* was described in 1920, only a few years after it was first recognized as a separate species.[60] A colonial physician, J. W. S. Macfie, experimented with possible local snail vectors as early as 1915,[61] the same year that the life cycle of *S. haematobium* was completely worked out.[62] Dr. A. Ingram, of the Medical Research Institute, also studied local vectors in the early 1920s.[63] There were experiments with tartar emetic injections as a possible cure, but without success.[64]

After this early spurt of activity, little was done for thirty years. Schistosomiasis was known to be common near Winneba and along the lower Volta;[65] important foci were later found in Bawku[66] and Zuarungu[67] districts in the Northern Territories. The disease was repeatedly acknowledged to be "commoner than supposed,"[68] and the cause of considerable ill health,[69] but few sought treatment. The urinary form of the disease was confused with gonorrhea by many Africans.[70] In the early 1950s, the newly constituted Medical Field Units conducted mass surveys in parts of Ashanti and the north. Examination of school children showed variable but frequently very high rates of infection, ranging from around 2 percent in some Ashanti towns to over 40 percent in Zuarungu and Bawku and over 50 percent in part of Brong-Ahafo.[71] Plans for the Volta Dam project and related irrigation works made systematic study essential, and a major investigation was begun in 1952.[72] Important foci of *S. haematobium* were found in northeastern Ghana, in a large area northeast of Accra, near the mouth of the Volta, and in scattered localities elsewhere in the country.[73] In Accra, 2.1 percent of persons autopsied had urinary tract damage caused by this parasite.[74] *S. mansoni* was much less common and was apparently restricted to a few small areas, such as Tarkwa and foci in Ashanti and the northeast.[75] Distribution of the disease was limited by the ranges of the snail hosts. Schistosomiasis clearly was "a major public health problem."[76]

Nothing was done by the colonial authorities to reduce the impact of schistosomiasis. As with other diseases discussed in this chapter, therapy reached only a tiny minority of patients. No effort was made to reduce transmission by either mass treatment or by eliminating snails, although, if the example of control measures in Egypt is applicable, neither policy would have had much lasting success.[77] Sanitary improvements probably had only a marginal impact. It is virtually certain that increased mobility allowed persons suffering from schistosomes to transmit the parasites to snail populations in previously uninfected areas. As the experiences of Egypt and the Sudan amply demonstrate, water resource development and irrigation projects are often responsible for spreading snail vectors and hence the disease,[78] but, since not much work was done along these lines in Ghana during the colonial period, this had little effect.

Specific clinical measures did almost nothing to alleviate the overall burden of the diseases spread in contaminated food, water, or soil. Incidence and distribution data are particularly deficient for the diseases in this group. Many individuals were saved from suffering and death, but only a small proportion of victims sought medical aid. More importantly, little headway was made in correcting the conditions which facilitated transmission. Adequate waste disposal and safe water supplies were massive problems which could not be confronted on a national scale without public cooperation and massive expenditure. It is not surprising that what progress was achieved was local, slow, and sometimes ephemeral.

Much more was done to improve sanitary conditions in urban areas than in the countryside. Public latrines were constructed in all the larger towns, and people who failed to use them were liable to fines. The pan latrine system was generally used, with septic tanks being introduced in some areas after the mid-1930s. Pans were collected daily and the excrement was dumped into the sea or buried. Piped water supplies were first introduced in 1914, when Accra's system began to function. Sekondi followed in 1917, Winneba in 1921, Cape Coast in 1928, Tamale in 1932, and Kumasi in 1934. By 1939, Saltpond, Elmina, and Koforidua had been added to the list.[79] Service was generally to public standpipes, but individuals could contract for connections into their homes if they wished to pay water rates. The public considered free water a right; attempts to levy a rate on water from communal taps met vigorous, although ultimately unsuccessful, African opposition.[80] Gradually, sanitary progress was also made in smaller towns, as in Larteh and communities in Ahafo.[81] Urban public health measures and attempts to provide adequate facilities for the growing towns, described in more detail elsewhere,[82] successfully reduced the incidences of many diseases associated with poor water and fecal contamination.

Conditions varied so greatly in rural areas that generalizations are difficult. At any given time and in any major region of the country, some villages were described as clean, with well-patronized pit latrines and good wells or springs, while neighboring villages might be filthy, with promiscuous defecation and urination, especially by children, and grossly polluted water supplies. For example, in Ashanti, medical and political officers tried to improve the sanitary situations by persuasion, coercion, and government assistance.[83] Chiefs and the general public were often eager for improvements,[84] and by 1921, village sanitation was "as a rule satisfactory,"[85] at least in parts of the region. In many villages in Western Ashanti, however, sanitation was virtually nil. The people obeyed orders to build latrines, but did not always use them. The impending arrival of a touring doctor stimulated hasty but temporary cleanups.[86] Moreover, even in the more cooperative areas, progress was not always permanent. In much of Ashanti, where sanitary conditions were considered better than in the cColony, a decline became evident during the depression because the chiefs could not afford to hire sanitation workers.[87] Local advances were reported in the Yendi and Ho areas of Togo,[88] but, observed one official, "progress is slow."[89] Conditions in the north ranged from "disgustingly dirty" in Gonja and Tallensi country to quite clean in villages near Tamale.[90] Primary responsibility for rural sanitation in the north was turned over to Native Authorities in 1935;[91] later claims of "great progress" under indirect rule were probably exaggerated.[92] Perhaps more representative of actual conditions was the complaint of the Senior Health Officer of the Western Province of the Colony that sanitary conditions were "most appalling" and that substantial improvement was unlikely. "It is heart-breaking work against an impassable barrier of indifference and open hostility."[93] The evidence is scattered and contradictory, but it is safe to conclude that overall advances in rural sanitation were incremental and erratic and that wide local variations did and do exist.

Not surprisingly, improvement of rural water supplies was also slow and irregular. While most emphasis was, understandably, placed on the towns, many wells were dug in rural areas by local administrators.[94] A few villages near large towns were connected to piped water supplies. In many places, such as in Ho District, water was inadequate in both quantity and quality; Africans complained frequently, and in the mid-1940s, the government bored many wells there.[95] Water was often scarce in the north, especially during the long dry season. Governor Alan Burns was horrified to discover during his 1946 tour of the north that women in the Yendi area had to walk as far as 4.5 miles from their homes to reach a watering place. Everywhere he went, chiefs and people begged for wells. "It is impossible to realize the seriousness of the situation," he wrote, "until one has visited the Northern Territories at the end of the dry season." Governor Burns had already been concerned about rural water supplies and had, despite wartime shortages, created a Temporary Water Supply Department in 1943. This agency, although hampered by lack of staff and supplies, had managed to complete 53 wells and seven dams by the time of the governor's tour, and had an equal number in progress. In addition, Native Authorities had over 1,000 projects in various stages of planning or completion. Despite these efforts, the situation in the north remained "desperate."[96]

By the early 1940s, colonial government had made a major committment to improve rural water supplies and, especially after 1945, many localities did get safe, ample, and convenient water.[97] However, the majority of the population received little or no benefit. In 1952, the government knew that wholesome water was still "one of the most urgent public health needs throughout the Gold Coast and in the

Northern Territories possibly the most urgent."[98] As late as the early 1970s, it was estimated that only 34 percent of the population had ready access to potable water.[99]

It is not really surprising that limited headway was made against the diseases transmitted by improper disposal of human wastes and by contaminated water. The medical authorities knew little about the incidence, distribution, and severity of most of them. Even if effective therapy had been readily available to the bulk of the population, curative measures alone would have been insufficient because of continuing re-infection. Prevention was essential, but this was impossible without fundamental changes in living standards and popular attitudes. Education and massive investments in facilities and staff were required over a long period of time, but governmental priorities, fiscal constraints, public indifference, and the sheer magnitude of the problems were barriers not easily overcome. Some real advances were made; they cannot be measured, but it is obvious that, on a national scale, both sanitation and water supplies were glaringly inadequate at the end of the colonial period. Ghana's situation was and is typical; few, if any, other African countries fared significantly better.

5

DISEASES TRANSMITTED BY THE RESPIRATORY ROUTE

Many important diseases are acquired by inhaling the pathogen into the respiratory tract on aerial droplets or dust. Pneumonia, tuberculosis, and cerebrospinal meningitis are important bacterial diseases spread in this manner, and acute viral diseases like influenza, smallpox, and measles are transmitted by the same respiratory route. Bacteria or virus may be shed by persons with clinical disease, or, in some cases, by healthy carriers who harbor the microorganisms but are not sick. In contrast to diseases with an insect vector or those spread by fecal contamination, there are no obvious measures to interrupt transmission of these conditions. Reduced crowding and improved ventilation of houses are often helpful, as are prompt isolation and treatment of victims, but artificial immunization is often the only effective means of control.

Pneumonia was one of the most common causes of death in colonial Ghana. The disease can be caused by a mycoplasma or by any of several bacteria and viruses, but the most common agent is *Diplococcus* (*Streptococcus*) *pneumoniae*. *D. pneumoniae* (and some other agents) are frequently found as inhabitants of the upper respiratory tract, where they apparently do no harm. Pneumonia generally develops when the host has become debilitated or has been weakened by a viral or other infection. Colds and minor upper respiratory tract infections often precede pneumonia. *D. pneumoniae* and other pathogens have many strains, which vary greatly in virulence.

Pneumonia cases were most frequent in Ghana during the first months of the year, especially when there was a strong harmattan[1] or after a mild "flu" outbreak.[2] Mortality was highest in males in the 25-45 year age group, particularly poor migrant workers in towns and in the mines, and among the very young, who were often weakened by malaria and worms. Fulminating cases, with death occurring in a matter of hours, were frequently noted.[3] Effective therapy was possible by late 1938, when sulpha drugs were first employed.[4] This advance was responsible for the dramatic decline in case mortality shown in table 15 (page 126). A further decline is evident after 1945, when penicillin was used to treat pneumonia.[5] The success of curative medicine is also indicated by the fall of the percentage of registered deaths from pneumonia and bronchitis from 13.6 percent in 1935 to 6.0 percent in 1941,[6] although, as table 40 (page 152) shows, they were always among the leading causes of death in urban areas with vital registration. In the absence of a vaccine, nothing specific could be done to prevent pneumonia.

Bronchitis grades into pneumonia, and diagnosis of the two conditions can be arbitrary. Both diseases are caused by a similar array of pathogens. Bronchitis was common, but (as is shown in table 16, page 127) case-mortality was very low and fell even further with the advent of sulpha drugs and antibiotics.

Influenza, an acute viral infection of the upper respiratory tract, was a common cause of sickness, but rarely of death, except in 1918-1919. During that great pandemic, a virulent strain of virus caused millions of deaths in Africa, both directly and as a precursor to severe pneumonia. The pandemic reached Ghana by sea and overland from Upper Volta and swept over the entire country between September 1918 and January 1919. Quarantines were tried, but there was no way to stop influenza. Therapy was also ineffectual; there still is no drug for the virus, and bacterial pneumonias were difficult to treat at the time. The political and medical arms of the colonial administration were, like governments around the world. powerless in the face of epidemic influenza. At least 80,000 to 100,000 people, roughly four percent of the population, died in the worst single demographic disaster in the recorded history of Ghana.[7]

Influenza struck hard only once, but tuberculosis was, year after year, a leading cause of death and a constant source of concern to the medical department. Tuberculosis is a complex, generally chronic disease caused by a bacterium, *Mycobacterium tuberculosis*. The most common form is pulmonary tuberculosis, or phthisis, a wasting disease of the lungs. Lesions may also develop in other parts of the body, including the bones, brain, spinal column, intestines, and lymph nodes. Transmission is usually by bacteria expelled from lungs of a victim in coughing or in sputum. Poverty, crowding, malnutrition, and dust in mines are positively correlated with tuberculosis. Populations vary greatly in their resistance to tuberculosis, apparently because of differing histories of exposure. In most societies, many more people are exposed to *M. tuberculosis* than ever acquire clinical symptoms. Bovine tuberculosis, caused by drinking milk from cattle infected with *M. bovis*, is very rare or non-existent in Ghana.[8]

Medical opinion was divided on how dangerous tuberculosis was for present and future public health. It was generally agreed that the disease was common, that most cases were not reported,[9] and that incidence was increasing. The rate of increase was disputed, with some seeing only a slow spread,[10] and hence a serious problem but not one requiring a special sense of urgency.[11] "The advance [of tuberculosis]," wrote a medical administrator in 1928, "although somewhat disquieting, is not yet of sufficient proportion to cause serious alarm."[12] In the 1920s and 1930s, the disease generally took a severe respiratory course which was quickly fatal. Most victims had an "almost complete absence of immunity," so case-mortalities were very high.[13] The symptoms were similar to those of "galloping consumption" in nineteenth century England,[14] suggesting that tuberculosis was being introduced into populations with little previous exposure.[15] Coastal Africans, who had had much longer contact with Europeans and their diseases, tended to have chronic cases, while northerners, who had only recently begun to interact with Europeans, had much more acute cases.[16] By 1949, resistance was apparently building up in all regions, as the acute, rapidly fatal course of the disease was less frequently seen.[17] The growth of resistance may also be reflected in an apparent levelling off of incidence in the last years of the period, a phenomenon which appears to be similar to the decline of tuberculosis in other world areas.[18]

Tuberculosis was especially prevalent among people in two environments: mines and urban slums; and, consequently, was at least two or three times more common in males than in females in most years. The disease was spread from these foci to rural areas by returning migrant laborers. Underground workers in the gold mines of southern Ghana were mostly recruited in the Northern Territories.[19] They were weakened by the long journey on foot to seek employment and encountered an unfamiliar climate, strange foods, and crowded living conditions. Fine quartz dust in the shafts damaged their lungs, resulting in many cases of silicosis and further reduction of their resistance to infection. Mining centers like Tarkwa reported very high tuberculosis death rates as early as 1914.[20] Two cases of dreaded yellow fever at Tarkwa in 1923 sparked a general investigation of public health in the mining areas. Good conditions prevailed at Prestea, where a company provided a "model village" to house its employees,[21] but the sanitary situation at the Tarkwa mines was so bad that special legislation was passed giving broad powers to public health officers.[22]

Miners who contracted tuberculosis were eligible for treatment in company hospitals, but many did not report at all or left soon after admission, preferring to go home to seek local treatment or to die among their family and friends.[23] Unable to force workers to stay in the hospital for what they knew was ineffective treatment, mine doctors tried to send groups of victims from the same areas home together under the care of a headman. Most of the returnees, all volunteers, had to walk hundreds of miles, but this gave them a better chance than staying in the mining areas, even if they remained in the hospital.[24] In one group, except for a headman, "there was no boy able to walk without a stick . . . none of them were fit in the ordinary sense of the word. They were a gang of invalids." Still, in the opinion of a mine doctor, members of such pathetic bands were better off than those who wasted away in hospital wards.[25] A committee appointed by Governor Guggisberg made recommendations which alleviated the problem. The government agreed to provide medical inspections of prospective mine workers, and the Chamber of Mines agreed that the companies would pay for recuperative stays in the Kumasi hospital for miners with medical discharges, and if they were still too weak to walk after treatment, would provide them with motor transport to their homes.[26]

In 1924, Professor W. J. Simpson was in the Gold Coast to study the plague epidemic, and he took time during his visit to investigate the mining areas as well. Simpson found poor sanitary conditions and a high incidence of tuberculosis and hookworm in many mines.[27] Some progress was made over the years,[28] but many miners continued to live and work in unsatisfactory conditions. Inadequate housing and a lack of bathing facilities characterized some mines; poor nutrition was common because of low wages, transportation problems, and high food prices fixed by rings of market women. Tuberculosis and other respiratory diseases continued to be much more prevalent than in the general population.[29] A major investigation begun in 1940 revealed that, despite some improvements in dust control,[30] respiratory diseases were still extremely serious. Of 1,002 miners given X-ray examinations, 46 had silicosis, 115 had tuberculosis, and another 19 suffered from both diseases.[31]

Tuberculosis also flourished in the slums of the growing cities.[32] Crowding, poor housing, lack of ventilation, and faulty diet made the urban poor, particularly migrants, especially vulnerable.[33] High tuberculosis rates were reported from most towns[34] and were closely linked with poverty. Exposure was general in urban areas by the 1930s, if the example of Saltpond is typical. In 1932, over 1,000 persons were given Mantoux skin tests, which showed that 71.6 percent had been infected with *M. tuberculosis*.[35] Clinical disease was obviously much less prevalent; the victims were mostly poor people with lowered resistance. Medical officials repeatedly stressed the strong association between poverty and tuberculosis, and were convinced that only better living conditions could reduce the prevalence of the disease.[36]

Population mobility helped spread the disease from the coast and urban areas throughout the whole country. Infection had probably been introduced to coastal peoples in pre-colonial times, but only in the twentieth century, with the rise of urbanization, mining, improved transportation, and labor migration were conditions favorable for rapid dissemination.[37] Men came to the mines and cities from all over Ghana to seek work; when they returned to their homes, they often brought tuberculosis and other diseases with them into previously unexposed areas.[38] In 1947, Mantoux skin tests of hundreds of villagers showed high exposure rates in the north. There were no more "virgin areas."[39] By the early 1960s, a majority of both rural and urban Ghanaians had been exposed to *M. tuberculosis* by age thirty; urban dwellers were only slightly more likely to have encountered the pathogen than country people. Fortunately, only a small percentage of infections resulted in clinical disease.[40]

The colonial medical service was unable to counteract the spread of tuberculosis or, prior to the early 1950s, cure its victims. Indeed, the absence of an effective cure until the introduction of isoniazid and other drugs at that time was a major factor in the propagation of the disease. Sufferers could not be detained in hospitals or in open-air "sanatoria" by compulsion;[41] they could leave at will, even if they were in a highly infectious state. Many victims never sought treatment and most of those who did come to hospitals or clinics were advanced cases for whom nothing could be done.[42] Hospitals thus acquired a poor reputation and even the few early cases, some of whom could have been helped, usually refused the long hospitalization necessary to cure the disease.[43] Like the moribund miners, they went home. Thus, neither incidence nor case-mortality are accurately represented in the clinical data presented in table 17 (page 128). A controversial vaccine, B.C.G., was developed in the 1920s and used in Europe, but not in Ghana.[44] Thus, the prevalence of tuberculosis resulted from socio-economic changes in the early decades of the twentieth century, coupled with the absence of effective measures of prevention and cure.

Cerebrospinal meningitis has caused great loss of life in Ghana (see table 18, page 129). The disease, caused by a bacterium, *Neisseria meningitidis*, is transmitted by sneezing and coughing patients. Except for scattered cases in Ashanti and an outbreak in Accra in 1947, epidemics were limited to the savanna country of the north and were parts of larger epidemics affecting wide areas in the Sudanic zone of West Africa.[45] Epidemics occur between January and April, when cold weather forces people to sleep inside and dry air weakens the effectiveness of the mucous membranes as a barrier to infection. The dark, crowded, poorly ventilated houses of northwestern Ghana facilitate the rapid spread of infection among their inhabitants. Between epidemic years, the disease may disappear from the country, persist in small endemic foci, or be maintained by organisms living in the mucous membranes of healthy carriers. Mortality in untreated cases ranges from 50 percent to over 90 percent.[46]

Cerebrospinal meningitis was first reported in Ghana in 1900 among carriers for the Ashanti Field Force in Cape Coast, many of whom had been recruited in East Africa.[47] It was unknown in northern Ghana until 1906, when a very severe epidemic hit the northwest. The outbreak lasted for three years and caused tremendous suffering and loss of life in Lawra, Wa, and Tumu Districts. This region was still only vaguely administered and despite a special investigation by Dr. A. E. Horn, the exact dimensions of the tragedy are unclear. At least 20,000 people must have died between 1906-08.[48]

No further cases were reported until 1919, when an epidemic struck in the same area and in Navrongo District, which had never been attacked before.[49] The disease reappeared in the northwest during the 1920 dry season, but did not spread east of Navrongo. Quarantines, isolating victims, and closing markets failed to halt the advance of the disease[50] and nothing could be done to cure patients beyond simple nursing.[51] There was a minor outbreak again in 1921. Altogether, over 4,000 deaths were recorded during the three-year period,[52] and the actual toll may have been considerably higher. The disease then entered another period of quiescence; only fifty-eight cases were detected from 1922 to 1938.

A new epidemic was evident in 1939, when over 800 cases were reported, and for the first time, there were many victims in the northeastern corner of the country. A higher than normal number of cases was recorded for the next several years, culminating in a major epidemic in the northwest in 1945-46, with over 10,000 cases. As in the past, funerals and other gatherings were banned, victims isolated in special camps, and markets and travel limited. These measures again had no results, but by 1945, in stark contrast to 1920, there was an effective cure. A sulpha drug, sulphanilamide, was employed with such success that mortality for treated cases fell to 8 percent. People had such confidence in this drug that patients were no longer hidden but eagerly brought forward for treatment. Chiefs were given pills and lists of symptoms so that possible victims could be treated at once while the medical authorities were being notified.[53] Unnecessary tragedies still could occur, however. An African assistant sent to check one remote village came back with a report that all was well. Later, it was discovered that he had never bothered to make the trip and that fifty-five people had died.[54]

There was an outbreak in Accra in 1947, with 225 cases and 36 deaths, mostly in the crowded Ussher Town and James Town sections.[55] In 1948, there were 11,000 cases, mostly in the northeast; and almost as many were recorded in 1949, evenly divided between the western and eastern sections of the far north.[56] Again, therapy with sulpha drugs in hospitals and special bush camps was highly effective; case-mortality in Kusasi in 1948 was only 7.3 percent.[57]

Cerebrospinal meningitis epidemics could not be predicted or prevented, and once they had started, their extension could not be limited by administrative measures. However, effective drugs were available in the 1940s; and this, plus aggressive action by mobile medical teams, reduced case-mortality from 60 percent or more to less than 10 percent.[58] The disease remained a serious threat to public health in northern Ghana, but the disasters of 1906-08 and 1919-20 were unlikely to be repeated.

Streptococcal infections cause a number of important pathological conditions. *Streptococcus pyogenes* has many strains with varying degrees of virulence. The organism is commonly carried in the upper respiratory tract and usually does no harm unless immunological defenses are weakened or a particularly virulent strain is encountered. Streptococcal disease in temperate countries frequently takes the form of sore throats or scarlet fever, but these conditions are not commonly seen in tropical countries. However, skin infections (erysipelas, pyoderma) are quite common, and, like "strep throat" and scarlet fever, can lead to such complications as middle ear infections, rheumatic fever, rheumatic heart disease, and glomerulonephritis.[59] Cardiac and kidney involvement are especially serious. Since lesions resulting from streptococcal infections are often difficult to distinguish from those caused by a number of other infections and non-infectious conditions, the amount of serious illness produced by *S. pyogenes* infections in Ghana cannot be determined. Crowding and poverty do favor streptococcal skin diseases. Table 19 (page 131) illustrates the point that even though scarlet fever was rare, streptococcal infections and their sequalae may have been quite important. Effective therapy became available in the late 1930s with the sulpha drugs and especially after 1945, when antibiotics came into use.

Diphtheria, a major cause of child mortality in nineteenth and early twentieth century Europe, was not frequently reported in Ghana. There were three cases in 1906, four between 1908 and 1923, and none recorded thereafter until a cluster of cases developed in Sekondi and Accra in 1930-31. The pathogen, *Corynebacterium diphtheriae*, was demonstrated in laboratory tests.[60] In 1935, skin tests showed that over 80 percent of persons in Accra under age twenty had been exposed to *C. diphtheriae*,[61] suggesting that since so many people had been at least carriers, the disease must have been much more common than supposed.[62] A 1954 survey showed that in Accra, over 40 percent of children under five had been exposed. Despite local medical opinion, diphtheria probably was a fairly widespread childhood disease in Ghana. "The chief reason for believing diphtheria to be of no account in West Africa," was, in the opinion of one doctor, "failure to look for it."[63] Immunization was effective but was not practiced in Ghana.

Whooping cough or pertussis was, as table 20 (page 132) indicates, much more frequently diagnosed. It was common among children in Accra[64] and in rural areas, although in 1954, it was acknowledged that little was known of its true incidence since only a small proportion of cases were treated or reported.[65] Two other diseases which primarily affected children, mumps and chickenpox, were also noted in clinical returns. Neither attracted much attention, and it seems reasonable to assume that they and their sometimes serious sequelae were more common than was realized. Urbanization and increasing intercommunication provided favorable conditions for the rapid and extensive transmission of diphtheria, pertussis, mumps, and chickenpox.

Although measles was not often treated in Ghana (and, indeed, attracted little notice from the medical profession), this viral disease has long been common[66] and was almost certainly a major cause of infant and child mortality. In fact, one experienced epidemiologist has suggested that measles "has probably cost the country more in terms of morbidity and mortality than all the major epidemics together." Recent data support this hypothesis. In 1970, over 45,000 cases and 200 deaths were reported; 273 deaths and over 95,000 cases were known in 1972.[67] The severity of measles is closely linked to the nutritional state of the patient; malnutrition makes what is usually a trivial childhood illness in developed countries into a killing disease in poor countries.[68] The potential toll of measles in Ghana is suggested by the only outbreak described in any detail: an epidemic in northeastern Ghana in April-June 1918. Prior to this epidemic, there had been a number of cases in the Tamale area during the last half of 1917, with at least eighteen deaths.[69] It is not clear whether measles spread into the northeast from Tamale or whether it came south from French territory in Upper Volta, which was also heavily afflicted.[70] In any case, measles ravaged the Bolgatanga area. It struck at the end of the dry season, when food reserves were always low, and 1918 was a particularly bad year, with widespread hunger. The epidemic was not known to the authorities until May 25, when the chief of Bolgatanga reported that many children were dying. The district commissioner learned of 188 deaths when he arrived the next day. A touring doctor came on May 28 and saw over 200 sick children, "many in a terribly emaciated condition." He and the D.C. were both responsible for several districts because of wartime staff shortages, so they were not able to learn much about the epidemic beyond the environs of Bolgatanga. A "few" deaths were noted at Gawri, and "many" at Zokko.[71] A death count of 425 was given in the Annual Report for the Northern Territories, mostly children who had little resistance because of the scarcity of food.[72] This figure is doubtlessly very conservative, and it is unclear whether it refers to Bolgatanga alone or to a wider area.

Serious loss of life must have accompanied other epidemics, such as an outbreak in Akuse in 1905 "which carried off a big section of the infant population," and one in Accra in 1916, which caused at least seventy deaths.[73] The authorities, however, learned little, partly because Africans often concealed cases to avoid the imposition of quarantines, as they did in the Axim area in 1936.[74] Measles vaccine was not developed until the 1960s, and there still is no specific therapy. However, good nursing reduced the chances of serious complications, and secondary bacterial infections were less dangerous after the discovery of the sulpha drugs, at least for the relatively few who sought treatment at infant welfare centres and other clinics. Cases treated are tabulated in table 20 (page 132). Comparative data on other countries would be extremely interesting.

Smallpox, an ancient and dreaded scourge, is now on the brink of world-wide extinction, thanks to mass vaccination campaigns and, since 1966, effective surveillance-containment techniques.[75] The virus can be transmitted by aerial droplets, direct skin to skin contact, and in clothes and bedding. Recovery conveys lifelong immunity, so major epidemics can occur only after intervals long enough to allow a new generation of susceptibles to appear. Smallpox was, in contrast to many of the diseases encountered in Ghana, well known to European physicians. While there was no specific therapy, prevention has been possible since the discovery of vaccination by Edward Jenner in 1798. Vaccination employs cowpox virus, which can cause a very mild disease, but produces immunity against smallpox. A weapon against smallpox was at hand; the problem was how to apply it.

Smallpox accompanied the earliest traders and was familiar on the coast,[76] in Ashanti, and in the far north[77] long before the colonial period. As in much of Africa,[78] many Ghanaian peoples tried to prevent smallpox by the practice of variolization: the direct innoculation of infective pus from the sores of a victim to healthy person in the hopes of inducing a mild case which would confer immunity. Variolization can be effective, but it can also result in serious infection and death and in contrast to vaccination, the innoculated person does acquire smallpox and can transmit the disease to others if he is not isolated. In the north, many peoples had practiced variolization "from time immemorial." Pus was generally put into an incision on the wrist.[79] Since people frequently travelled to other villages for innoculation, the practice contributed to the spread of the disease.[80] Epidemics often stimulated indigenous preventive measures, which sometimes made the outbreaks more widespread. For example, in 1901, the Axim branch of the Aborigines Rights Protection Society, complaining about the lack of medical aid furnished by the colonial government against smallpox, reported that local people "have been resorting to a primitive way of innoculating their healthy friends and relatives with the virus from small-pox patients, who have been lucky to have had the disease in a mild form, with dire consequences in most cases."[81] Variolization was blamed for the spread of smallpox in Ashanti in 1910,[82] in the Eastern Province in 1911, Wa District in 1916,[83] and in Accra in 1920, when the work of a woman who innoculated on the forehead caused many deaths.[84] In 1930, two mallams doing arm-to-arm innoculations in the Yendi area were allegedly responsible for 600 cases and 44 deaths.[85] Variolization did provide protection for individuals, but even allowing for possible bias on the part of Western doctors,[86] the practice sometimes caused deaths and the further dissemination of the disease. Vaccination was much safer for the individual and the community, and–if properly done–much more effective.

Smallpox notifications and vaccinations are shown in table 21 (page 133). As Scott points out, however, even this acute, well-known disease was considerably under-reported, especially before the 1930s.[87] Indeed, surveys have shown that smallpox in West Africa was grossly under-reported even in the 1960s.[88] Nonetheless, it is clear that there were major outbreaks in 1900-1902, 1924-26, and lesser epidemics at other times. The high figures in many of the years after 1940 reflect, in part, more accurate notifications. Smallpox was almost always present in Ghana, either in conspicuous epidemics or in small outbreaks in isolated areas. Case mortalities ranged from under 10 percent to over 50 percent, depending in large measure on the type of virus involved,[89] and the extent of previously acquired immunity.

The 1899-1902 epidemic was especially severe along the coast. The government, acting through the chiefs, tried to isolate victims and vaccinate the general public, but neither policy was very successful, as people resisted isolation and there were not enough vaccinators.[90] Not all chiefs would cooperate,[91] although their receipt of 1d for each of their subjects who was vaccinated had some effect.[92] The population was frequently apathetic or hostile, and the arrival of the vaccinator in a village was sometimes a signal for a general exodus.[93] Furthermore, the glycerinated lymph supplied from England was "largely inert." Much of it spoiled in the tropical climate, increasing the skepticism of many Africans about European medical efforts.[94] The fiasco of the impotent vaccine was remembered, and in later years, when smallpox broke out, people in some villages were eager for vaccination, but in others, the population fled.[95]

Problems with vaccines were not completely solved until the introduction of freeze-dried vaccine in 1957. Lanolated lymph preparations from the Lister Institute in England were usually employed and were fairly satisfactory if promptly used.[96] It was often adequate in Ashanti if sent in thermos flasks, but was of little value by the time it had made the long journey to the Northern Territories.[97] One frustrated northern M.O. got only 20 percent positive vaccinations with nine-month-old lymph; another batch gave 36 percent, but he ran out before he could protect an endangered population.[98] Vaccine was prepared in the Medical Laboratory in Accra from 1910 to 1913. It was safe but impotent.[99] Dried vaccine was supplied to the north after 1921 with somewhat better results.[100] Proposals were made in 1926 for a special laboratory in Nigeria to make vaccine for all of British West Africa, but the facility did not function until 1938.[101]

The number of vaccinations rose steadily after the Accra epidemic of 1920. Except in response to outbreaks, little had been done previously, because of lack of staff[102] as well as undependable lymph, so even the colony's capital was unprotected. Two hundred and sixty-four cases were found in Accra and its environs in 1920; sixty-eight persons (26 percent) died. An energetic M.O.H., P. S. Selwyn-Clarke, isolated victims, vaccinated and observed their contacts, and launched a successful mass innoculation campaign. Special attention was paid to school children, Kru laborers, ships' passengers, traders, and other travellers. In all, almost 77,000 people were vaccinated within a twenty-mile radius of the city.[103] Although the quality of the vaccine "was very variable and unless kept on ice its potency seemed to be lost fairly quickly,"[104] about 90 percent of the vaccinations were reportedly successful. Selwyn-Clarke's efforts to educate the people included a pamphlet distributed through the chiefs and schools entitled "Vaccination or Smallpox," which explained the procedure and had grisly photographs to show what happened to those who evaded the needle.[105] The vaccination campaign was successful, and thanks to a high rate of re-vaccination in later years, Accra never again suffered more than a few scattered cases of smallpox.

The success of immunization in Accra encouraged large-scale protective efforts throughout Ghana when a major epidemic began in 1924. This epidemic lasted two years and primarily affected the northern half of the country. Mass vaccination, perhaps aided by quarantines and by punishments for those who concealed cases,[106] reduced the impact of the epidemic. By the early 1930s, despite technical and administrative problems, a substantial proportion of Ghanaians were protected against smallpox by routine vaccination campaigns. Severe outbreaks could still occur; for example, there were fifty-six deaths in Bawku and seventy-nine in Navrongo-Zuarungu in 1947,[107] but vaccination and surveillance had greatly reduced the dangers of smallpox, and it became almost unknown in urban areas.

The communications revolution allowed more rapid smallpox transmission within the country, and porous colonial frontiers permitted the disease to enter Ghana from neighboring territories, but preventive medicine more than compensated for this, at least by the 1930s. As with cerebrospinal meningitis, and (to a lesser extent) pneumonia, colonial medicine had a positive impact on public health. However, except for aid to individual sufferers, little or nothing was accomplished against most other diseases spread by the respiratory route, partly because appropriate drugs and vaccines were unavailable.

Throughout Africa, enhanced mobility in the twentieth century caused rapid propagation of disease transmitted by the respiratory route. Cerebrospinal meningitis was mostly restricted to arid or semi-arid areas, but influenza accompanied travellers everywhere. Concentration of people in cities or in work sites like mining, logging, or construction camps was almost inevitably followed by high incidences of pneumonia, bronchitis, and tuberculosis. Miners employed underground, as in the Gold Coast, were especially susceptible. Bovine tuberculosis was not common in the Gold Coast because very few people drank milk, but it may have become a problem among pastoral groups in Eastern Africa and other places where milk was important in the diet. Finally, considerable attention has been given to smallpox vaccination, not only because of its intrinsic importance but also because vaccination is a useful index of medical activity, even in the early twentieth century. If a colonial medical service was not at least trying to protect people against smallpox, it probably was not doing very much at all.

6

OTHER INFECTIOUS AND NON-INFECTIOUS DISEASES

Most infectious diseases are transmitted to man by the three major routes thus far considered: arthropod vectors, improper disposal of excreta, and inhalation. Several important diseases, however, are spread by other means. Direct physical contact is essential for venereal diseases and yaws and may be a mode of transmission for leprosy and tropical ulcer. Some pathogenic bacteria are acquired by ingestion, handling diseased animals, or in soil-contaminated wounds.

Leprosy, because of the fear and revulsion it evoked in Europeans, attracted much more attention than its public health importance or the possibilities for successful therapy could justify. The disease is caused by *Mycobacterium leprae*, a close relative of the agent of tuberculosis. Leprosy is not a highly contagious disease, but the mode of transmission is still unclear. Close, prolonged contact is usually necessary for infection; skin to skin and aerial droplet routes are both possible. Crowding, poverty, and dirt favor the spread of leprosy.

The basic control method employed by the colonial authorities was the segregation of victims into special centers where they could be treated and would not be a danger to others. The notion of a leper colony as a separate and at least partially self-sustaining community goes back to ancient times and was widely adopted in medieval Europe. Educated Africans came to share these beliefs and urged the government to get unsightly and allegedly dangerous lepers off the streets.[1] Before leper colonies could be created, however, it was necessary to determine how many victims there were. Governor Hugh Clifford's personal interest caused the Northern Territories administration to assess the prevalence of leprosy in 1913. D.C.s were instructed to question the chiefs to learn how many lepers there were, ascertain public attitudes toward the disease, and report on the possibilities of erecting camps in their districts.[2] The resulting reports indicated that the disease was not common.[3] Although some people knew that leprosy was contagious, victims were cared for within the family. Intimate contact was avoided, but there was no special effort to isolate lepers.[4] Fatalism was widespread. "They see so much of the painful side of life," wrote one D.C., "that they look upon all sickness, including leprosy, as one of the ordered conditions of existence."[5] The situation did not seem to require special measures, and none were taken.

High-level official concern revived a decade later, and another survey of northern D.C.s was taken in 1925. This time, in addition to determining the prevalence of leprosy and public attitudes toward it, the local administrators had to report on the best site for a leper colony in their district.[6] Few D.C.s wanted one. They reported low incidence of the disease,[7] lack of space for a settlement,[8] and stressed popular opposition to compulsory isolation of victims.[9] "The healthy population look on lepers with complete indifference," wrote the D.C. of Wa, "except in some very advanced cases when a separate house is provided and food given in a separate dish." The chiefs would "passively resist" any segregation scheme, and a strong force of guards would be needed to confine lepers to special settlements.[10]

Eastern Dagomba was the only district which responded positively. Dr. Helen Hendrie, M.O. at Yendi, was concerned about an apparent increasing incidence of leprosy, and a colony was authorized near Yendi.[11] Governor Guggisberg was delighted, praising Dr. Hendrie's leprosy work and noting that she had achieved "admirable results" despite "conditions that were far from ideal."[12] In October 1926, Dr. F. H. Cooke, the M.O. at Ho, established a voluntary camp in response to a strong local demand for treatment. Here, as at Yendi, patients were given periodic moogrol injections and were encouraged to farm or engage in crafts to the best of their ability.[13]

Continuing interest in leprosy was due in part to the efforts of a private philanthropic society in the United Kingdom, the British Empire Leprosy Relief Association. Leprosy was, at least until the post-World War II period, the only disease in Ghana which had such an interest group in the metropole. The organization sent a leprosy specialist, Dr. M. B. D. Dixey, to Ghana in 1928 to study the prevalence of the disease and to propose measures to combat it. Dixey travelled widely, seeking out and treating lepers, and observing the care given in special camps and the outpatient departments of hospitals. His visit also stimulated Governor A. R. Slater to order another round of surveys by district commissioners.[14] These inquiries, plus Dixey's work, showed that leprosy occurred throughout the Gold Coast. Five hundred and fifty-three cases were known in the Colony, 859 in Togo (mostly near Ho), 1,056 in Ashanti, and 1,702 in the north. Only 2,161 of the 4,170 known cases were being treated. The real prevalence was estimated to be at least four times the number of confirmed cases.[15] Dixey recommended the compulsory registration of lepers, but this policy was rejected because the medical department considered it impractical and only likely to result in more concealment of victims.[16]

Another representative of the Association toured the country in 1936.[17] Dr. E. Muir visited leper settlements at Accra, Ho, Yendi, and Kumasi, and was generally pleased by what he saw. About 400 people, a third of whom were considered highly infectious, were voluntary inmates and hence no longer a danger to the public. They were well cared for, but, unfortunately, nothing could really be done for them. Muir proposed another major survey, with special attention to the north. Hopefully, missionaries could be induced to establish agricultural settlements for lepers.[18]

Little changed over the next twenty years. As is shown in table 22 (page 000), the number of patients rose after 1945, probably because the expanded medical services reached a higher proportion of the victims. The leprosy settlements were, not surprisingly, "all dismal and depressing,"[19] but they did provide refuge for hundreds and therapeutic benefits to at least a few. In the late 1940s, accurate prevalence figures were still impossible to obtain; leprosy was considered likely to be much more common "than generally imagined."[20] Indeed, surveys in the early 1950s revealed that over 2 percent of the population of Gonja, Lawra, and the Konkomba areas were afflicted.[21] The reduction in cases treated after 1952 could suggest a real reduction in prevalence, as the Medical Field Units and the expanded network of hospitals and clinics should have detected a higher proportion of total cases than were found in earlier surveys. However, over 21,000 lepers were known to the health authorities in 1967.[22]

Colonial medical measures, despite considerable effort and concern, could do little to effect the incidence or severity of leprosy. Isolation did reduce transmission, but only a small proportion of victims lived in leper colonies. Treatment is, even today, a long, difficult process. Moogrol, the only drug available until the mid-1930s, was not very effective. Sulphones were subsequently used, with somewhat better results. Injections, however, did not produce a rapid cure, and many patients, discouraged by slow or inapparent progress, left the colonies or stopped visiting outpatient clincs. Therapy, like isolation, had little effect on the prevalence of leprosy. Rising living standards may have had some beneficial impact.

Venereal diseases were well established in Ghana long before the twentieth century, especially along the coast. They spread across the country after 1900, thanks to social changes and increasing mobility. Gonorrhea, caused by the bacterium *Neisseria gonorrhoeae*, was the most common venereal disease. Control was, and is, complicated by the fact that many infected females show no clinical symptoms but can still transmit the disease. It is a common cause of female sterility. Syphilis is a complex disease which can cause damage to a number of organs over a period of many years. The agent, a spirochete called *Treponema pallidum*, is very closely related to the pathogen of yaws, *T. pertenue*. Yaws was extremely common, and because the causative organisms are so similar, victims of yaws acquire partial immunity against syphilis.[23] This probably explains why syphilis has been less common than gonorrhea in Ghana and has spread more slowly. Two less important venereal diseases also deserve mention. Lymphogranuloma venereum was rarely diagnosed, but soft chancre was fairly common, with at least a few dozen recorded cases in most years. It is possible that soft chancre was substantially underdiagnosed.[24]

The medical authorities were well aware of the importance of venereal diseases and their impact on the health and fertility of the population. Gonorrhea was known to be widespread in Kumasi and other major towns before World War I.[25] Syphilis was common in some southern towns but not in rural areas or in the north,[26] except among soldiers and porters.[27] Clinical records and surveys of prisoners showed a high gonorrhea rate in Accra,[28] so in 1920 a special clinic for the free treatment of venereal diseases was opened in the Victoriaborg section under an African physician, Dr. C. E. Reindorf. Reindorf treated hundreds of cases annually and gave lectures and published pamphlets in Ga and Twi to encourage attendance.[29] The popular clinic was moved to larger quarters at Korle Bu in 1927. Speakers at the dedication ceremony there, including Governor Guggisberg and the eminent African educator J. K. G. Aggrey, urged the chiefs and public not to hide venereal diseases in shame but to seek help and to continue treatment until they were cured.[30]

The Accra clinic did not, of course, serve more than the capital and its environs. Elsewhere, syphilis and gonorrhea were spreading. M.O.s around the country, in response to a request from the colonial office, supplied data on gonorrhea among selected groups in 1922 and 1923. Over 7,000 male prisoners, policemen, soldiers, and inmates of the colonial lunatic asylum were examined; about 6.9 percent had gonorrhea. The highest incidence was among police (12 percent); prisoners were second (9 percent).[31] These special groups were not considered representative, but the survey results did suggest widespread infection. The M.O. at Ho found that over half of his patients had venereal diseases. Old cases, chronic gonorrhea and tertiary syphilis, were alarmingly common, and he estimated, perhaps excessively, that one-fifth of the population of southern Togo was infected.[32] Many victims preferred traditional treatments to government clinics, but some indigenous cures, such as vaginal tampons covered with red pepper or other irritants, were quite dangerous.[33]

Venereal diseases were widespread in southern Ghana, especially in the larger towns, by the early 1920s. Several factors contributed to their dissemination to the rest of the country. Thousands of young men left their homes and families to seek work in the towns and in the mines and cocoa farms. Since they were usually away for months or years, they augmented the clientele for prostitutes. Indeed, many prostitutes were also labor migrants. Women from southern Togo went to Accra and other towns in the Colony.[34] In 1930, the *Gold Coast Independent*, complaining that prostitutes and brothels in Accra "are swelling in numbers daily," observed with some self-righteousness that many of the women were Nigerians or other foreigners.[35] Miners in Tarkwa had the services of prostitutes from as far away as Calabar.[36] Urbanization, social disruption, uneven economic development, and more mobile populations created conditions in which casual or commercialized sex became more prevalent. Syphilis and gonorrhea were transmitted to new areas as soldiers, laborers, prostitutes, traders, and lorry drivers travelled to and from the towns and about the countryside.

Venereal diseases gradually advanced northward in the 1920s and 1930s. For example, these diseases were rare in the Yendi area in the 1920s, except among traders. Most cases were found along the new motor roads.[37] Syphilis was still rare there in 1937, but gonorrhea was spreading rapidly. Even the isolated Konkomba of Eastern Dagomba District, who were still unaffected in 1928,[38] had a few cases by 1937. Kete Krachi had some gonorrhea but very little syphilis in 1937; remote Kusasi still had very little of either.[39] Gonorrhea, and to a lesser extent syphilis, were beginning to increase in the far northern districts of Navrongo and Zuarungu by the late 1920s. Introduced by returning migrants, they were called "the Kumasi disease."[40] Venereal diseases spread slowly in the north; for the most part, only peddlers, drivers, men who had travelled to the south, and their immediate contacts, were affected.[41] Meanwhile, incidences remained high in the coastal towns, and control and treatment had little result. The influx of troops and laborers during World War II further complicated the situation.[42]

Effective syphilis treatment was available early in the twentieth century. Paul Ehrlich's "magic bullet," neosalvarsan, was one of the very few specific antimicrobial drugs available before the late 1930s. Neosalvarsan and related drugs were reasonably effective if patients took the full course of shots. Penicillin, introduced after World War II, was even more potent. Treatment of gonorrhea was much less effective until the introduction of sulpha drugs.[43] Sulpha-resistant strains of gonococcus were encountered by 1945,[44] but penicillin proved highly successful.[45] Mass antibiotic therapy directed against yaws undoubtedly contributed to a reduced prevalence of both syphilis and gonorrhea after 1953. Thus, venereal diseases—with resulting chronic illness, sterility, and (especially for tertiary syphilis) sometimes lethal sequalae—spread rapidly during the colonial era. Even more "social" than most diseases, their distribution and prevalence were profoundly influenced by socio-economic changes. The medical authorities recognized the problem and, as table 23 (page 135) indicates, saw increasing numbers of cases, but they had no technical capability to retard further spread of these diseases except for treating victims, thus rendering them non-infectious to others. Many more males were treated than females, partly because of care given to prisoners and soldiers.

The sexual disparity for gonorrhea also reflects the fact that many female cases are asymptomatic. Therapeutic measures did not begin to catch up with the problem until after 1945, when antibiotics became a powerful weapon against the venereal diseases.

Yaws is caused by a bacterial agent, *Treponema pertenue*, which, as described above, is very closely related to the organism which causes syphilis. Yaws is usually contracted by direct contact with skin lesions of a victim. Transmission is favored by hot, humid conditions, crowding, and dirt. It is associated with poverty and poor personal hygiene, especially in places where seasonal water shortages preclude bathing.[46] Yaws is a chronic disease whose course varies widely from victim to victim. Many recover after suffering ugly skin lesions; in other cases, disabling lesions of the feet, hands, and bones develop. A few patients suffer gangosa, or destructive lesions of the nose and upper lip. Yaws is rarely fatal by itself, but it is a frequent cause of sickness, disfigurement, and crippling.

Yaws was extremely common in Ghana and, as table 24 (page 136) indicates, was one of the most frequently treated diseases. Most regions were affected to some degree, but incidence varied greatly. In the north, cases were rare in Bawku District but very common in Lawra and among the Konkomba.[47] In parts of Western Ashanti, 10 percent of the adult population had advanced (tertiary) cases.[48] Children were so commonly attacked in some areas that many parents, especially in Ashanti, considered yaws as a normal condition of childhood and either saw no reason to seek medical assistance or else waited until late symptoms developed.[49] Many believed that adults suffered more severely if they did not contract yaws as children, so early symptoms were often welcome, and in some districts, healthy children were deliberately innoculated.[50]

Such fatalism was encouraged by the ineffectiveness of "traditional" remedies, which included dressings of pepper, copper sulphate, and nut oil, and bathing with a special root infusion. Early western medicines, potassium iodide and mercury, were not much better. In 1920, therapy was revolutionized when Dr. Reindorf of the Accra venereal diseases clinic began treating both syphilis and yaws with arsenicals. Two neoarsenobillon (N.A.B.) injections given fourteen days apart gave spectacular results in many children; advanced cases required a longer series of shots.[51] This treatment became very popular and, together with hygienic improvements, soon made yaws rare in the capital. Dr. Helen Hendrie tried N.A.B. in conjunction with mercury in the Yendi area with great success.[52] People developed great faith in N.A.B. injections; some believed that it could cure almost anything. Unfortunately, many patients stopped attending outclinics after the overt symptoms subsided and experienced relapses because they did not receive a complete series of shots. N.A.B. was the first "wonder drug" employed in Ghana; the popularity of injections and the prestige of the medical department rose precipitously. The former phenomenon, at least, has continued; many Ghanaians still consider injections an essential part of therapy for almost any complaint.[53] Yaws injections dispelled the hostility of villagers at Asamankese in 1926, making it possible for investigators to study the yellow fever epidemic there. Promising trials at Tamale made people in that region eager for treatment.[54] In late 1925, Dr. Hendrie began trials with sobita (sodium bismuth tartarate) in the Yendi area. Results were extremely encouraging, despite the fact that she had difficulty convincing the chiefs that she had to check the progress of all patients, even those who considered themselves cured and saw no reason to see the doctor again.[55] Sobita seemed effective against all but some advanced cases, was easy to administer, and seemed to produce less pain and fewer side effects than N.A.B. Moreover, it was much cheaper. N.A.B. was, however, still useful for tertiary yaws and for a few cases which resisted sobita.[56] Other bismuth compounds were tried, but none proved as effective as sobita.[57] Both N.A.B. and sobita remained in use, and their relative merits were debated for years, but mass treatment would have been prohibitively expensive without the cheaper bismuth compound.[58] Therapy and the greater degree of personal cleanliness made possible by improved water supplies were responsible for rapid progress against yaws in major towns like Accra, Cape Coast, Koforidua, and Kumasi. By the early 1930s, the disease was largely a rural problem.[59] The medical department was euphoric, and by 1937 the D.M.S. expressed the hope that yaws could be eradicated "at some not far distant date."[60] Declining case loads in 1938 and 1939 were interpreted as indicating decreasing prevalence.[61]

There were, however, problems. Many remote regions had not been reached by the medical services, and yaws was rife in some of them. Serious side effects were sometimes noted, and sobita proved more painful than N.A.B.; a switch back to arsenical drugs in some places produced a surge of new patients.[62] Many people were apparently discouraged by clinic fees; when shots were made free, cases soared again.[63] More serious was the problem of relapses, which was especially important because a high percentage of patients failed to complete the series of injections necessary to destroy all of their *T. pertenue* parasites. In Lawra, a deposit system proved useful: patients paid one shilling for their first shot and received it back after they had completed their second or third shot.[64] This system, however, could not be used after free treatment was introduced.

In 1943, a major yaws campaign was approved for the Yendi region. It was an experimental plan using mobile teams in a very remote and difficult area. A sum of £8,140 was allocated.[65] In 1944, 6,487 cases were treated, but a re-survey showed a 10.6 percent relapse rate after six months. The first year of the campaign did produce valuable experience, and the needs of the mobile teams convinced the administration to improve the road network, especially in the Konkomba areas.[66]

The campaign was greatly expanded in 1945, when almost 21,000 patients were treated with a new bismuth drug.[67] However, the program proved very expensive, and relapse rates remained disturbingly high. Governor Alan Burns, despite his skepticism about the scheme, allowed the experiment to continue.[68] Operations were extended in Dagomba country in 1946; the area was surveyed, and over 20,000 cases were treated. In 1947, the yaws and trypanosomiasis mobile teams were combined, and in 1950, they were merged into a new rural health care system, the Medical Field Units. Work continued in Dagomba, and the campaign was extended to the Ejura and Nkoranza regions of Ashanti.[69]

Thousands of patients were cured, but relapses remained frequent, and new cases continued to appear in large numbers. By the early 1950s, it was obvious that yaws was still highly endemic in Eastern Dagomba, despite the extensive efforts of 1944-49.[70] Arsenic and bismuth drugs failed to fully cure all patients and did not affect the large number of persons who harbored *T. pertenue* but who did not, at least at the time a survey team visited their village, display overt symptoms. Mass treatment did reduce suffering and temporarily slowed transmission, but the results were undone in a matter of months.

Yaws was defeated by a second wonder drug. Penicillin was first tried in Winneba in 1944, with excellent results.[71] However, partly because of expense, the antibiotic was not used in the mobile campaign until 1952, when it was given to victims with severe nasal ulcerations.[72] Mass treatment remained dependent on the old bismuth and arsenic drugs until late 1953, when penicillin came into general use.[73] Then, all children were considered latent cases and were given penicillin injections, a policy pioneered in Haiti to reduce the reservoir of *T. pertenue* in the population.[74] The M.F.U. teams examined hundreds of thousands of villagers. In 1955, the World Health Organization began to supply penicillin.[75] An effective, easy-to-administer drug which cured quickly and eliminated inapparent infections, penicillin was the ideal weapon for the virtual elimination of yaws in Ghana[76] and other tropical countries.

Yaws was so ubiquitous in Ghana that it is doubtful whether increased mobility had any significant effect on its distribution. Better living conditions, particularly improved water supplies, contributed to a gradual reduction in prevalence, especially in the cities. From the mid-1920s on, the popularity of therapy ensured that thousands of people were cured or at least relieved of symptoms. Transmission was at least temporarily reduced in regions where large numbers of patients were treated with bismuth or arsenic drugs. Widespread and sustained progress was not achieved until after 1953, but medical efforts in the pre-penicillin era made a real contribution to public health. Extensive use of penicillin probably also reduced the incidence of syphilis and gonorrhea, although it is possible that the virtual erradication of yaws will reduce immunities against treponemes and allow syphilis to spread more easily.

Colonial health care personnel spent a great deal of time treating cutaneous tropical ulcers. This condition was very common, as the figures for new cases in table 25 (page 137) show. Each patient had to have his lesions cleaned and dressed periodically, often over a period of months. Ulcers were rarely fatal unless complicated by secondary infections, but they could incapacitate a victim for months.[77] The etiology of tropical ulcer remains obscure. It frequently develops at the site of a minor wound and is most common among poorly nourished rural people. Tropical ulcer was almost never seen in people with good diets, such as policemen, prisoners, or others with regular employment.[78] A number of microorganisms are regularly found in the lesions. Most of these are opportunistic invaders, but there may be a specific microbial agent. The condition is not normally infectious, but there is evidence that it can under some circumstances be transmitted from person to person. In Ghana, therapy and improved diets probably had a small but positive impact. Anti-microbial drugs were helpful in controlling secondary infections.

Three other bacterial diseases deserve brief mention, although none was a major cause of morbidity or mortality. Anthrax attacks sheep and cattle and can be contracted by people who handle the skins or carcasses of diseased animals or eat their flesh. Small but deadly outbreaks were occasionally detected. For example, eight people died at Zongoiri in Bawku District in 1915, and ten cases with three deaths resulted from eating an infected bullock at Tarkwa in 1947.[79] Veterinary measures, meat inspection, and prompt cremation or burial in quicklime of animals dying from anthrax helped reduce transmission. Anthrax responds to some sulpha drugs and to penicillin, which was successfully employed in the Tarkwa outbreak.

Tetanus occurs when *Clostridium tetani*, a common soil bacterium, gains entrance to a wound. The organism produces a deadly neurotoxin, which causes lockjaw. Tetanus was, and still is, very difficult to treat, as the case-mortality tables in table 26 (page 138) indicate. Fortunately, the disease was relatively uncommon. Immunization by an antitoxin was discovered in the late nineteenth century and was widely employed in Europe during World War I. Prophylaxis was not, however, widely practiced in Ghana.

Food poisoning became more common during the twentieth century, especially in urban areas where many people bought meals from street vendors or at chop bars. Unsanitary food handling and storage allowed bacteria of the genus *Salmonella* to produce gastroenteritis in unwary diners. *Salmonella* infection may make a victim very sick, but the disease is usually self-limiting. Botulism, a rare but much more deadly condition, is caused by ingesting food containing toxin produced by an anaerobic bacterium, *Clostridium botulinum*. It is generally acquired from improperly preserved foods in sealed containers, so the growing popularity of imported tinned and bottled foods increased the risk of botulism poisoning. Public health authorities tried to regulate restaurants and chop bars and frequently condemned spoiled food; their efforts certainly had some impact. Few statistics on food poisoning were published prior to 1953; most *Salmonella* cases were presumeably listed under non-specific gastroenteritis or diarrhea when they were detected. In the period 1953-55, an average of 352 cases and 6 deaths were reported annually for "Food Poisoning; Infection and Intoxication."

The great scarcity of dentists in the colonial period makes it difficult to assess trends in tooth and gum diseases. The government dentist reported in 1914-15 that the teeth of Accra school children were "generally good";[80] but five years later, he complained of a high rate of cavities and periodontal disease in children in Accra, Sekondi, Cape Coast, and Kumasi. In contrast, examinations revealed few problems in students in Tamale, Gambaga, Wa, and Navrongo, because the traditional diet was not being altered in the north.[81] In the towns of the south, imported foods such as white bread, sugar, and polished rice were blamed for the rising incidence of cavities, but most rural people continued to have good teeth.[82] In Ghana, as in other countries, change to a more "modern" diet, especially perhaps an increase in sugar consumption, produced a regression in dental health.[83]

Non-infectious diseases had a very important impact on health in Ghana in the 1900-1955 period, but their contributions to morbidity and mortality tended to be obscured by the tremendous burden of microbial and helminthic infections. Non-infectious diseases result from such diverse factors as genetic disabilities, metabolic disturbances, aging, stress, poor nutrition, or trauma. Cardiovascular, endocrine, neoplastic, and other non-infectious conditions were often poorly diagnosed, even after such vague categories as "senile decay" or "general debility" fell into disuse. Furthermore, many pathological conditions of the heart, liver, digestive tract, kidneys, and other organs can have multiple etiologies and may be caused by infectious as well as non-infectious diseases. Nephritis, for example, may result from malaria and several other infections, as well as organic causes.

The public health significance of non-infectious diseases has doubtlessly been increasing during the period under consideration. In Ghana, as in other countries, two factors have contributed to this phenomenon. One is the whole spectrum of socioeconomic change. Urbanization, industrialization, chemicals and pollutants, dietary changes, stress, motor vehicles, and other accoutrements of modern society have not yet altered the disease environment of Ghana as much as they have affected the developed countries, but considerable change has occurred. Equally if not more important has been a slow but definite aging of the population. In developed countries, preventive and therapeutic advances, particularly against infectious diseases, have lowered mortality rates, especially for infants and cihildren, and have helped to raise life expectancies to and beyond the proverbial three score and ten.[84] Inevitably, diabetes, cancers, strokes, heart disease, and other pathological conditions which are more likely to develop in older people have become greater public health problems. Mortality reduction has been much less dramatic in Ghana, but, as will be argued in a later chapter, death rates have declined and life expectancy has been rising. As fewer persons have died of malaria at age two, smallpox at four, or cerebrospinal meningitis at twenty, more have lived long enough to succumb to cancer at fifty or heart attacks at sixty. The trend seems clear. Medical intervention and other factors will gradually reduce the toll exacted by communicable diseases, and Ghana's disease environment will become more like those in the developed countries. Hence, the relative brevity of this discussion of degenerative, metabolic, neoplastic, and other non-infectious diseases is not due to their lack of importance. Rather, it is a function of the overwhelming significance of infectious diseases and the measures taken against them, and the lack of data on non-infectious diseases, due partly to lact of interest and inadequate methods of diagnosis and treatment. The Medical Department was, quite rightly, primarily concerned with diseases of microbial etiology.

Three groups of conditions will be more fully discussed elsewhere and will only be mentioned here. The health problems of mothers during pregnancy, childbirth, and the immediate post-partem period were extremely important. Prematurity and various ill-defined diseases of early infancy were responsible for heavy loss of life. Many maternal and infant deaths were, of course, caused by microorganisms. Well-defined nutritional diseases like beri-beri or scurvey were not common, but most diets were deficient in animal protein, and kwashiorkor was first described in Ghana. Nutrition is a vital factor in the general health of any community; poor nutrition reduces resistance to the acquisition of most infections and makes their course more severe. As will be described in the following chapter, nutritional changes have had an important influence on health in Ghana.

Cardiovascular disease was frequently detected. Data for Accra are probably the most accurate because the major colonial hospital and the best (and for many years the only) pathology laboratory were located there. Diseases of the heart and blood vessels were major causes of death. A survey of records of 3,645 autopsies conducted in Accra from 1921 to 1953 showed that 12.8 percent had evidence of cardiovascular disease.[85] During most of the colonial era, little could be done for most patients besides nursing care and advice on lifestyles. Drugs and surgery helped some individuals but had little impact on overall mortality. As noted above, streptococcal infections can lead to cardiac disease. Syphilis can produce aneurisms and other severe diseases of the aorta; these conditions were fairly common in persons autopsied in Accra.[86] Stress is frequently linked to hypertension and cardiovascular disease in western societies, and it seems plausible that cultural and socio-economic changes, together with the general stresses of urban life, have made many Ghanaians more susceptible to these conditions. Zulu residents of Durban, South Africa, both recent immigrants and life-long city dwellers, develop high blood pressure much more frequently than their rural counterparts.[87] Hopefully, different political circumstances have made Ghana's cities less stressful than those in South Africa, but hypertension was "not uncommon" in Accra in the early 1950s,[88] and it is reasonable to expect that cardiovascular problems will become more prevalent.

Cancers were diagnosed from the beginning of the century but were not commonly treated as late as the mid-1950s (see table 27, page 139). It is unlikely that smoking or chemical pollution was sufficient to influence cancer rates, and therapy was not advanced enough to give lasting help to more than a handful of victims. Better diagnosis is the most likely explanation for the rising case loads after

1953. Except for the probable influence of a gradual increase in the number of older people, there is no evidence to suggest changes in the real incidence of neoplastic diseases.[89]

Colonial physicians encountered a wide range of diseases of the abdominal region, including such cosmopolitan difficulties as appendicitis (an infection), gastric ulcers, gall bladder problems, intestinal obstructions, hernias, enlarged prostate, endometriosis, and cirrhosis of the liver. Dietary problems, including alcoholism, played a role in some of these diseases, as did aging. Nephritis was, as described in a later chapter, fairly common; many cases resulted from malaria, yellow fever, or streptococcal infection. In addition, arthritis, anemia, constipation, prickly heat, abcesses, snakebite, fungal diseases, chigger fleas, goitre, and a host of other infectious and non-infectious conditions, vague or well-defined, tragic or trivial, common or rare, were treated in hospitals and clinics. For some, medicine, surgery, skilled nursing, intravenous feeding and other therapy saved lives; cures or symptomatic relief improved the happiness and productivity of many more. Tens of thousands were assisted every year, but the effect on the overall health of the population was small, because only a minority of the population had access to, or the inclination to use, modern medical facilities.

One area in which medical intervention clearly was effective was the treatment of victims of traumatic injuries. Indeed, as table 28 (page 140) indicates, people injured in accidents, assaults, or by poisons, animals, the elements, or other external causes, consistently accounted for a high percentage of total cases treated. Case-mortality figures are made slightly higher by the fact that this classification included a few examples of the only condition which physicians were not allowed to treat: judicial execution. Injured people were more likely to go or be taken to a hospital or clinic than those suffering from less spectacular ailments. Moreover, physicians and surgeons found it relatively easy to demonstrate their very real skills on people who had been cut, stabbed, shot, hurt in falls, or run down by cars. Their ability to close wounds, repair fractures, and prevent sepsis were widely appreciated. Modern medicine saved lives and limbs, but, on the other hand, modernization made some kinds of traumatic injuries more likely. Table 29 (page 141) suggests the recent public health importance of two of these.

For a final category of diseases, psychological disorders, colonial medicine had little to offer. Limited resources and the primitive state of psychiatry meant that not much could be done for the insane. A colonial lunatic asylum was established in Accra in 1887. It was moved to Christiansborg Castle in 1899 and was transferred a few years later to its present site on Castle Road.[91] In 1914, there were already over one hundred inmates. The minority, who were not considered "maniacal and dangerous," were kept busy gardening, cleaning, or in crafts.[92] The institution held over 200 people in the early 1920s and was overcrowded, despite some recent expansion.[93] The asylum was suitable only for custody, not treatment; indeed, many M.O.s refused to send patients for fear that the asylum would only make them worse. Furthermore, it was too close to the Ridge residential area, so whites were sometimes disturbed by the nocturnal clamorings of the inmates.[94] The director, H. L. Mooney, seems not to have been well qualified to deal sympathetically with his patients; he thought that the high frequency of "dementia praecox" cases might reflect the "simian" characteristics of West Africans.[95] A qualified Alienist Officer was employed beginning in 1929, and conditions seem to have improved somewhat. In 1942, a D.M.S.S. who rarely had anything positive to say about his department found that the institution was well-managed and that the patients, although overcrowded, were clean and adequately fed. Despite the psychiatrist's lack of equipment, he was able to cure some of his patients.[96]

By 1951, the colonial mental hospital averaged 730 patients a day. "The institution remains unsatisfactory. . . . [It] remains what it was designed to be—a lunatic asylum of the old type."[97] A second, more modern hospital remained on the drawing boards.[98]

There has been considerable debate on the question of whether social change or "modernization" increases the rate of mental illness in "traditional" societies. It is obviously impossible to answer the question with Ghanaian data, although it seems plausible that disturbed persons became more conspicuous and perhaps more difficult for their families and friends to control in customary ways. Some insane people went to the cities, where they begged in the markets or roamed the streets naked, blocking traffic, annoying respectable citizens, and, on occasion, committing crimes.[99] Colonial medical services could offer little but custodial care for such unfortunates and the removal of violent individuals from society. Ghanaians with psychological problems were much more likely to consult and be helped by "traditional" healers, many of whom were sympathetic and highly competent practitioners. These healers performed very valuable social functions;[100] their failures often ended up in the government asylum.

Thus, of all the conditions described in this section, medical intervention was effective only with yaws, traumas, and some other conditions requiring surgery, and, to a lesser extent, syphilis and gonorrhea. In contrast to wide regions of Equatorial Africa, where gonorrhea has been implicated in the high level of female sterility,[101] venereal diseases apparently had little affect on fertility in Ghana, at least at the national level. Better living standards may have reduced the prevalence of some diseases, such as yaws and tropical ulcer. Many non-infectious diseases of body and mind are still poorly understood and remain difficult to prevent or cure in Ghana and throughout the world.

7

THE DEMOGRAPHIC CONSEQUENCES AND CAUSES OF THE CHANGING EPIDEMIOLOGICAL SITUATION

The preceding chapters have shown that there have been substantial changes in the prevalence of at least some of the major diseases which have afflicted Ghanaians during the colonial era. Presumably, these changes have had an impact on the size and growth of the population. This chapter assesses the contributions of preventive and therapeutic medicine and socio-economic factors to one of the most important phenomena in the recent history of Ghana: a dramatic increase in human numbers.

Ghana's rate of demographic growth during the first fifty-five years of the twentieth century was significantly higher than that for the continent as a whole.[1] Immigration from other African territories contributed to this growth, and a small proportion of the increase might have been caused by higher birth rates, but the most important factor was declining mortality. Studies of mortality in England and Wales and rural America have shown that medical technology played a relatively minor role in reducing death rates from most diseases.[2] There has, however, been considerable debate over the causes of declining mortality in underdeveloped countries, with some authors arguing that modern medicine has been more important than improved living standards.[3] An assessment of Ghana's experience, however tentative, may contribute to this debate and will shed light on the nature of the country's colonial past.

Demographic and medical data for Ghana, as for other African territories, are deficient in many respects. Census results are generally unreliable, vital registration was confined to a few urban centers and was often indifferently enforced, colonial health services reached only a fraction of the population, and disease conditions in some remote areas were almost unknown. It is likely that valuable demographic information will be found in Roman Catholic and possibly other mission records, but parish registers would cover only very small areas and would pertain to groups who were monogamous and perhaps otherwise unrepresentative.[4] Hence, we cannot accurately determine the size of the population or its age composition; vital rates and causes of death can only be surmised from incomplete and sometimes imprecise registration and hospital data, a few special surveys, and general impressions of health conditions.

Vital registration began in 1912 with the Births, Deaths, and Burials Ordinance, which was applied to sixteen towns. New registration areas were proclaimed over the years, but there were none in Togo or the Northern Territories until 1929. In

1940, about 9 percent of the population lived in 35 towns designated as registration areas;[5] in 1960, the 36 registration areas, all urban, covered about 12 percent of the population.[6] It must be stressed that registration was applied only to certain towns and was never attempted in rural areas. Registration was never complete, despite occasional fines for evasion. Births were widely underreported, and pregnant women sometimes returned to their home villages to have their babies. Urban deaths might be increased by an influx of destitute migrants or sick people going to city hospitals; conversely, moribund town-dwellers might go home to rural areas and die unregistered. Indeed, while colonial vital statistics are often useful and informative, it will be repeatedly stressed in this chapter that they must be used with caution. Even today, birth and death registration has been characterized as "defective and highly unreliable."[7] It is probably true that, as a student of English historical demography has suggested, no underdeveloped country today keeps vital records "with the accuracy of the parish priests and parish clerks even of Stuart England."[8]

Censuses were taken in 1891, 1901, 1911, 1921, 1931, 1948, 1960, and 1970. The 1901 census was the first to attempt to cover the entire country as it was then constituted, but substantial areas of the north were omitted. Mandated Togo was included from 1921. The 1931 census was the first in which the population was individually enumerated; the 1948 census was the first to be based on house-to-house enumeration rather than on totals for villages and towns. The censuses were not very accurate, although they improved over the decades. According to one modern writer, prior to 1948, "available demographic statistics were of such dubious quality that no plausible population estimates could be based on them."[9] This may be too pessimistic, but the first reasonably accurate census was not held until 1960.[10]

Colonial census takers were under no illusions that they were making a precise count. The 1911 census left out much of the northeast and undercounted elsewhere.[11] The 1921 enumeration was better organized, but accurate maps, trained staff, and public cooperation were often lacking. In Tumu District, chiefs brought in beans, groundnuts, and stones to represent various age and sex categories.[12] In another northern district, high rainy-season vegetation hid many compounds. Once located, the head of the household would frequently

> sit in front of his compound and tell you blandly that he and he alone is the only inhabitant, while his wives and children are climbing out at the back, in full view of you, and running into the corn.[13]

"In short," wrote the census director, "it is difficult to imagine conditions more unfavorable to an accurate or even comparatively reliable enumeration."[14] The 1931 census was described as a great improvement, but the possibility of a 2-10 percent undercount was admitted.[15]

Data for sex and age are even more suspect than the overall counts. In some areas, women were hidden from enumerators.[16] More importantly, since few people in a non-literate society know their exact ages, census-takers frequently had to guess. Until 1960, ages were reported for categories such as 0-5, 6-15, 16-45, and over 46. Even so, misclassification was easily possible; for example, adolescent girls being counted as adults. In extreme cases, as in Wa District in 1921, where even the enumerators did not know how old they were, the age tables were "absolutely and entirely fictitious."[17] Reliable age data, which could be used to estimate fertility and mortality rates, are unfortunately lacking.

Although population data for Ghana are deficient in many respects, they are superior to what are available for Sierra Leone,[18] Nigeria,[19] and for many of the former French colonies.[20] Indeed, Gold Coast demographic material is probably better than that for most African territories in the colonial period. Censuses were flawed, and the long 1931-48 gap is frustrating, but major trends can be established. Population estimates for census years are shown in table 30 (page 141). Table 31 (page 142) gives year-by-year estimates which have been used to produce the per capita figures presented in earlier chapters; these annual estimates are based on arithmetic projections from flawed data for census years, so they are no more than convenient approximations. Table 32 (page 143) shows intercensal growth rates, calculated on the assumption that all growth was due to biological increase. Because this ignores immigration, and (more importantly) because population figures are uncertain, especially for the earlier censuses when undercounting was substantial, growth rates are only illustrative. It is clear, however, that population has been increasing throughout the twentieth century, with a marked acceleration evident after 1948.[21] Growth rates in the north have lagged behind more prosperous regions. It is quite possible that the population has been growing in much of Ghana since the mid-nineteenth century or earlier, although perhaps at lower rates.[22] Population growth must be due to one or more of the following factors: net immigration, more births, or fewer deaths.

The Gold Coast, as one of the most prosperous West African territories, attracted more people as immigrants than it lost as emigrants. Towns, mines, and cocoa farms drew people from Upper Volta, Togo, Nigeria, and virtually every other country in West Africa. Among the permanent settlers were Moba colonists from Togo, who began settlements in what was then bush country in Kusasi in the 1920s, and Lobi farmers, who moved into Gonja and Wa from the Ivory Coast.[23] Political pressures also produced many immigrants. High taxes, forced labor, compulsory cash crop cultivation, military conscription, and other aspects of French colonial rule induced tens of thousands to seek refuge in the Gold Coast. Thousands of Sanwi fled to southwestern Ghana before 1918; during the late 1920s and early 1930s, an estimated 80,000-100,000 people moved from Upper Volta to the Northern Territories.[24] However, as table 33 (page 143) shows, migration can only explain a small percentage of Ghana's growth. Even in the period 1948-1960, foreign-born Africans and their Ghana-born children account for only one-fifth of total growth. Slow growth rates in the Northern Territories are at least partially due to labor migration to the Colony and Ashanti.

There is little reliable information on fertility in the pre-independence period, but the evidence suggests that birth rates have always been very high and have increased only marginally, if at all, in the twentieth century. Caldwell argues that precolonial West Africa was probably

> the most unhealthy major region in the world. Death rates were almost certainly the world's highest (presumably close to 50 per thousand with a life expectancy at birth under 20 years), and population numbers were sustained only by equally high birth rates, achieved only by placing great cultural and social stress on high fertility values.[25]

Birth registration data are presented in table 34 (page 144). While evasion of registration was common, especially in the early years that the ordinance was in force in any given town, compliance tended to improve with time.[26] The crude birth rates shown are fairly steady and reasonably high, considering problems of underreporting and the relatively low proportion of women in some towns.[27] Crude rates are measured against the total population, and as will be discussed later, some official population figures are inaccurate. Male/female birth ratios were well below the 1.05/1.00 expected in large populations and which were in fact recorded in Ghana in 1963-67.[28] This may suggest higher male fetal death rates and/or bias against recording male deaths. Recorded crude birth rates are consistent with a pattern of continuing high fertility and are well above comparable crude death rates.

Special surveys also suggest that high fertility rates have existed for decades. For example, in 1924, 1,000 women seeking medical treatment for themselves or for their children in Koforidua were questioned on their reproductive histories. Ages of the mothers could not be accurately determined; they seemed to have an "average age" of 25-30 years and had given birth to a total of 3,666 children. The 72 women "over 40," with presumably completed families, had produced 493 live infants, or 6.8 per mother.[29] Fertility histories were collected from 5,854 "old" women during the 1931 census. Two hundred seventy-one were barren; the others had given birth to an average of 5.6 live children.[30] Reproductive histories were also collected in 1938-39 from women with completed families in conjunction with nutrition surveys. One hundred fifty-four women in northeastern Ghana had given birth to an average of 5.4 children, suggesting a crude birth rate of about 40/1,000.[31] An anthropologist found completed family sizes among Tallensi women in Zuarungu District of 6.2 children per mother in 1934 and 6.0 in 1973.[32] In three forest villages in the Akim area, 66 mothers averaged 7.5 births[33] for a crude birthrate of about 53.6/1,000. In four coastal villages, 83 mothers averaged 7.1 births,[34] implying a crude birthrate of 50.7/1,000. The samples in these surveys were small, and in 1938-39, barren women may have been excluded. In addition, experience with retrospective surveys has shown that reproductive histories may be intentionally or inadvertently falsified; in particular, stillbirths and children dying in infancy may be omitted.[35] The results do, however, suggest that fertility rates have been high for at least the last several decades.

The continued high percentage of children in the population, shown in table 35 (page 145), also suggests that fertility levels have been at or near contemporary levels for some time. Indeed, the age structure of the population has remained remarkably stable for decades. Demographers can use age distribution and model life tables to determine birth rates provided that (1) ages are accurately recorded, (2) mortality or growth rates are known, and (3) a published life table accurately describes the population. Although these conditions really do not exist for Ghana, Caldwell has used the method, with seemingly reasonable mortality assumptions, to produce "purely speculative" estimates of crude birth rates. He suggests figures of 48/1,000 in 1921, 50/1,000 in 1948, and 52/1,000 in 1960.[36] Increases, if real, could be explained by general health improvements, which would reduce the number of stillbirths and the number of potential mothers left as widows. Another student of Ghanaian demography is even more skeptical of pre-1960 data but agrees that fertility and crude birth rates have changed little since at least 1945.[37]

Although data are scanty, it seems that at most, rising birth rates could only be responsible for a small fraction of the population increase between 1901 and 1960. Since neither immigration nor an increased birth rate are sufficient explanations, declining mortality against a background of continuing high fertility must be the most important factor in demographic growth.

Ideally, studies of mortality should be based on data from a comprehensive death registration system in which causes of death are certified by physicians using standardized criteria. Such data, which are fairly recent even in Western countries, do not exist for Ghana, now or in the past. Since national figures have never been compiled, mortality rates can only be estimated for a limited number of registration areas, all urban, and from overall population trends. Causes of death can only be inferred from general disease conditions and from hospital and registration information on a small portion, primarily urban, of the total population.

Mortality data for registration areas are presented in table 36 (page 146) and table 37 (page 148). Deaths were more frequently reported to the authorities than births, but evasion was common, especially in the first few years that the Registration Ordinance was applied to a town. Uncertain base populations are an even more serious problem for determining crude death rates (C.D.R.). Registrars usually made population estimates for inter-censal years by assuming that growth continued at the same rate as between the two preceding censuses. For example, the population of a town in 1938 would be determined by adding seven times the average annual increase between 1921 and 1931 to the 1931 census figure. In 1940, this method was given up as totally unrealistic, and the same base population was used for 1940-47, even though it was obvious that urban areas were growing rapidly. The revised population estimates presented here were obtained by interpolation between the immediately previous and subsequent censuses; i.e., the 1938 figure is calculated by adding seven times the average annual increase between 1931 and 1948 to the 1931 base. This method better reflects the accelerating pace of urbanization, but towns did not necessarily grow at steady rates, and the census results were themselves imprecise. Hence, the revised crude death rates are only rough approximations. It is clear, however, that Ghana's towns were not the demographic sumps that towns were in nineteenth century Europe; births consistently exceeded deaths.[38]

Male deaths were consistently far in excess of female deaths. Males were more numerous in towns because of selective migration, so their greater number of deaths in part reflects a larger population at risk. However, sexual imbalance was not pronounced enough to explain the entire disparity. In 1931, the urban sex ratio was 1.22 males per female, but 1.71 males died for every female. By 1948, the urban male/female ratio had fallen to 1.11 to 1, but the death ratio in 1950 (1948 figures are not available) was 1.44 to 1.[39] Males had higher death rates largely because they constituted a disproportionate percentage of the economically and socially marginal segments of urban populations.

Registration reports give age at death in eight categories for 1920-38 and 1950-55. Unfortunately, as the censuses prior to 1960 give ages only in four broad categories, the age composition of registration area populations is uncertain, and it is impossible to determine age-specific death rates. Table 36a (page 147) and table 36b (page 148) show age at death as a percentage of all deaths for both sexes, while table 37 (page 149) shows the ratio between male and female deaths at various ages. The high proportion of deaths in the 25-45 age group is noteworthy. The disproportionate ratio of male/female deaths in this category is, as described above, partly due to the sizes of the groups at risk and partly due to the severe health problems facing poor migrants. The decline in mortality in this age group in the 1950s probably reflects improved urban health conditions. Infant mortality (24 hours to 1 year) was also very high, with males, not surprisingly, being more vulnerable. The increase in the proportion of infant deaths in the 1950s was probably due to a larger population at risk. Significantly, child deaths (1-5 years) were nearly as numerous. Infant and child mortality will be discussed in detail below. Relatively few people lived long enough to die in the over-65 category, but females had a great advantage. In fact, this is the only age group in which females died in greater numbers than males.

Crude death rates remained remarkably stable between the mid-1920s and 1955. It seems probable, however, that more complete registration to some extent masks a real improvement in urban mortality. There are no comparable data for rural areas, but rural C.D.R.s have almost certainly been higher than urban ones. Caldwell has used age data from the census and stable population analysis to produce very rough national C.D.R. estimates of 38/1,000 in 1921, 24/1,000 in 1948, and 23/1,000 in 1954. Life expectancy at birth was estimated at 28 years in 1921, 39.5 years in 1948, and 52.5 years in 1954.[40] Assuming that the crude birth rate has remained at about 50/1,000 over this period, it is obvious that declining mortality has produced a widening gap between births and deaths which has been the primary cause of Ghana's increasingly rapid demographic growth. Although vital registration figures show no appreciable mortality decline, population increase provides clear evidence of falling death rates.[41]

A number of medical and non-medical factors might explain declining mortality. On the medical side, preventive measures may have reduced exposure to potentially lethal pathogens. Therapy may have contributed directly by saving lives or indirectly by curing people so that they could not infect others. Conversely, non-medical factors may have played a major role. Selective pressures may have produced less virulent microorganisms or more resistant human populations. Stable administration may have reduced mortality from slave raids and wars. Nutrition, particularly animal protein intake, may have improved. Economic growth may have enabled a significant number of Ghanaians to enjoy a higher standard of living. The remainder of this chapter will be devoted to a discussion of the relative importance of these factors.

As McKeown and his associates have demonstrated in England and parts of Europe, knowledge of trends in specific causes of death is extremely useful in seeking explanations for declining mortality. However, even in Europe and America, reliable information on cause of death dates only from the mid-nineteenth century at best, and even twentieth century records are often lacking or faulty.[42] Not surprisingly, Ghanaian data are much worse. Two sources are available; registration reports and medical records based on hospital deaths and mortality in epidemics. These sources are partially overlapping, since most hospitals were in registration areas and deaths of patients presumably were reported accurately. Both have a strong urban bias and so may not reflect conditions in the country as a whole. Furthermore, registrars often had to assign causes of death without the aid of a medical diagnosis. Causes were sometimes deduced from post-mortem appearance or statements of survivors. Eighty-eight percent of all deaths in Accra were medically certified in 1925-25, but only 48.5 percent of the total in all registration areas were so documented.[43] The situation did improve, and by 1929, causes were certified by physicians in two-thirds of all deaths.[44] However, even when a doctor determined a cause, accurate diagnosis or deciding which of several co-existing diseases killed a patient was often difficult. Thus, information on specific causes of mortality is limited to a small and atypical segment of the population and is not very precise.

Since we cannot know disease-specific mortality with any degree of accuracy in 1955 (or 1981, for that matter), let alone in 1900, it will be much more difficult to explain declining mortality in Ghana than in a country like England, and the answers must be both more vague and more tentative. Information on the prevalences of particular diseases and the measures taken against them will be used freely to support the data on disease-specific mortality, and some very broad generalizations will have to be made on non-medical factors. Two special categories of mortality—maternal and infant and child—will be discussed first, followed by an assessment of specific diseases, a discussion of non-medical factors, and an appraisal of the overall contribution of modern medicine to Ghanaian health and population growth between 1900 and 1955.

It is unlikely that medical measures had much affect on maternal death rates, at least until after 1945. The Accra maternity hospital, the first of its kind, was not opened until 1928; the first trained midwives did not begin to practice until the early 1930s. Most women wanted to give birth at home, preferring familiar customs and the care of relatives at this difficult time.[45] Ante-natal and post-natal care became increasingly popular, but hospitalization or the government midwife were not usually considered necessary unless there was serious trouble during labor; hence, the high case-mortality rates shown in table 38 (page 150).[46] Medical intervention affected only a small percentage of pregnancies. Even with the conservative assumption of a crude birth rate of 45/1,000, about one mother in 10,000 got hospital care in 1925, and about 1 in 1,000 attended an outpatient clinic. These figures rose slowly: 1.5 percent were in-patients and 9 percent were out-patients in 1935; 4 percent were in-patients and 30 percent had out-patient care in 1950. The handful of trained midwives had little impact until the late 1940s, except in a few large towns. In Accra, for example, roughly 40 percent of all births were attended by government midwives in 1937 and 1938.[47] Even as late as 1968, over three-fourths of all births in the urban registration areas were assisted only by "traditional" attendants.[48] Government medical services did provide care for difficult cases, and (as the in-patient figures suggest) many lives must have been saved from the 1930s on. However, the numbers involved were too small to have more than a marginal demographic effect. The published maternal mortality rates suggest little if any real progress, even in the towns. Rates ranged from 11.1 to 23.8 deaths per 1,000 live births between 1938 and 1955, without any definite trend.

Infant and child mortality rates have always been very high in Ghana. Since accurate infant mortality rates (I.M.R., deaths 0-1 year per 1,000 live births) depend on good birth and death registration, the data in table 34 (page 144), which, of course, apply only to towns, must be treated with caution. Births were less completely reported than deaths, so I.M.R.s were sometimes artificially inflated, especially in the early years of registration. For example, Accra's official I.M.R. was 483/1,000 in 1918, 405/1,000 in 1920, 259/1,000 in 1925-26, and 113/1,000 in 1930, the general level where it remained until after 1950. While public health and medical care produced some improvement during the 1920s, more complete birth registration explains most of the apparent progress.[49]

The only information on rural infant mortality comes from a few special surveys. Data from some of these are presented in table 39 (page 151). As discussed above with fertility, the surveys were based on retrospective case histories, and the women questioned may well have omitted some infant deaths. Figures from Koforidua in 1924 and the 1968-69 national demographic survey are presented for comparison. Ages at death were imprecise; frequently, deaths were categorized as "infant" if the child died before being able to walk. Three facts are clear, despite the inadequate data. There were significant regional differences in infant mortality, with the poorer north having especially high rates. Towns had significantly lower rates than rural areas. Finally, neither registration nor survey data suggest a decline in I.M.R. prior to 1955.

Stillbirth figures are given in table 34 (page 144). Reporting of stillbirths was probably even less accurate in both registration and in retrospective surveys. Very substantial under-reporting is likely; on the other hand, babies who lived a few minutes or a few hours may have been assigned to this category. While no great confidence can be placed in the numbers, it is clear that stillbirth rates were consistently several times higher than in developed countries, indicating poor health among pregnant women.

Very heavy mortality among young children (ages 1-5) is shown in table 36a (page 147) and table 36b (page 148) and table 37 (page 149) for registration areas, and in the rural data from the retrospective surveys. The 1968-69 sample surveys also revealed very high death rates for young children (1-4), especially in the second year of life; and in two of three surveys, child deaths actually exceeded infant deaths.[50]

The causes of infant and child mortality in poor tropical countries like Ghana were, and are, diverse and complex. Even more than for adults, several co-existing conditions often contributed to death. Genetic defects, poor maternal health, prematurity, birth injuries, and infection of the umbilical cord (neonatal tetanus) were prominent causes of death for fetuses and very young infants. Babies and toddlers were exposed to the entire spectrum of infectious diseases, with malaria, diarrheal diseases, respiratory tract infections, measles, and whooping cough being important causes of death. Children passed through an especially critical period between roughly six and eighteen months. During this time, the child lost maternal antibodies against malaria and other diseases and could only develop his own as a result of infection. He was challenged by a rapid succession of bacterial and viral infections of the digestive and respiratory systems. Crawling babies were vulnerable to soil-transmitted helminths like ascaris and hookworm. Nutritional problems were often crucial. The baby lost a vital source of protein and other nutrients during weaning; mother's milk was often replaced by starchy gruels. Malnutrition, often accompanied by anemia due to malaria, hookworm, or faulty diet, retarded growth and reduced resistance to infection during what has been aptly described as the "weaning crisis."[51] Weanling diarrhea, an often fatal syndrome which resulted in large numbers of infant deaths in developed countries into the early twentieth century, seems to be associated with poor nutrition. The usual bacteria and amebae can be responsible, or diarrhea may be caused by organisms which are not normally pathogenic in well-nourished children.[52] No specific pathogen could be detected in most cases, but recent research has suggested that a virus is the most common cause.[53]

Infant and child mortality was, as colonial physicians were quite aware, intimately linked to the most basic problems of hygiene, nutrition, and disease. Only a broad attack on all of these problems could reduce the tragic loss of young lives. The Infant Welfare Centre movement, described in chapter 2, was one response to this challenge. Poor diet, especially lack of protein after weaning, was a major concern, because there was no indigenous dairy industry, and meat and fish were expensive. Dr. Cecily Williams' discovery of kwashiorkor,[54] a grave condition caused by extreme protein deprivation, gave an extra sense of urgency. Medical officials advocated the introduction of dairy cattle and even the importation of European milking goats, but animal diseases frustrated such efforts.[55]

The only alternative seemed to be imported milk in powdered or condensed form. It has become evident in recent years that bottle feeding is a dangerous innovation in African conditions and should be discouraged in favor of natural nursing. Bottle feeding, seen by many women as a symbol of prestige and modernity, could be beneficial if properly done. However, because milk is expensive, it is often highly diluted, thus depriving the baby of essential protein. More importantly, since the water, bottles, or nipples are very likely to become contaminated, artificial feeding frequently leads to infection.[56] These drawbacks more than make up for any possible benefits, unless the mother cannot nurse.[57] Such problems were not evident in the 1930s, when tinned milk proved able to cure and prevent kwashiorkor and seemed to be an invaluable supplement to the diets of older babies. Several firms regularly advertised condensed and powdered milk for babies in the local press, beginning in the mid-1920s,[58] but at first these products were probably used only by a few well-to-do urban Africans, who perhaps were able to use ample quantities and to prepare milk properly. Dr. Williams was so enthusiastic about the potential value of tinned milk that she unsuccessfully urged an official endorsement of Nestlé's product to encourage more general use.[59] Dr. F. M. Purcell, equally impressed by clinical experience with malnourished children, proposed that infant welfare clinics issue free milk to mothers.[60]

Such suggestions were never implemented, and it is not clear how widespread the substitution of bottle feeding for breast feeding had become by 1955. Probably the process had not gone very far. However, it is clear that infant and child nutrition were still crucial problems at the end of the colonial era and remain so today. The ratio of child to infant deaths, especially the ratio between second year and first year deaths, has been suggested as an index of a society's nutritional state. Deaths in the 1-4 age group average about fifteen percent of infant mortality in developed countries,[61] but the ratio approaches 1/1 in Ghana. Child mortality is perhaps Ghana's most crucial health challenge. Infant mortality rates in the 1960s were ten to fifteen times those of developed countries, but child death rates were fifty to sixty times greater than in developed countries.[62]

Statistical data, plus the sheer complexity of the factors involved and their intimate relationships to poor living conditions and very difficult medical problems, suggest that little was accomplished in the colonial era to prevent the wastage of the new-born, infants, and children. Certainly, the basic problems were not solved, but some incremental progress was made. Modest advances in care in the ante-natal period and during childbirth must have had some impact on stillbirths and deaths of very young infants. Infant Welfare Centres, malaria control, public health measures, and therapy began to have at least a marginal effect in some areas by the 1920s; rising case-loads suggest that medical factors became more meaningful in a demographic sense in the 1930s and especially after 1945. Malnutrition continued to be common, but as will be argued later, gradual dietary improvements influenced all age groups, including the very young. Slowly declining infant and child mortality appears to have been an important component of population growth, especially after 1948.[63] As with overall mortality, our knowledge of conditions in the country as a whole is much too meager to measure changes in infant and child mortality rates directly. In the cities, better reporting of vital events probably masks a real decline in mortality among the young, as well as for the general population. Both medical and non-medical factors made contributions to the saving of lives among mothers, infants, and children, but any kind of quantitative assessment is impossible.

The effects of therapeutic and preventive medicine on morbidity and mortality from various diseases have already been discussed in previous chapters; this section will briefly summarize the demographic consequences of actions against major specific causes of death. Two factors which limited the impact of medical measures must be kept in mind throughout the discussion. First, relatively few Ghanaians sought western medical care until the 1920s, and even then, the percentage of the population attending hospitals and clinics rose slowly. Not until 1941 did as many as one person in ten receive treatment (see table 6, page 115, and table 7, page 117). Second, the limits of contemporary medical knowledge and capabilities hindered progress. Without cheap, effective drugs and vaccines for mass use, rapid health improvements were impossible in the absence of extensive socio-economic change.

Malaria was by far the greatest threat to life and well-being among the insect-vectored diseases. Indeed, success against malaria would have reduced mortality more than the conquest of any other disease. Unfortunately, although the mode of transmission and an effective prophylactic and curative drug were known in 1900, malaria remained a major cause of death, even in urban areas (see table 40, page 152). Vector control and chemical prophylaxis had little lasting impact, but the sheer number of cases treated indicates that therapy saved hundreds, perhaps thousands, of lives every year, especially after the late 1920s (see table 9, page 119). Yellow fever, louse-borne relapsing fever, and plague were not major killers, although effective control measures against the last two probably prevented more widespread outbreaks. Trypanosomiasis was a serious threat in parts of the north during the 1930s and 1940s, and vector control doubtlessly prevented thousands of cases. Since the disease is usually fatal, treatment saved thousands of lives annually during this period (see table 10, page 120).

The record against diseases spread by fecal contamination and impure water was much less impressive. Therapy, especially perhaps emetine for amebic dysentery, did help a small percentage of the victims of enteric infections, but little real progress was possible without extensive and costly improvements in sanitation and water supply. Gold Coast Africans were "so far as their persons are concerned . . . remarkable cleanly," an early medical observer noted, "but in their mode of life, houses, and surroundings generally, they are indescribably filthy."[64] While the last part of the quotation requires modification today, there is still a striking contrast between personal and environmental sanitation which, among many other factors, ensures a continuing high incidence of many of the diseases in this group. Piped water, latrines, and other public health measures did convey substantial benefits on town-dwellers, so, despite crowding and poverty, births easily outdistanced deaths in the growing cities (see table 34, page 144, and table 36, page 146). Even in urban areas, however, table 40 (page 152) shows that enteric diseases were serious, though declining, causes of death throughout the colonial period.

Tuberculosis and the pneumonia group of diseases were also major causes of death in cities, as indicated in table 40 (page 152). Therapy for tuberculosis was generally ineffective until the early 1950s, but sulpha drugs in the late 1930s and antibiotics after 1945 were potent weapons against pneumonia. Indeed, table 15 (page 126) shows that case mortality rates were roughly cut in half between the early 1930s and early 1940s, so improved therapy prevented hundreds of deaths per year. Similarly, new drugs drastically reduced the toll in cerebrospinal meningitis epidemics in the far north after the Second World War. Smallpox, another disease spread by the respiratory route, was contained to some extent by large-scale vaccination after 1920; it was the only disease for which immunization had a significant public health impact.

The spread of venereal disease easily outran medical countermeasures until the advent of sulpha drugs, effective against gonorrhea, and especially penicillin, a powerful cure for both gonorrhea and syphilis. Anti-yaws campaigns reduced the incidence of this chronic and disabling disease, but probably had little impact on mortality.

Given the weak data, it is obviously impossible to calculate the number of lives saved by medical measures, either against these major causes of death or against the array of less-frequently lethal conditions discussed in previous chapters. Such an exercise would perhaps be possible for Accra and other cities with reasonably good death registration data, but on the national level it would be futile to try following the trail blazed by McKeown for England and Wales or Mandle for British Guiana. It is, however, tempting to make one brief and very tentative quantitative foray. If Caldwell's suggestions of crude death rates of roughly 38 per 1,000 in 1921 and 24 per 1,000 in 1948 are accepted,[65] there would have been about 97,000 deaths in 1921 and 106,000 in 1948, or, extrapolating from these figures, something like 100,000 deaths per year in Ghana during the intervening period. Therapy for malaria, trypanosomiasis, respiratory diseases, traumatic injuries, and other life-threatening conditions certainly prevented thousands of deaths annually from at least the late 1920s. If, for sake of argument, we assume that 4 percent of all patients received life-saving treatment, some 2,300 deaths would have been averted in 1921 and almost 32,000 in 1948. There is, of course, nothing magic about the 4 percent figure, but an examination of the disease returns suggests that it is not implausible, at least for 1948. If the crude death rate of 38 per 1,000 was still prevailing in 1948, there would have been around 168,000 deaths that year, or about two-thirds higher than calculated from Caldwell's estimate for 1948. Even if 4 percent is too high a proportion for patients' lives saved by therapy, medical intervention plus preventive measures might well account for half or more of the total mortality reduction by the late 1940s.

While no particular credence can be placed on the figures discussed above, they do suggest that, at least by the 1940s, medical measures did play a very substantial role in reducing mortality. Other factors, however, also contributed to declining crude death rates. A slightly younger population structure had some effect, although this was minimized by continuing high infant and child mortality. Non-medical factors are clearly involved as well, and, as in Europe and North America, they may have played a crucial role in reducing the incidence of and mortality from infectious diseases. Discussion must now turn to these factors.

A non-medical factor which could have effected mortality is a change in the virulence of one or more major infectious diseases. Such changes can occur by gradual natural selection for milder strains of pathogens which do not kill their hosts or stimulate strong immunological defenses, or by sudden mutation. Mutant microbes could, of course, also be more deadly than earlier strains. Selection could also work on the hosts. The most genetically vulnerable individuals would tend to die off, leaving later generations with a higher percentage of people with genetically determined defenses against the disease. Such evolutionary forces have obviously been at work for centuries in Ghana.

Genetic changes in the pathogen probably played a role in the decline of trypanosomiasis in the 1940s, but it is impossible to say how much. Influenza viruses undergo frequent mutations which allow them to cause epidemics in populations with acquired resistance to older strains. A particularly virulent mutant caused enormous loss of life in 1918-19; the relatively benign nature of influenza in Ghana since then (at least until 1957) was largely due to the absence of severe new forms of the virus. Scarlet fever has undergone major fluctuations in virulence in Europe over the last two centuries,[66] but the disease has never been significant in Ghana. Genetic resistance against tuberculosis has probably increased somewhat in Ghana, and the same could be true for measles,[67] but, for these and other diseases, selection for more resistant people is probably much less important than the population's living standards, general physical condition, and epidemiological experience. Previous exposure, especially to diseases like smallpox, measles, and yellow fever (which convey long-lasting immunities on survivors) reduced the pool of susceptible individuals and hence retarded the spread of epidemics. Major shifts in the biological balance between man and his pathogens cannot be ruled out, but, with the exception of influenza, such changes have probably had little demographic impact during the short period of five-and-a-half decades under consideration here.

Stable administration would logically be considered favorable to population growth, but the demographic blessings of the "Pax Coloniale" can be overestimated and the costs underestimated. Termination of slaving and warfare, physical security (allowing more extensive use of arable land), abolition of internal trade barriers, better transportation, and, of course, medical services, would be beneficial. Conversely, bloody "pacification" campaigns, heavy labor demands, forced delivery of forest or farm products, resettlement schemes, and enhanced opportunities for the spread of infectious diseases, would retard growth and could precipitate substantial population declines. Indeed, the early decades of colonial rule were marked by demographic stagnation or regression in much of Africa. This phenomenon began in the 1890s, at least in East Africa, and was not reversed until 1930 or thereabouts in some places.[68] Ghana, perhaps in common with other areas in West Africa, does not follow this pattern. Population growth seems to have been continuous since at least the mid-nineteenth century in most of the country, with more rapid growth during the colonial years.[69] The country's early epidemiological history, its relative wealth, and the comparatively benign nature of British rule, set it apart from, for instance, East Africa or French Equatorial Africa. Some aspects of the colonial era, such as rapid urbanization, labor migration, and faster transportation, did help increase mortality, but not nearly enough to offset gains from natural increase and immigration.

British rule over the entire territory which now constitutes the Republic of Ghana did establish peace between previously hostile states. Caldwell, in a stimulating essay on Africa's population history, has argued that warfare was a major check on growth prior to the colonial period. Direct casualties, the extraction of slaves, and disruption of agriculture took a heavy toll until European powers intervened.[70] It is difficult to generalize about the destructiveness of African wars, and, while this hypothesis has some validity for places like southern Chad and southern Sudan, it has little relevance for Ghana. The winding down of the Atlantic slave trade and the relatively, if not entirely, peaceful conditions which prevailed in southern Ghana during the last three-quarters of the nineteenth century, indicate that wars caused few direct or indirect casualties in most of the forest and coastal regions.[71] Wilks has suggested that metropolitan Asante's population declined from c. 500,000 in the early nineteenth century to c. 350,000 between 1910 and 1920. Even if losses of this magnitude did occur in the core provinces, however, migration southward into the Colony was probably more important than mortality caused by wars and internal strife.[72] Northern Ghana did experience considerable fighting and unrest late in the century, with much loss of life and, probably, substantial depopulation in some regions.[73] Chokossi raids in the northeast in the 1860s and 1880s,[74] the predatory activities of Zabarima bands under Babatu and other leaders in the northwest from the 1870s to the establishment of British control, and the brief forays of Samori after 1895, seem to have been very destructive.[75] The northwestern corner of the country, which also suffered thousands of deaths from cerebrospinal meningitis (1906-1908), influenza (1918-19), and perhaps other epidemics, may well have experienced a demographic decline in the late nineteenth and early twentieth centuries typical of most of Africa. However, except for these far northern districts, the British found little local fighting to suppress, so this aspect of colonial rule had only a small impact on mortality.

Other possible demographic benefits of stable, unified administration will just be mentioned here, as they will be discussed in the following sections. The administration, eager to increase trade, removed commercial barriers between formerly independent states and revolutionized the transportation system. This permitted diseases to spread more rapidly, but it also stimulated a growing trade in foodstuffs, which encouraged greater production. This, plus improved distribution, resulted in better nutrition and the alleviation of local famines.[76] Veterinary, and, perhaps to a lesser extent, agricultural services, contributed to these ends. The British regime's efforts to encourage production and trade, however halting, did assist many Ghanaians to achieve real advances in living standards. And, of course, the government did provide at least the beginnings of a modern health service.

The impact of diet on the general health of a population can hardly be overestimated. Inadequate intake of specific nutrients may result in well-defined deficiency diseases; for example, lack of vitamin B-1 causes beri-beri, scurvy results from shortages of vitamin C, and lack of vitamin D causes rickets. More commonly, diets deficient in vitamins, minerals, or proteins containing essential amino acids, produce general loss of vigor. Malnourished individuals are less energetic, less productive, and have less resistance to infectious and non-infectious diseases. Poor nutrition weakens pregnant and nursing women and may have a crucial impact on fetal survival and the size and health of their babies. Protein and vitamin deficiencies in young children can retard physical and mental growth.

The strong synergistic relationship between a host's nutritional state and his resistance to infectious diseases is especially crucial in poor tropical countries like Ghana. Malnutrition and infection reinforce each other; the combined effects are generally more severe than the symptoms of either condition in isolation would suggest. Infection may trigger a nutritional crisis, or a disease may take a more serious course in a poorly nourished host.[77] For example, diarrhea may stimulate kwashiorkor in children with diets deficient in protein, while malnourished children sometimes acquire diarrhea from common intestinal organisms which are not normally pathogenic.[78] Tuberculosis takes a more acute course in persons with poor diets, especially those deficient in protein and vitamin A. Conversely, tuberculosis interferes with crucial metabolic processes and may induce shortages of these substances.[79] Measles is a serious, sometimes lethal disease in malnourished children, and the disease can precipitate kwashiorkor.[80] Chronic malaria and hookworm are common causes of anemia, but people with good diets may harbor these parasites with few or no clinical symptoms. Mortality from bronchopneumonia is higher in those suffering protein deficiencies,[81] as is the incidence of tropical ulcer.[82]

Indeed, although the biological mechanisms which link nutritional state and resistance to infection are complex and not fully understood, and the relationships between nutrition and some viral diseases are still unclear,[83] nutritional factors may be assumed to influence all the diseases of bacterial, protozoan, or helminthic etiology found in Ghana.

Few details are available on nutritional patterns and dietary changes in Ghana. With some exceptions among the poorest urban residents and seasonal dearths in parts of the north, total caloric intake apparently was generally adequate. There was an over-dependence on carbohydrates: cassava, maize, plaintains, and yams in the south; millet and sorghum in the north. The most crucial and widespread problem was the shortage of animal protein.[84] Vitamin deficiencies were common but, except perhaps for lack of vitamin A in the north, were not usually severe enough to produce specific diseases. Unlike most Europeans prior to the twentieth century, most Ghanaians had access to fresh fruits and vegetables throughout the year. Urban dwellers often had close ties with the countryside and its produce. Abundant sunshine insured production of vitamin D in the skin; hence, again in contrast to urban Europe in the nineteenth century, rickets was extremely rare. Although specific deficiency diseases such as beri-beri, scurvy, and pellagra were known, and heightened medical interest resulted in the discovery of more cases,[85] none were very prevalent. Kwashiorkor, a protein-deprivation syndrome frequently seen in recently weaned children, was an exception. This disease, which was first described by Cecily Williams in Accra children, seems to have been fairly widespread. Diets with chronically inadequate quantities of specific vitamins and, especially, animal protein were a much more significant problem than starvation, gross protein-calorie malnutrition, or specific deficiency diseases. Children, pregnant and lactating women, poor laborers, and inhabitants of some densely populated districts in the far north were most vulnerable.[86]

The medical authorities were well aware of the importance of nutrition. As early as 1920, the Health Branch prepared a simple leaflet explaining good dietary habits and distributed copies to chiefs and school children.[87] Departmental annual reports regularly noted the general lack of animal protein and fats and seasonal shortages of fresh fruits and vegetables in some areas and advocated steps to improve fishing, agriculture, and stock-raising.[88] "There is probably no more ready method of relieving much of the worst effects of endemic diseases," observed one D.M.S., "than through improved nutrition."[89] Indeed, by the mid-1930s, there was a growing medical consensus that better health in Ghana and in Africa in general would depend in large measure on more nutritious diets.[90]

In 1936, a Colonial Office circular dispatch pointed out the significance of nutrition throughout the Empire and urged that colonies form special committees to investigate local conditions.[91] The Gold Coast government created a committee chaired by the D.M.S., which included the D.D.H.S., the Analytical Chemist, the Senior Pathologist, the Secretary for Native Affairs, the Principal of Achimota, and the Directors of the Education, Agriculture, and Veterinary Departments. The committee met for the first time on May 5, 1937, discussed meat, fish, and milk supplies, and agreed to appoint a research officer to conduct nutritional surveys in various regions of the country.[92] Its final report, largely the work of its research officer, Dr. F. M. Purcell, was an important document which clearly demonstrated what had long been suspected: that nutritional conditions varied widely in different zones of the Gold Coast.[93] The report, together with Purcell's other accounts of his investigations,[94] provides invaluable information on diet, general health conditions, fertility, and infant mortality in the north, the forest area, and the coast. Little could be done during the war to correct the problems Purcell demonstrated; indeed, he resigned in disgust in 1944, but a full-time nutritionist was added to the department in 1946.[95]

Purcell's study showed that the most critical situation was in the northern tier of districts which now comprise the Upper Region. It had long been recognized that the last months of the dry season, April through June, were often "a period of semi-starvation" there because stored food stocks ran low or were exhausted;[96] indeed, the "hungry season" is still an almost annual phenomenon in parts of the north.[97] Lack of fruit was linked to an apparent deficiency of vitamin A in 1931; red palm oil, a rich source of this vitamin, was distributed through Native Authorities.[98] Anthropological studies among the Tallensi in the mid-1930s showed that both poverty and cultural practices were responsible for low meat consumption. Game and fish were scarce, and cattle, sheep, and goats were not slaughtered for food but only eaten when sacrificed for special ritual occasions. Eggs were not eaten, and women could not eat chickens. Guinea fowls were the only domestic animals killed specifically to be consumed.[99]

Purcell worked in Northeast Ghana from July to October 1939 while he was also responsible for an anti-trypanosomiasis team, and briefly revisited the area in 1940. He was able to examine, weigh, measure, and question hundreds of people in South Mamprussi, Kusasi, Zuarungu, and Navrongo Districts, and did a little work in Lawra. He was unable to perform detailed analyses of foodstuffs, but he and his assistants recorded sample diets in selected compounds which confirmed that the people were "practically vegetarians." Groundnuts were an important source of protein for children.[100] During the wet season, caloric intake ranged from 1,500 to 3,000 or more per day, but often fell below 1,500—even to 500-1,000—in the dry season, and vitamins A, C, and some of the B-group were deficient then.[101] Goitre was common in the Sandema area of Navrongo District.[102] The major nutritional problems were the scarcity of protein and "the widely prevalent state of semi-starvation caused by lack of every kind of food," especially during the dry season.[103]

Purcell had studied nutrition in forest villages since 1935, when he was M.O. at Oda. Here he found that people ate a "great excess" of carbohydrates but got plenty of vegetables, fruit, and vitamin A-rich palm oil. The greatest problem was animal protein. Meat from goats, chickens, or game was scarce and mostly consumed by wealthier persons. Eggs were "rarely" eaten. The collection of terrestrial snails made a small contribution. The major source of protein was dried or salted fish, which was imported from the coast. Fish was cheap, but supplies were seasonal.[104] Clinical cases of well-defined deficiency disease were rare, except for kwashiorkor in young children, a condition which was well-known to traditional practitioners. Purcell noted that this deadly syndrome was often precipitated by attacks of measles, whooping cough, or bacillary dysentery, and urged government distribution of tinned milk to ensure adequate protein for post-weaning infants.[105] In a later survey at the cocoa village of Akokoase, Purcell found better nutrition because fish was more plentiful,[106] but, as at Oda, stress from disease often produced symptoms of malnutrition.[107]

Inhabitants of the fishing villages of Dnelukope, Pram Pram, Nungua, and Senya Beraku were not very cooperative with Purcell's survey teams, but they seemed to be the best nourished population in the colony. They had plenty of protein in the form of fish and were prosperous enough to buy agricultural produce from their neighbors. Fishermen had noticeably better physiques and far fewer signs of malnutrition than people living a short distance inland.[108]

Purcell's surveys in the late 1930s showed that, except in the far north, daily caloric intake was generally adequate, although too much was in the form of carbohydrates. Specific vitamin deficiency diseases were rare. Cooking with palm oil insured adequate amounts of vitamin A; rickets was almost unknown because ample sunshine ensured that people could manufacture vitamin D; and fresh fruits and vegetables provided vitamin C in quantities sufficient to prevent scurvy. Diets were often monotonous, and some children, pregnant women, and poor people did border on malnutrition.[109] The greatest problem everywhere, except among fishing populations, was lack of animal protein.

Similar conditions were found in forest villages in the post-war years. At Kwansakrom, a village on the south edge of the forest only fifteen miles from the sea, investigators noted in 1950 that "too little protein was eaten." Here, as almost everywhere else in the country, goats were not milked and cows' milk was not available. Of fifty 1-5 year olds examined, twenty-three (46 percent) showed signs of malnutrition.[110] At a village near Kumasi and at another village eight miles from Accra, another researcher found diets "poor or inadequate to the extreme," with too much starch and too little fat and protein. The people kept chickens and turkeys, but neither poultry nor eggs were regularly eaten. Smoked or dried fish from the coast, eaten in small quantities, was the major source of animal protein.[111]

Details of changes in nutrition during the twentieth century are scarce, and, as the surveys cited above suggest, there were important regional differences. It is also clear that persons with higher incomes were able to buy better food, notably meat and fish. Unfortunately, although the quantity and quality of foodstuffs had crucial effects on health conditions, lack of historical research means that trends in food supplies can only be discussed in tentative and impressionistic terms. Three factors are involved: food importation; production from animal husbandry, fishing, and agriculture; and the distribution of food within the country.

Large quantities of foodstuffs were imported during the colonial period, but since customs returns were often aggregated under the heading "Foodstuffs, Alcoholic Beverages, and Tobacco," the nutritional impact is difficult to assess. However, figures for processed meat and fish are available for the 1920s and 1930s, and (as shown in table 41, page 000) several pounds of animal protein per capita were imported annually. While most was doubtlessly consumed by a few relatively prosperous town dwellers and cocoa farmers,[112] the quantities are large enough to have been nutritionally significant. However, not all imported foods had a beneficial effect on health. In the 1920s, medical authorities were concerned that too much reliance was being placed on canned foods with dubious nutritional value.[113] The growing popularity of polished rice, which lacked the outer layer rich in B-vitamins, was also viewed with alarm.[114] White bread, produced from imported flour, was widely consumed in parts of southern Ghana in the late 1930s and was increasingly popular after 1945.[115] Problems caused by the widespread use of tinned milk, advocated by many doctors as an answer to the post-weaning nutritional crisis, have been described above.

Colonial authorities were, quite rightly, anxious to improve the meat supply. "Any money spent on giving the people of the country an adequate meat supply so necessary to a balanced and sufficient diet," wrote the head of the Veterinary Service, "is more than repaid by improved health. Without this necessity, nutritional disorders and deficiency diseases are common and the body is in a state of prediliction to all kinds of disease."[116] While this statement was part of an argument by the Veterinary Department for a larger share of the colonial budget, it contains much truth. The government encouraged importation of live cattle, sheep, and goats overland from French West Africa, and a small seaborne trade from Nigeria and Cameroun. Animals from the north were inspected for disease, and their movement southward, in lorries or on the hoof, was facilitated by government roads, watering places, and tsetse control efforts. Herds in the Northern Territories had been decimated by rinderpest during World War I, and—largely because of trypanosomiasis—cattle-raising was impossible in the south, except on the dry coastal plains east of Accra. By the early 1930s, energetic work by the Veterinary Department had controlled rinderpest and bovine pleuropneumonia, and, after the end of epizootic disasters, Ghanaian herds began to increase. Local production, however, rose much slower than demand, and, especially for beef, the Gold Coast was dependent on imports from Upper Volta and other French territories. There is little data on domestic production of small stock and poultry, but, as described above, per capita consumption remained low, although it may have gradually risen over the decades. The Veterinary Department accomplished little with sheep and goats but did some locally useful work encouraging hog raising and in control of diseases of chickens. Together with the Agriculture Department, some progress was made in introducing improved animal breeds, but attempts to establish a dairy industry failed.[117] Slaughtering data may provide an index of meat supplies in major cities; figures for 1948 suggest that 10.7 pounds of meat were available per person in Accra, and 25 pounds per person in Kumasi.[118]

Fish has been the primary source of animal proteins for most Ghanaians, but little is known about the history or productivity of the indigenous fishing industry. Large quantities of preserved fish, especially tinned sardines, have been imported since early in the century. The development of trade in fresh-water fish from the Niger River was made possible by colonial roads; by 1953-54, an estimated 4,000-5,000 tons were imported annually in lorries.[119] Coastal canoe fishermen provided the bulk of the local catch. After the adoption of improved nets about 1900, the basic technology of the industry remained unchanged until large motor craft with long cruising ranges were introduced in 1954. Canoe fisheries were largely seasonal; 80 percent of the annual catch was made during the June-September herring season.[120] Landings were sold to women traders, who smoked most of the catch and sold it in towns or inland markets. Early in the century, Accra women headcarried sixty-pound loads of fish as far inland as Kororidua, Kibi, and Dodowa. The advent of lorries by c. 1920 eliminated this form of trade but permitted larger quantities of fish to reach markets further inland.[121] Only a tiny volume of fish reached Kumasi prior to 1903, but Fanti traders took advantage of the opening of the rail line in that year to increase sales. In 1908, 544 tons of fish reached the city, still far below the demand.[122] In addition to the sea fisheries, people caught small quantities of fresh water fish in ponds and streams. Ewe fishermen followed the Volta system far into the Northern Territories; they exploited waters avoided by local populations because of the danger of onchocerciasis.[123]

It is impossible to determine the amount of fish caught or consumed in the pre-1940 period because the colonial government took almost no interest in the industry. In 1936, the government applauded the efforts of a former teacher at Achimota to introduce traps for crabs and lobsters and to improve the curing of fish,[124] but fisheries work did not begin until 1941-42, and a Fisheries Department was not created until 1945. On the basis of a small sample survey, total marine landings in 1942 were estimated at approximately 23,000 tons; in 1954, the domestic catch was estimated at 20,000 tons.[125] Perhaps 20,000 tons is a reasonable upper limit for the average annual production of the traditional canoe industry. The catch was probably lower in the early years of the century, as it seems likely that the expansion of the market made possible by improved transportation stimulated production to its technological limits by 1920 or so. In 1954, about 11,000 tons of fish were imported by sea, 4,000 tons by land, and 20,000 tons caught locally, for a total of 35,000 tons. Even if it is assumed that the annual catch in the late 1920s and early 1930s was in the order of 20,000 tons, it is clear from the data in table 41 (page 153) that fish imports had become much more important by the 1950s. By 1954, annual per capita consumption, with the obviously incorrect assumption that all Ghanaians had equal access to fish, was about 12.6 pounds. In 1962, per capita fish consumption was estimated at 25.9 pounds; meat consumption was less than half this figure (14.3 pounds). Household surveys in 1961 showed higher figures: average daily per capita fish consumption of 0.15 pounds in urban areas and 0.11 pounds in rural areas, for totals of 55 pounds and 40 pounds, respectively. Demand was, and probably always has been, highly income elastic.[126] Thus, while it is impossible to give specific figures, it is reasonable to assume that fish consumption rose during the colonial era because of imports and because by 1920 or so better transportation extended the areas in which fish could be sold, thus encouraging increased production as well as wider distribution of this much-needed source of animal protein.

Roads and railroads facilitated the movement of agricultural produce as well as animals and fish. Foodstuffs were sold locally or at distant markets in the mining areas and growing towns. Fruit and vegetable production was stimulated around urban centers. Accra was provisioned with shallots from Keta, groundnuts from northern Ashanti, and yams from Dagomba country.[127] Seasonal food shortages in densely populated northern districts were alleviated by grain shipments from more fortunate regions.[128] The spread of cassava, rich in calories although extremely poor in vitamins and proteins, may have played a role somewhat analogous to that of maize and the potato, new crops which apparently stimulated population growth in Europe.[129] Since almost no research has been done on any aspect of Ghanaian agricultural history except for cocoa, the extent of the development and diversification of food production and the role of the colonial government and its agricultural officials in this process are unclear. Despite the emphasis placed on cocoa and other cash crops, however, agricultural extension and growing markets probably had a substantial beneficial effect. Rapid transportation of bulky produce enhanced the quantity, quality, and variety of foodstuffs available to consumers and greatly mitigated the effects of local deaths from drought or locusts.

Thus, while the data are scanty and further research on food and nutrition is essential, it is probable that most people were generally able to improve their diets over the colonial period. Importation, production, and transportation of foods prevented outright starvation when local crops failed and allowed most Ghanaians to enjoy a more reliable and more nutritious supply of food. While diets typically were still high in starch and low in animal protein in the mid-1950s, better nutrition was a very important (although unquantifiable) factor in improved health and reduced mortality. Whether this is true for other African countries remains unclear; there probably was considerable regional and temporal variation.

Health conditions are closely correlated with incomes and general living conditions. Prosperity enables people to obtain an array of goods and services which not only increase their comfort but will also reduce the prevalence and severity of diseases. More and better food is one obvious example; improved housing is another. Warmer and dryer homes, additional living space per person, and better ventilation retard the transmission of respiratory diseases. Domestic rodent and insect pests are reduced by the substitution of metal roofs for thatch, cinder blocks for mud and wattle, and cement floors for beaten earth. Cheap textiles provide clothing and blankets for protection against cold and damp; possession of extra sets of clothes allows more frequent laundering. Shoes and sandals prevent hookworm infection. Tables, simple stoves, and pots with covers help reduce the danger of contaminated food and drink. Soap facilitates personal hygiene and the cleansing of clothes and utensils. Persons with higher incomes had more access to doctors, medicines, and transportation to health centers. In a more tangible but extremely important area, money is needed for school fees and supplies. A family with even one educated member, or with a child in school, is exposed to new ideas on health and hygiene.

Unfortunately, it is extremely difficult to measure past living standards in Ghana. Economic historians have had little interest in such questions, and there will be no attempt here to do more than suggest some approaches and to venture a common-sense judgement. The most direct approach is to construct indices of incomes and consumer prices to determine changes in purchasing power over the years. The British administration did collect data on prices for food, housing, and other necessities from time to time, especially with the censuses. However, prices are almost all for towns, and there is little information on incomes other than salaries paid to government workers and some other wage earners, so the evidence pertains to only a small fraction of the total population. Studies on Accra show a general rise in real wages from 1901 to 1938, a substantial decline during the war, and an improvement in the early 1950s.[130] The figures suggest only a modest overall rise in real income for Accra workers in the colonial period. More research could be done in other cities[131] and in the mining and cocoa areas, but there are real limits to what can be learned.

Another method would be to examine import statistics for changes in quantities of consumer goods with implications for health. Such a study would be helpful, but there are serious methodological difficulties. Goods are frequently aggregated into large categories which may be re-classified from time to time and are often difficult to break down into specific items. The distribution of goods within the country presents further complications. How much, say, corrugated iron roofing was used by the government, or what percentage of imported soap was consumed by expatriates and a few wealthy Africans? Did imported cloth reach rural villages? If so, who could afford it?

A third approach is simply impressionistic. General descriptions in documents, the press, contemporary writings, and secondary works, together with the rising volume of trade, the spread of cocoa cultivation, and the increase in salaried employment, suggest a slow but substantial increase in living standards for most Ghanaians between 1900 and 1955. Progress was not steady; there were good years and bad. Nor was prosperity evenly distributed among geographical regions or among individuals. The entire north and many rural areas lagged far behind the cocoa zones and the coastal towns. Enormous income gaps developed between large-scale cocoa farmers and urban professionals on one hand and subsistence farmers and under-employed migrant laborers on the other. Despite urban slums in the south and overcrowded, exhausted lands in parts of the north, however, poverty was gradually ameliorated for most Ghanaians. The rising level of economic activity, led by cocoa and gold, permitted more and more people to purchase foodstuffs and consumer goods in the marketplace. Regardless of whether "development," "underdevelopment," or "growth without development" characterized the colonial economy in the long run, and regardless of whether things might have been done in a more efficient or more equitable way, one immediate consequence of economic change was that millions of Ghanaians were able to improve the comfort and healthiness of their lives.

The net consequences of all of these non-medical factors for health conditions are difficult to judge. Increased intercommunication enhanced risks of exposure to new pathogens and/or heterologous strains of familiar organisms but also permitted more efficient food distribution and easier access to medical care. Genetic accommodation between host and parasite populations played a small but positive role with tuberculosis and perhaps other diseases. Higher living standards reduced exposure to many infections, while better diets strengthened resistance against most endemic and epidemic diseases. Improved nutrition was especially crucial because so many people suffered simultaneously from more than one chronic disease as well as from frequent attacks by acute infections. European and American experience[132] suggests that better living conditions and more abundant, reliable, and nutritious foods were responsible for much of the reduction in morbidity and mortality, especially in the first three decades of the century. Further research is essential on the changing material conditions of life for various groups in the Ghanaian population, but there are limits about what can be learned about influences on health in the past, as even today it is very difficult to measure mortality in Africa or to determine the importance of specific causes of death, let alone explain regional differences in medical, environmental, or socioeconomic terms.[133]

Studies of Africa's colonial experience usually pay scant attention to matters of health and disease, but they frequently at least mention a sort of demographic race between negative forces unleashed by colonial regimes, such as the rapid spread of epidemics and exploitive labor practices, and the beneficial impact of modern medicine. Characteristically, scholars describe population declines in the late nineteenth and early twentieth centuries until a time, usually around 1920-1930, when administrative reforms and medical measures reduced death rates and the population began to grow. This concept is not new; it was, for example, advanced by Lord Lugard and extensively developed by a pioneering student of African demography, R. R. Kuczynski.[134] The idea seems very plausible and, in broad outline, is consistent with the known facts, although there are bound to be important local variations.

Ghana is such an exceptional case. The population grew during the early colonial period, indicating that, biologically at least, the beneficial aspects of British rule more than balanced negative factors. By the early 1930s, the greater volume and speed of human mobility had led to the widespread dissemination of venereal diseases and tuberculosis, aided the spread of cerebrospinal meningitis and trypanosomiasis in the north, and allowed plague and louse-borne relapsing fever to enter the country. Migrants to the mines and cities paid an especially heavy price in life and health. With some regional differences in timing, however, medical and non-medical factors compensated for heightened epidemiological risks. Indeed, in contrast to most African territories, Ghana was a biological "success story"[135] both before and after c. 1920-30. While clinical and registration data are not comprehensive enough to demonstrate major changes in overall morbidity and mortality, and we cannot adequately assess fluctuations in specific major causes of illness and death, the fact of population growth, together with the medical evidence, shows conclusively that, however unevenly and incompletely, the disease burden was slowly being alleviated.

In Ghana, as in eighteenth and nineteenth century Europe,[136] population growth has resulted in part from the control of major demographic crises due to disease and/or famine, and in part from gradual improvements in health conditions. Twentieth-century Ghana suffered surprisingly little from major epidemics. Indeed, the age of great epidemics, if there was one in Ghana, was past, and most major health problems were those associated with poverty and a tropical environment. Diseases of affluence still affected only a tiny minority. The reasons for Ghana's relatively fortunate experience with great epidemics are complex and somewhat obscure. Geography probably played a major role. Except for pandemic influenza in 1918-19 and for smallpox, the most destructive epidemics were restricted to the savanna country of the north. Louse-borne relapsing fever, cerebrospinal meningitis, and trypanosomiasis occurred in devastating epidemics in the savanna zone of western and central Africa, but were inconsequential in the forest regions of southern Ghana where the bulk of the population lived. Conditions for the dissemination of these diseases were much more favorable in the semi-arid north than in moister regions nearer the coast. Immunities resulting from previous disease exposure and good medical work were doubtlessly beneficial, but ecological factors were probably more significant. Indeed, it would be interesting to test the hypothesis that throughout West Africa, major epidemics caused much higher mortality in the savanna zone than along the coast.

Thus, spectacular epidemics were not the greatest threats to life and health in Ghana; less dramatic endemic infections took a much higher toll. J. W. S. Macfie described the overall disease environment in 1922. He admitted that the medical department was just beginning to render significant assistance to the African population and that official returns were too spotty to measure disease incidence with any degree of accuracy, but he could identify the most significant causes of morbidity and mortality. Yellow fever and trypanosomiasis were not major killers, syphilis was not common yet, and typhus, leishmaniasis, and cholera–rampant in some tropical countries–were unknown. The number one menace was clearly malaria, with hookworm, in his view, holding second position. The other crucial diseases included yaws, gonorrhea, dysentery, pneumonia, tuberculosis, tropical ulcer, and other helminthic infections, excluding schistosomiasis.[137] This list, with some modifications, is valid for the entire 1900-1955 period. Knowledge of the prevalence and distribution of most of these conditions remained fragmentary, even though Kuczynski's assertion that "the only decisive change that has occurred" in understanding African health conditions prior to the 1940s "is that our knowledge of health and mortality in the larger towns has increased considerably"[138] is exaggerated.

Medical progress was real, but painfully slow. Funds, staff, and hospitals were scarce. Preventive and therapeutic efforts were concentrated in the towns, which received far more medical assistance than the countryside. Understanding of the behavior of many diseases was only acquired after extensive clinical experience and research. The lack of effective drugs was a critical limitation on therapy. As late as 1935, specific antimicrobial drugs existed only for the protozoa which cause malaria, amebic dysentery, and trypanosomiasis, and for the spirochetes responsible for syphilis, yaws, and relapsing fever. There was no way to attack most pathogenic bacteria directly until the discovery of sulpha drugs in the late 1930s and the antibiotics during and after World War II.

Preventive measures were also hampered by technical and financial barriers. Except for smallpox, yellow fever, and tetanus, useful vaccines were not developed for most diseases until the 1950s and later. Vector control was extremely expensive and ineffective until the introduction of DDT and other persistent insecticides in the mid-1940s, and progress has been slow and spotty even with these powerful chemicals. Safe water supplies and sanitary disposal of human wastes have long been recognized as essential, but provision of such amenities to the majority of the population has proven to be beyond the capabilities of both the colonial and independent governments.

Slow, uneven advances in living standards played a vital role in alleviating the burden of disease. Better nutrition was especially important in increasing host resistance to malaria, worms, and other chronic endemic diseases, but its significance in regard to acute infections such as measles, pneumonia, and tuberculosis should not be underestimated. Preventive and curative medicine made a larger contribution to mortality reduction in Ghana, and presumably in the rest of Africa, than in developed countries, but non-medical factors were always crucial. Until the mid-1920s, when colonial medicine began to have a significant and growing impact, non-medical factors were the major sources of progress. By 1940 or so, modern curative and preventive medicine was effective enough to be primarily responsible for improved health and an accellerating rate of population growth.[139]

This interpretation, which stresses the strong contribution of nutrition and other non-medical improvements to mortality reduction, is somewhat at variance with commonly-held views on the role of scientific medicine. For example, Mandle's fine study of mortality reduction in another tropical country, British Guiana, stresses the dominant role of colonial medical activities. Improved water supplies, better waste disposal, advances in pre- and post-natal care for mothers and infants, therapy, and, after 1945, an effective program to control malaria vectors with DDT, accounted for a substantial fall in all major causes of death.[140] However, Guiana had a much smaller population, most of which was concentrated along a narrow coastal strip, so sanitary and medical improvements were much easier to introduce than in Ghana. Guiana's health and mortality data are certainly far superior to the scattered and frustrating figures compiled in the Gold Coast. Gradual improvements in living conditions may have been much more meaningful in a relatively prosperous and mildly-ruled country like the Gold Coast; the contribution of modern medicine was probably proportionally much more significant in other, less fortunate colonies, even though physicians and public health workers faced a far more difficult situation in most of Africa than that in small, compact Guiana.

Progress in Ghana must not be exaggerated. Major epidemics had been contained by 1955, but most endemic diseases, including malaria, remained substantially uncontrolled. Life expectancy was still very low compared to developed countries, and infant, child, and maternal mortality rates were appallingly high. The continuing ubiquity of parasitic worms is an outstanding example of the limitations of clinical medicine in poor tropical countries.[141] Costs in well-being, resistance to subsequent infections, and productivity vary among individuals and are extremely difficult to measure.[142] Adequate nutrition and good general health reduce the damage caused by helminthic infestations, but they are a major burden on public health and will remain so for the foreseeable future.

Since the mid-1950s, antibiotics have allowed cheap, effective mass treatment of yaws, venereal diseases, pneumonia, and some other conditions, while vaccines have eliminated smallpox and reduced the dangers from other viral diseases. The numbers of clinics, doctors and other health-care personnel, and patient-attendances have risen dramatically. However, despite impressive gains on many fronts, recent experience has only confirmed what many colonial physicians recognized decades ago; that substantial and sustained advances in general levels of health are impossible without major improvements in living conditions. Better food, clothing, housing, education, water, and sanitation were responsible for much of the progress made prior to 1955; poverty and ignorance remain greater barriers to good health than shortages of doctors or clinics.

TABLE 1[1]

African Population by Area of Origin, 1931

Area of Residence

Percentage of Population Originating in:	Colony			Ashanti	Northern	Togoland	
	Western Province	Central Province	Eastern Province		Territories	Northern	Southern
Colony - Province of Origin	90.1	90.3	87.5	----	----	----	----
Colony - Other Province	9.1	1.6	0.8	3.5	0.2	0.1	3.8
Ashanti	1.1	0.6	1.1	80.1	0.2	0.1	0.1
Northern Territories	2.6	1.1	0.9	3.9	91.1	0.7	0.4
Togoland	----	0.2	1.2	0.2	----	84.1	88.7
Other British W. Africa[2]	3.0	2.5	3.0	2.7	0.9	1.1	1.7
Other[3]	6.1	3.7	5.5	9.2	7.7	13.9	5.3
Total Population	284,902	431,384	855,076	578,978	717,275	168,142	125,529

[1]Calculated from Kuczynski, Demographic Survey, I, p. 423.
[2]Mostly Nigeria.
[3]Mostly French West Africa

TABLE 2

Government Physicians, 1906-1954

Year	Total Physicians[a]	Population per Physician[b]	Cases Treated per Physician
1906	41	47,073	-
1907	44	44,022	758
1908	44	44,181	847
1909	n.a.	-	-
1910	n.a.	-	-
1911	n.a.	-	-
1912	51	39,686	905
1913	60	34,717	822
1914	59	36,288	878
1915	53	41,509	914
1916	51	44,275	939
1917	48	48,250	1,088
1918	46	51,630	1,271
1919	45	54,067	1,292
1920	41	60,780	1,424
1921	43	59,302	1,332
1922-3	43	60,721	1,647
1923-4	49	54,551	1,576
1924-5	45	60,756	1,821
1925-6	65	43,015	1,499
1926-7	61	46,836	1,718
1927-8	70	41,686	1,892
1928-9	81	36,790	2,649
1929-30	92	33,054	2,699
1930-1	93	33,366	2,902
1931-2	82	38,585	3,148
1932-3	63	51,381	3,796
1933-4	63	52,556	3,960
1934	63	53,714	4,038
1935	65	53,200	4,177
1936	67	52,701	4,613
1937	72	50,056	4,556
1938	74	49,703	4,351
1939	68	55,162	4,709
1940	72	53,125	4,737
1941	71	54,901	5,536
1942	71	55,944	5,618
1943	70	57,786	7,027
1944	68	60,559	7,320
1945	68	61,647	7,772
1946	68	62,721	7,526
1947	71	61,113	8,615
1948	78	56,564	10,182
1949	86	53,547	9,710
1950	84	57,119	9,593

TABLE 2

Government Physicians, 1906-1954

Year	Total Physicians[a]	Population per Physician[b]	Cases Treated per Physician
1951	98	50,929	8,217
1952	114	45,474	9,094
1953[c]	97	55,433	8,588
1954[c]	n.a.	-	-

Sources: Compiled from M.D.A.R., R.M.H., and the Dominion Office and Colonial Office List. There are small discrepancies between these sources for several years. Staff for several years calculated by reported changes (resignations, appointments) when previous year was known.

Notes:

a. Includes Sr. M.O.s, M.O.Hs, M.O.s, African M.O.s, Woman M.O.s, and Specialists, including pathologists. Dentists, radiographers, and alienists were excluded, as were full-time administrators. Actual strength was somewhat lower, due to leaves of absence, resignations, and appointments during the course of a year.

b. These and all other calculations involving total populations are based on estimates shown in Table 31.

c. Assuming 8 full-time administrators.

TABLE 3

Medical Department Expenditures, 1900-1955

	Year	Medical Dept.[a]	Total Gov't Spending	% to Medical Dept.	Medical Spending per capita
	1900	17,754	214,948	8.3	.01
	1901	25,285	331,113	7.6	.01
	1902	27,715	469,405	5.9	.02
	1903	34,410	541,705	6.4	.02
	1904	36,181	585,763	6.2	.02
	1905	36,054	577,281	6.2	.02
	1906	34,537	589,896	5.9	.02
	1907	35,245	575,415	6.1	.02
	1908	40,405	597,253	6.8	.02
	1909	43,268	626,197	6.9	.02
	1910	52,931	657,318	8.1	.03
	1911	69,998	725,441	9.6	.04
	1912	84,919	816,089	10.4	.04
	1913	94,560	910,273	10.4	.05
	1914	104,316	1,048,800	9.9	.05
	1915	116,565	1,082,617	10.8	.05
	1916	115,892	1,146,936	10.1	.05
	1917	115,425	1,172,202	9.8	.05
	1918	117,499	1,186,909	9.9	.05
	1919	139,255	1,689,121	8.2	.06
	1920	205,219	2,060,173	10.0	.08
	1921	224,872	2,763,413	8.1	.09
Jan-Mar	1922	56,200	724,396	7.8	---
	1922-3[b]	221,828	2,558,488	8.7	.08
	1923-4	220,094	2,692,792	8.2	.08
	1924-5	257,150	3,007,298	8.6	.09
	1925-6	277,484	3,222,033	8.3	.10
	1926-7	268,934	3,261,638	8.2	.09
	1927-8	221,384	2,374,087	9.3	.08
	1928-9	306,804	2,553,423	12.0	.10
	1929-30	358,294	2,692,012	13.3	.12
	1930-1	369,083	2,872,385	12.8	.12
	1931-2	320,144	2,700,469	11.6	.10
	1932-3	285,170	2,647,486	10.8	.09
	1933-4	278,124	2,302,061	12.1	.08
	1934	282,258	2,334,844	12.1	.08
	1935	293,431	2,603,096	11.3	.09
	1936	312,413	2,337,357	13.4	.09
	1937	339,721	2,701,522	12.5	.09
	1938	349,981	3,020,234	11.6	.10
	1939	357,556	3,213,921	11.1	.10
	1940[c]	366,992	3,872,912	9.5	.10
	1941[c]	360,049	2,908,961	12.4	.09
	1942[d]	385,759	4,126,167	9.3	.10
	1943[c]	428,460	4,360,346	9.8	.11
	1944[d]	470,393	4,436,744	10.6	.11
	1945[e]	496,643	5,427,057	9.2	.12
	1946	519,694	5,497,168	9.5	.12
	1947	596,351	8,992,843	6.6	.14
	1948	755,430	9,639,688	7.8	.17
	1949	890,378	11,237,930	7.9	.19
	1950	965,020	14,012,606	6.9	.20
	1951	1,037,794	32,904,023	3.2	.21
	1952	1,607,544	37,130,469	4.3	.31
	1953	1,818,597	43,436,492	4.2	.34
	1954	1,904,293	43,686,929	4.4	.34
	1955	2,345,686	48,822,007	4.8	.41

Sources: M.D.A.R., R.M.H., G.L.A.R., CSO 11/6, 726/32, Memorandum of D.M.S.S., 14 June 1932. The latter document tabulates expenditures from 1900. Figures from different sources often vary slightly.

NOTES: a. Excludes veterinary expenditures 1910-1920.
b. April 1 - March fiscal year, 1922-1934.
c. Calculated from figures for the first 10 months of the year.
d. Calculated from figures for the first 9 months of the year.
e. Calculated from figures for the first 7 months of the year.

TABLE 4

Allocation of Funds Within the Medical Department

Year	% to Medical Branch	% to Health Branch	% to Laboratory Branch
1900	85.1	14.9	
1901	87.0	13.0	
1902	82.5	17.5	
1903	83.0	17.0	
1904	85.3	14.7	
1905	87.7	12.3	
1906	92.1	7.9	
1907	91.3	8.7	
1908	91.1	8.9	
1909	89.2	10.8	
1910	85.0	15.0	
1911	73.5	26.5	
1912	61.2	38.8	
1913	61.0	39.0	
1914	54.1	45.9	
1915	54.4	45.6	
1916	52.7	47.3	
1917	50.6	49.4	
1918	51.0	49.0	
1919	54.5	45.5	
1920	n.a.	n.a.	
1921-2	53.2	46.8	
1922-3	55.4	41.7	2.9
1923-4	54.0	43.7	2.2
1924-5	48.0	50.0	2.0
1925-6	51.6	45.2	3.1
1926-7	59.7	35.6	4.7
1927-8	52.2	42.2	5.6
1928-9	56.4	38.9	4.6
1929-30	53.1	42.2	4.8
1930-1	53.0	42.0	5.1
1931-2	52.0	43.4	4.5
1932-3	54.5	42.7	2.9
1933-4	55.8	41.5	2.3
1934	56.5	41.0	2.5
1935	57.6	39.9	2.5
1936	57.9	39.7	2.4
1937	59.2	38.6	2.2
1938	57.4	40.6	2.0
1939	57.7	40.3	2.0
1940[a]	59.3	39.0	1.7
1941[a]	57.5	41.0	1.5
1942[b]	59.6	38.7	1.6
1943[a]	59.4	39.3	1.3
1944[b]	53.8	43.9	2.2
1945[c]	52.9	44.8	1.3
1946	54.8	42.8	1.4
1947	57.0	40.0	1.6
1948-55	n.a.	n.a.	n.a.

Sources: C S O 11/6, 726/32, Memorandum of D.M.S.S., 14 June 1932; M.D.A.R.

Notes. a) Calculated from figures for the first 10 months of the year.
b) Calculated from figures for the first 9 months of the year.
c) Calculated from figures for the first 6 months of the year.

n.a. signifies not available

Pre-1910 figures for "Health Branch" are expenditures for "Sanitation."

TABLE 5

Government Hospitals and Hospital Beds

Year	Hospitals	Beds	Persons/Bed	Year	Hospitals	Beds	Persons/Bed
1900	5	n.a.	-	1941	39	1486	2623
1904	9	n.a.	-	1942	39	1575	2522
1909	9	n.a.	-	1943	38	1626	2488
1912	22	n.a.	-	1944	38	1626	2533
1914	21	n.a.	-	1945	33	1600	2620
1926-7	34	712	4013	1946	33	n.a.	-
1927-8	39	783	3727	1947	33	1610	2695
1928-9	39	825	3612	1948	33	1708	2583
1929-30	43	952	3194	1949	33	1765	2609
1930-1	40	1061	2925	1950	33	1866	2571
1931-2	40	1069	2960	1951	33	n.a.	-
1932-3	40	1041	3110	1952	34	n.a.	-
1933-4	39	1097	3018	1953	n.a.	2242	2398
1934	39	1114	3038	1954	n.a.	2233	2494
1935	39	1150	3007	1955	n.a.	2422	2379
1936[a]	38	1183	2985				
1937	38	1223	2947				
1938	38	1241	2964				
1939	38	1186	3163				
1940	39	1390	2752				

Sources: M.D.A.R., G.C.A.R., R.M.H.

Note: a. Seven of the hospitals listed were reserved for Europeans until 1936; 6 from then until 1942, and 5 from 1943 to 1946 when separate hospitals were abolished.

TABLE 6

New Patients Treated and Hospital Deaths, 1900-1955

	In-Patients			Out-Patients			All Cases			Deaths		
Year	Male	Female	Total	M	F	Total	M	F	Total	M	F	Total
1900												
1901												
1902[a]			1,311									150
1903[b]			2.767			over						146
1904[b]			2,060			21,000						129
1905[b]			1,958									135
1906[b]			1,949									109
1907[c]			2,276			31,086			33,362			113
1908			3,031			34,223			37,254			500
1909			3,413			43,747			47,160			232
1910			3,009			40,823			43,832			271
1911			2,788			39,543			42,331			184
1912			3,837			42,331			46,168			257
1913			3,543	34,926	10,858	45,784			49,327			242
1914			3,592	36,678	11,513	48,191			51,783			239
1915			3,138			45,323			48,461			219
1916									47,913			282
1917									52,229			281
1918									58,444			524
1919									58,131			304
1920									58,385			414
1921									57,263			383
1922-1st Quarter									20,231			89
1922-3									70,821			382
1923-4									77,224			475
1924-5									81,957			797
1925-6									97,443			862
1926-7			11,284	65,946	27,581	93,527			104,811			700
1927-8			11,804	84,803	35,839	120,642			132,446			980
1928-9			12,573	128,934	73,098	202,032			214,605			1,045
1929-30			15,162	142,310	90,853	233,163			248,325			1,432

TABLE 6 Cont'd.

Year	In-Patients Male	In-Patients Female	In-Patients Total	Out-Patients M	Out-Patients F	Out-Patients Total	All Cases M	All Cases F	All Cases Total	Deaths M	Deaths F	Deaths Total
1930-1			17,960	154,387	97,534	251,921			269,881			1,327
1931-2			17,634	142,028	98,455	240,483			258,117			1,409
1932-3			20,291	128,621	90,209	218,830			239,121			1,434
1933-4			21,876	131,462	96,139	227,601			249,471			1,634
1934			21,100	141,800	91,467	233,267			254,367			1,668
1935			23,411	147,330	100,749	248,079			271,490			1,841
1936			24,916	165,940	118,190	284,130			309,046			2,082
1937			26,188	172,459	129,396	301,855			328,043			2,247
1938			25,867	174,163	121,908	296,071			321,938			1,945
1939			25,878	171,917	122,422	294,339			320,217			2,066
1940			25,922	182,833	132,284	315,117			341,039	1,262	581	1,843
1941			29,920	209,569	153,559	363,128			393,048	1,647	709	2,356
1942	19,964	8,699	28,663	198,887	171,348	370,235	218,851	180,047	398,898	1,585	621	2,206
1943	20,389	9,929	30,318	247,754	213,828	461,582	268,143	223,757	491,900	1,738	798	2,536
1944	19,759	11,758	31,517	258,872	207,365	466,237	278,631	219,123	497,754	1,689	760	2,449
1945	21,891	12,666	34,557	277,730	216,232	493,962	299,621	228,898	528,519	1,753	844	2,597
1946	22,839	13,370	36,209	286,412	189,159	475,571	309,251	202,529	511,780	1,665	844	2,509
1947	25,949	15,423	41,372	327,040	243,240	570,280	352,989	258,663	611,652	1,903	945	2,848
1948	37,678	20,965	58,643	401,946	333,637	735,583	439,624	354,602	794,226	2,020	1,136	3,156
1949	35,514	21,625	57,139	439,455	338,494	777,949	474,969	360,119	835,088	2,041	1,327	3,368
1950	35,353	23,254	58,607	431,288	315,943	747,231	466,641	339,197	805,838	2,019	1,131	3,150
1951	40,956	25,762	66,718	443,535	295,051	738,586	484,491	320,813	805,304	1,885	1,183	3,068
1952	35,222	25,317	60,539	565,460	410,741	976,201	600,682	436,058	1,036,740	1,696	1,251	2,947
1953	34,204	29,496	63,700	468,472	300,862	769,334	502,676	330,358	833,034	1,737	1,421	3,158
1954[d]	37,285	32,048	69,333	277,361	179,949	457,310	314,646	211,997	526,643	2.071	1,352	3,423
1955[d]	29,776	27,629	57,405	273,776	146,347	420,123	303,552	173,976	477,528	1,673	1,301	2,974

Source: M.D.A.R., R.M.H.

Notes: [a]1902; Hospitals at Accra, Cape Coast, Keta, Elmina, and Axim.
[b]1903-6; Above, plus Sekondi and Kumasi.
[c]1907 on; all hospitals.
[d]1954-5; excludes Medical Field Units.

TABLE 7

Total Cases Treated as a Percentage of the Total Population, 1907-1955

Year	Percentage	Year	Percentage
1907	1.7	1932-3	7.4
1908	1.9	1933-4	7.5
1909	2.4	1934	7.5
1910	2.2	1935	7.9
1911	2.2	1936	8.8
1912	2.3	1937	9.1
1913	2.4	1938	8.8
1914	2.4	1939	8.5
1915	2.2	1940	8.9
1916	2.1	1941	10.1
1917	2.3	1942	10.0
1918	2.5	1943	12.2
1919	2.4	1944	12.1
1920	2.3	1945	12.6
1921	2.2	1946	12.0
1922-3[a]	2.7	1947	14.1
1923-4	2.9	1948	18.0
1924-5	3.0	1949	18.1
1925-6	3.5	1950	16.8
1926-7	3.7	1951	16.1
1927-8	4.5	1952	20.0
1928-9	7.2	1953	15.5
1929-30	8.2	1954	9.5
1930-1	8.7	1955	8.3
1931-2	8.2		

Sources: M.D.A.R., R.M.H.

Note: [a]1 April 1922-31 March 1923.

TABLE 8

Attendances at Infant Welfare Centres, 1925-1955

Year	Children	Pregnant Women	Year	Children	Pregnant Women
1925-6	20,327		1941	139,069	43,083
1926-7	28,982		1942	142,993	49,104
1927-8	61,749	2,010	1943	149,594	54,843
1928-9	71,826	5,436	1944	147,660	63,373
1929-30	112,675	13,370	1945	192,683	74,121
1930-1	135,745	23,414	1946	168,903	72,912
1931-2	106,861	19,462	1947	194,778	85,011
1932-3[a]	74,317	18,826	1948	189,156	87,729
1933-4[a]	74,160	18,873	1949	194,561	96,187
1934	121,059	21,795	1950	187,380	83,453
1935	110,039	28,744	1951	173,887	61,739
1936	107,900	18,205	1952	172,712	63,875
1937	140,774	34,669	1953	n.a.	n.a.
1938	106,729	46,483	1954	153,513	n.a.
1939	93,012	40,993	1955[b]	189,409	n.a.
1940	105,797	40,823			

Source: M.D.A.R., R.M.H.

Notes: a. Does not include missions.
b. Does not include Northern Territories
n.a. signifies not available

TABLE 9

Malaria Cases Treated, 1900-1955

Year	Cases Treated[a]	Malaria as % of all Cases Treated	Year	Cases Treated[a]	Malaria as % of all Cases Treated
1900[b]	112		1929-30	18,924	7.6
1901	242		1930-1	24,972	9.3
1902	316		1931-2	30,011	11.6
1903	533		1932-3	20,317	8.5
1904	487		1933-4	25,538	10.2
1905	409		1934	24,535	9.6
1906	394		1935	25,815	9.5
1907	2,369	7.1	1936	25,125	8.1
1908	2,561	6.9	1937	30,522	9.3
1909	2,994	6.3	1938	28,938	9.0
1910	2,765	6.3	1939	30,651	9.6
1911	2,310	5.5	1940	31,949	9.4
1912	2,282	4.9	1941	38,234	9.7
1913	2,576	5.2	1942	38,358	9.6
1914	2,729	5.3	1943	47,066	9.6
1915	2,748	5.7	1944	50,207	10.1
1916	3,607	7.5	1945	48,896	9.3
1917	3,501	6.7	1946	47,825	9.3
1918	3,168	5.4	1947	51,234	8.4
1919	3,741	6.4	1948	78,831	9.9
1920	4,696	8.0	1949	104,484	12.5
1921	5,935	10.4	1950	87,625	10.9
Jan-Mar 1922	1,797	8.9	1951	100,428	12.5
1922-3	7,497	10.6	1952	137,111	13.2
1923-4	5,945	7.7	1953	129,120	15.5
1924-5	5,206	6.4	1954	64,975	12.3
1925-6	6,567	6.7	1955	70,548	14.8
1926-7	6,430	6.1			
1927-8	8,957	6.8			
1928-9	16,043	7.5			

Sources: Malaria Cases Treated, 1900-1955. Includes a small number of blackwater fever cases.
<u>M.D.A.R.</u>, <u>R.M.H.</u>

Note: [a]Returns for 1900-1906 are very incomplete. See Table 6.

TABLE 10. Yellow Fever, Louse-Borne Relapsing Fever, and Trypanosomiasis: New Cases Treated and Deaths

Year	Yellow Fever[a] Cases	Yellow Fever[a] Deaths	Relapsing Fever[a] Cases	Relapsing Fever[a] Deaths	Trypanosomiasis Hospital Cases	Trypanosomiasis Cases Notified[b]	Trypanosomiasis Hospital Deaths
1900	0		0		0	0	
1901	0		0		0	0	
1902	2		0		0	0	
1903	0		0		0	1	
1904	0		0		0	6	
1905	0		0		0	7	
1906	0		0		0	3	
1907	0		0		0	34	
1908	0		0		0	16	
1909	0		0		0	45	
1910	15	14	0		0	52	
1911	9	5	0		0	83	
1912	10	3	0		0	104	
1913	20	7	0		0	57	
1914	19	9	0		0	12	
1915	2	2	0		0	17	
1916	6	5	0		0	8	
1917	5	5	3[c]	0	12	12	6
1918	4	1	0	0	0	10	
1919	11	7	0	0	0	14	
1920	2	1	96[c]	0	27	27	3
1921	4	3	0	0	8	8	3
Jan-Mar 1922	5	1	1[c]	0	3	3	0
1922-3	22	15	72	0	15	15	0
1923-4	13(19)	10	158	3	5	6	2
1924-5	10	7	44	2	25	26	0
1925-6	8	5	2	1	36	37	5
1926-7	86	20	52	4	67	67	11
1927-8	45(87)	16	97(156)	2	55	59	4
1928-9	2	2	18	2	55	94	13
1929-30	0	0	118	8	116	121	24
1930-31	2	1	341	10	239	224	17
1931-32	26	9	22	3	241	250	28
1932-33	3	2	25	3	680	685	47
1933-34	1(7)	0	47	2	1128	1179	81
1934	2	2	0	0	1883	1973	114
1935	7	4	3	0	3680	3885	116
1936	3	3	0	0	4466	4820	134
1937	73(75)	40(69)	0	0	4934	5599	156
1938	18(15)	12(15)	0	0	4849	5611	151
1939	2	1(2)	0	0	4764	6826	156
1940	0(2)	0(2)	0	0	5473	6165	142
1941	4	4	0	0	4003	5630	172
1942	1	1	3	1	3683	4758	127
1943	1(2)	1(2)	0	0	3340	4500	125
1944	0(1)	0(1)	1	0	3894	4872	112
1945	5	4	0	0	3727	5059	80
1946	0	0	0	0	3256	4226	58
1947	0	0	1	0	3169	4477	60
1948	0(2)	0	3	1	2330	3312	41
1949	12(22)	5(10)	10	0	1239	2200	47
1950	13	2(4)	11	0	1708	2586	27
1951	41(25)	12(15)	11	0	1054	2498	23
1952	8(6)	8(6)	0	0	770	2348	12
1953	0	0	0[d]	0	156	1480	7
1954	1(2)	1	1	0	306	992	16
1955	3(7)	1(6)	0	0	280	710	31

Sources: M.D.A.R; R.M.H., David Scott, Epidemic Disease in Ghana, p. 45, p. 125, p. 142.

[a]Inpatients and outpatients; deaths are for inpatients. Figures in parenthesis represent total notifications, i.e., all cases known to the authorities, whether treated or not. Notification figures are given only in cases where they are significantly more comprehensive than case totals.

[b]Persons treated as outpatients or otherwise known.

[c]These figures may be erroneous as there is no other indication of relapsing fever in these years. See Scott, p. 142-5.

[d]Clinical returns give 185 cases, but this must be a printing error (Scott, p. 145).

TABLE 10a[85]

Filarial Diseases, 1953-5

Year	W. bancrofti		Loa loa		other and unspecified (excluding O. volvulus)	
	cases	deaths	cases	deaths	cases	deaths
1953	166	0	9	0	82	1
1954	219	0	12	0	170	1
1955	52	0	1	0	578	2

TABLE 11

Dysentery, Diarrhea and Enteritis, and Typhoid and Paratyphoid Fevers; Cases Treated and Hospital Deaths, 1902-1955

Year	Dysentery[a]		Diarrhea and Enteritis		Typhoid and Paratyphoid[b]	
	Cases	Deaths	Cases	Deaths	Cases	Deaths
1902[c]	50	14	58	12	0	0
1903	56	10	810	5	0	0
1904	82	23	34	1	1	0
1905	111	22	24	1	2	1
1906	95	15	n.a.	n.a.	2	0
1907	259	9	n.a.	n.a.	4	1
1908	471	20	n.a.	n.a.	6	1
1909	327	14	n.a.	n.a.	0	0
1910	477	25	n.a.	n.a.	2	1
1911	367	19	1,455	16	8	0
1912	545	29	1,370	7	4	2
1913	848	30	n.a.	5	7	1
1914	785	15	n.a.	1	7	1
1915	621	21	n.a.	8	21	4
1916	533	12	1,806	13	6	0
1917	510	9	1,340	7	10	1
1918	412	15	1,472	7	6	0
1919	455	12	1,436	10	9	0
1920	823	20	1,662	8	11	1
1921	708	26	1,651	10	41	0
1922-3[d]	1,173	28	2,460	9	27	0
1923-4	550	19	1,805	16	34	2
1924-5	689	22	1,640	20	27	6
1925-6	929	21	2,482	14	8	4
1926-7	899	39	2,534	9	84	4
1927-8	1,000	43	2,718	21	27	1
1928-9	2,103	47	5,294	25	66	6
1929-30	2,234	40	5,749	24	51	13
1930-1	1,496	41	6,631	37	83	14
1931-2	1,602	45	4,790	33	48	12
1932-3	1,415	39	4,398	31	78	9
1933-4	1,423	38	4,083	35	128	10
1934	1,186	29	4,820	21	72	12
1935	1,219	46	4,713	27	57	12
1936	1,831	56	5,708	58	105	9
1937	2,100	57	6,083	49	127	21
1938	1,540	44	5,829	33	99	9
1939	1,848	31	5,747	30	79	10
1940	1,757	49	6,541	17	177	22
1941	1,587	44	5,742	33	196	27
1942	1,607	80	6,560	32	125	19
1943	1,832	56	7,299	57	158	16
1944	1,841	45	7,648	46	178	28
1945	2,106	43	9,848	46	238	31
1946	2,441	52	10,256	50	216	26
1947	3,316	54	14,908	49	285	44
1948	5,053	50	21,417	92	516	37
1949	6,078	48	29,592	64	422	49
1950	7,918	87	28,267	75	366	40
1951	8,555	69	28,687	63	649	60
1952	32,714	65	49,176	74	462	37
1953	12,804	112	32,237	83	443	31
1954	7,653	127	13,039	119	722	40
1955	5,121	68	7,556	91	683	45

Sources: M.D.A.R., R.M.H.

Notes: [a]All forms. No systematic attempt was made to distinguish between amebic and bacillary forms until 1924-5; even after that date there was always a large category labelled "other and unclassified."

[b]Often lumped together, sometimes under the term "enteric fever."

[c]Returns for 1902-1906 are very incomplete. See Table 6.

[d]Fifteen months.

TABLE 12

Acute Poliomyelitis

Year	In-Patients Admissions M	F	Total	Deaths M	F	Total	Out-Patients M	F	Total	All Cases M	F	Total
1926-7			2				2		2			4
1927-8			0					1	1			1
1928-9			4				9	3	12			16
1929-30			0				2	4	6			6
1930-1			1				23	7	30			31
1931-2			8				15	6	21			29
1932-3			1				8	9	17			18
1933-4			3			1	23	9	32			35
1934			3			1	7	2	9			12
1935			0				6	4	10			10
1936			5				7	5	12			17
1937			3				11	1	12			15
1938			2				7	7	14			16
1939			3				8	1	9			12
1940			4		1	1	6	4	10			14
1941			2		1	1	7	2	9			11
1942		1	1				7	2	9	7	3	10
1943	1		1				1	1	2	2	1	3
1944	3	3	6				4	6	10	7	9	16
1945	3	3	6		1	1	1	5	6	4	8	12
1946	11	2	13	2	1	3	5	4	9	16	6	22
1947	9	9	18	2	1	3	14	6	20	23	15	38
1948	19	9	28				28	22	50	47	31	78
1949	7	3	10				10	1	11	17	4	21
1950	7	2	9				49	29	78	56	31	87
1951	11	4	15				44	16	60	55	20	75
1952	15	4	19		2	2	47	16	63	62	20	82
1953	9	5	14	5	4	9	6	9	15	15	14	29
1954	24	2	26	2	0	2	13	6	29	37	8	45
1955	34	14	48	1	1	2	4	3	7	38	17	55

Source: Acute Poliomyelitis. Not reported prior to 1926-7.
M.D.A.R., R.M.H.

TABLE 13

Total Helminthic Infections Treated and Hospital Deaths, 1902-1955

Year	Cases	Helminthic Infections as % of cases treated	Deaths	Year	Cases	Helminthic Infections as % of cases treated	Deaths
1902[a]	41		0	1929-30	5,037	2.0	5
1903	95		0	1930-1	4,780	1.8	32
1904	144		0	1931-2	5,768	2.2	40
1905	78		0	1932-3	5,578	2.3	31
1906	65		0	1933-4	5,477	2.2	39
1907	1,765	5.3	0	1934	4,851	1.9	24
1908	1,785	4.8	2	1935	5,632	2.1	18
1909	1,619	3.4	0	1936	8,839	2.9	27
1910	1,572	3.6	1	1937	8,200	2.5	37
1911	1,890	4.5	1	1938	8,172	2.5	39
1912	1,946	4.2	1	1939	7,095	2.2	25
1913[b]	2,709	5.5	3	1940	7,976	2.3	15
1914[b]	2,844	5.5	5	1941	7,512	1.9	25
1915	2,266	4.7	2	1942	7,741	1.9	19
1916	1,494	3.1	2	1943	7,645	1.6	50
1917	1,985	3.8	6	1944	9,221	1.9	27
1918	1,673	2.9	4	1945	9,149	1.7	52
1919	2,542	4.4	8	1946	12,547	2.5	66
1920	1,928	3.3	4	1947	15,091	2.5	47
1921	2,217	3.9	2	1948	25,683	3.2	58
1922-3[c]	3,213	3.5	4	1949	28,398	3.4	57
1923-4	2,483	3.2	2	1950	25,645	3.2	109
1924-5	3,552	4.3	4	1951	24,171	3.0	53
1925-6	3,753	3.9	7	1952	22,885	2.2	18
1926-7	2,809	2.7	4	1953	30,325	3.8	47
1927-8	3,264	2.5	14	1954	22,148	4.2	45
1928-9	3,638	1.7	7	1955	20,767	4.3	60

Source: M.D.A.R., R.M.H.

Notes: a. Returns for 1902-1906 are very incomplete. See Table 6.
b. Returns lumped under "Parasitic"; includes some cases of sand fleas (Tunga penetrans) and other insect infestations.
c. Fifteen months.

TABLE 14 Specific Helminthic Infections, 1953-5.

Parasite		1953	1954	1955
Ascaris	cases	7183	7887	8552
	deaths	16	19	23
Guinea Worm	cases	2657	1746	1714
	deaths	0	0	5
Hookworm	cases	4067	6395	4346
	deaths	13	8	8
Schistosomes[a]	cases	4947	5764	3020
	deaths	7	7	12
Tapeworms[b]	cases	984	964	777
	deaths	0	1	2

Source: R.M.H.

Notes: a. Both *S. haematobium* and *S. mansoni*.
b. Both *T. saginata* and *T. solium*.

TABLE 15

Pneumonia Cases and Deaths, 1902 - 1955

Year	In-Patients	Hospital Deaths	Case Mortality Rate - %[a]	Total Cases	Pneumonia as % all cases treated
1902[b]	41	13	31.7	n.a.	
1903	78	25	32.1	n.a.	
1904	46	19	41.3	n.a.	
1905	24	9	37.5	n.a.	
1906	23	8	34.8	n.a.	
1907	n.a.	n.a		n.a.	
1908	n.a.	n.a.		n.a	
1909	n.a.	n.a.		n.a.	
1910	n.a.	n.a.		n.a	
1911	97	29	29.9	514	1.2
1912	106	30	28.3	596	1.3
1913[c]	95	23	24.2	252	0.5
1914[c]	109	36	33.0	252	0.5
1915[c]	83	27	32.5	212	0.4
1916	n.a.	54		427	0.9
1917	n.a.	25		301	0.6
1918	n.a.	71		566	1.0
1919	n.a.	28		381	0.7
1920	n.a.	51		1,157	2.0
1921	n.a.	52		480	0.8
Jan.-Mar. 1922	n.a.	17		205	1.0
1922-3	n.a.	80		787	1.1
1923-4	n.a.	91		681	0.9
1924-5	n.a.	74		661	0.8
1925-6	n.a.	99		878	0.9
1926-7	408	75	18.4	783	0.7
1927-8	403	129	32.0	962	0.7
1928-9	664	183	27.6	1,665	0.8
1929-30	636	199	31.3	2,942	1.2
1930-1	525	157	29.9	1,590	0.6
1931-2	534	181	33.9	1,891	0.7
1932-3	494	182	36.8	1,190	0.5
1933-4	562	173	30.8	1,416	0.6
1934	550	172	31.3	1,251	0.5
1935	707	223	31.5	1,500	0.6
1936	698	236	33.8	1,560	0.5
1937	915	294	32.1	2,088	0.6
1938	639	182	28.4	1,481	0.5
1939	810	147	18.1	1,849	0.6
1940	633	127	20.1	1,651	0.5
1941	811	128	15.8	1,760	0.4
1942	867	140	16.1	1,939	0.5
1943	1,254	241	19.2	2,642	0.5
1944	1,322	239	18.1	2,531	0.5
1945	1,379	216	15.7	3,725	0.7
1946	1,499	188	12.5	3,084	0.6
1947	1,562	229	14.7	3,684	0.6
1948	2,791	254	9.1	7,140	0.9
1949	2,870	304	10.6	7,910	0.9
1950	2,616	256	9.8	6,598	0.8
1951	3,017	261	8.7	7,199	0.9
1952	3,067	284	9.3	8,100	0.8
1953	2,516	252	10.0	7,320	0.9
1954	2,638	290	11.0	5,560	1.1
1955	2,349	275	11.7	5,181	1.1

Sources: M.D.A.R., R.M.H.
Pneumonia Cases and Deaths, 1902-1955 - all forms, including bronchopneumonia.

Notes: [a]Percentage of hospital patients who died.
[b]Returns for 1902-1906 very incomplete. See Table 6.
[c]Bronchopneumonia not included.

TABLE 16

Bronchitis and Influenza Cases Treated 1902 - 1955

Year	Bronchitis			Influenza	
	Cases	Bronchitis as % of all cases treated	Hospital Deaths	Cases	Hospital Deaths
1902[a]	40		2	0	0
1903	60		2	0	0
1904	89		3	2	0
1905	53		2	0	0
1906	62		4	6	0
1907	2,785	8.3	3	5	0
1908	2,701	7.3	3	0	0
1909	3,631	7.7	4	5	0
1910	3,398	7.6	3	6	0
1911	2,867	6.8	4	2	0
1912	4,236	9.2	3	0	0
1913	n.a.		1	2	0
1914	n.a.		2	2	0
1915	n.a.		5	77	0
1916	3,863	8.1	4	27	0
1917	3,703	7.1	5	280	0
1918	3,161	5.4	5	7,756[b]	240[b]
1919	4,581	7.9	10	127	4
1920	4,010	6.9	8	884	3
1921	1,676	2.9	13	184	1
Jan.-Mar. 1922	1,294	6.4	0	69	0
1922-3	5,614	7.9	3	243	0
1923-4	5,393	7.0	4	192	0
1924-5	3,990	4.9	10	246	2
1925-6	6,268	6.4	10	547	5
1926-7	5,284	5.0	16	218	0
1927-8	7,457	5.6	20	452	0
1928-9	10,779	5.0	14	863	5
1929-30	12,545	5.1	20	693	0
1930-1	14,166	5.2	7	396	0
1931-2	11,105	4.3	14	1,269	1
1932-3	10,186	4.3	6	563	3
1933-4	11,907	4.8	14	492	2
1934	10,967	4.3	26	326	2
1935	12,362	4.6	29	1,331	0
1936	11,746	3.8	16	292	3
1937	15,176	4.6	16	676	3
1938	12,232	3.8	9	182	0
1939	14,761	4.6	10	961	0
1940	14,189	4.1	9	431	1
1941	13,988	3.6	10	332	0
1942	15,782	4.0	17	260	0
1943	19,934	4.1	14	557	1
1944	19,530	3.9	13	476	4
1945	21,792	4.1	15	492	3
1946	18,525	3.6	16	167	1
1947	25,129	4.1	20	327	3
1948	31,673	4.0	8	463	1
1949	41,786	5.0	9	421	3
1950	31,341	3.9	21	1,577	0
1951	36,251	4.5	14	1,305	0
1952	62,980	6.1	30	764	1
1953	42,531	5.1	15	465	7
1954	12,401	2.4	12	1,425	0
1955	11,810	2.5	16	291	0

Sources: M.D.A.R., R.M.H.

Notes: [a]Returns for 1902 - 1906 are very incomplete. See Table 6.
[b]During the 1918 epidemic, influenza caused at least 80 - 100,000 deaths.

TABLE 17

Tuberculosis Cases Treated and Deaths, 1902 - 1955

Year	Respiratory Cases	Respiratory Deaths	Case Mortality Rate - %[a]	Non-Respiratory Cases	Non-Respiratory Deaths	All Tuberculosis Cases	All Tuberculosis Deaths	Tuberculosis % of all cases treated
1902[b]						6	4	
1903						4	1	
1904						10	5	
1905						7	5	
1906						25	7	
1907						n.a.		
1908						n.a.		
1909						n.a.		
1910						n.a.		
1911						191	10	0.5
1912						134	13	0.3
1913						141	15	0.3
1914						271	21	0.5
1915						274	19	0.6
1916						281	25	0.6
1917						258	24	0.5
1918						236	33	0.4
1919						269	24	0.5
1920						355	36	0.6
1921						336	41	0.6
1922-3[c]						515	46	0.6
1923-4						398	64	0.5
1924-5						392	51	0.5
1925-6						555	76	0.6
1926-7	504	80	15.9	186	12	690	92	0.7
1927-8	675	104	15.4	210	17	885	121	0.7
1928-9	867	114	13.1	322	18	1,189	132	0.6
1929-30	958	126	13.2	236	22	1,194	148	0.5
1930-1	1,027	146	14.2	241	13	1,268	159	0.5
1931-2	1,056	138	13.1	251	23	1,307	161	0.5
1932-3	997	145	14.5	189	18	1,186	163	0.5
1933-4	987	165	16.7	174	17	1,161	182	0.5
1934	1,046	182	17.4	161	24	1,207	206	0.5

TABLE 17

Tuberculosis Cases Treated and Deaths, 1902 - 1955 (Cont'd)

	Respiratory			Non-Respiratory		All Tuberculosis		
Year	Cases	Deaths	Case Mortality Rate - %[a]	Cases	Deaths	Cases	Deaths	Tuberculosis % of all cases treated
1935	1,053	196	18.6	170	20	1,223	216	0.5
1936	1,345	221	16.4	218	27	1,563	248	0.5
1937	1,172	207	17.7	183	15	1,355	222	0.4
1938	1,214	226	18.6	200	25	1,414	251	0.4
1939	1,318	244	18.7	213	27	1,531	271	0.5
1940	1,508	214	14.2	146	8	1,654	222	0.5
1941	1,755	285	16.2	267	18	2,022	303	0.5
1942	1,936	302	15.6	401	29	2,337	331	0.6
1943	2,032	334	16.4	270	35	2,302	369	0.5
1944	2,046	309	15.1	362	37	2,408	346	0.5
1945	1,996	284	14.2	448	17	2,444	301	0.5
1946	1,987	248	12.5	305	17	2,292	262	0.4
1947	2,438	309	12.7	508	44	2,946	353	0.5
1948	2,519	242	9.6	743	28	3,262	270	0.4
1949	2,025	231	11.4	407	24	2,432	255	0.3
1950	2,032	213	10.5	276	12	2,308	225	0.3
1951	2,268	149	6.6	342	31	2,610	180	0.3
1952	2,211	189	8.5	990	68	3,201	257	0.3
1953	2,210	132	6.0	403	30	2,613	162	0.3
1954	3,503	165	4.7	1,658	48	5,161	213	1.0
1955	1,918	85	4.4	412	36	2,330	121	0.5

Sources: M.D.A.R., R.M.H.

Notes: a. Deaths as percentage of all cases treated, in-paitnet and out-patient.
b. Returns for 1902 - 1906 are very incomplete, see Table 6.
c. Fifteen months, Jan. 1922 - Mar. 1923.

TABLE 18

Cerebrospinal Meningitis Cases and Deaths, 1906-1955

Year	Cases	Deaths	Year	Cases	Deaths
1906	?	est. 20,000	1939	839	151
1907	?	est. 8,000	1940	149	46
1908	?	est. 6,000	1941	26	11
1909-18	0	0	1942	255	140
1919	1,041	986	1943	644	187
1920	?	2,984	1944	1,061	900
1921	?	89	1945	10,368	1,199
1922-3[a]	2	2	1946	719	156
1923-4	4	2	1947	1,297	219
1924-5	2	2	1948	11,002	868
1925-6	14	14	1949	10,943	193
1926-7	3	2	1950	1,029	166
1927-8	0	0	1951	1,077	205
1928-9	4	3	1952	317	80
1929-30	1	1	1953	281	57
1930-1	3	3	1954	134	26
1931-2	3	3	1955	173	45
1932-3	0	0			
1933-4	2	1			
1934	0	0			
1935	1	1			
1936	0	0			
1937	0	0			
1938	4	4			

Sources: R.M.H., 1953, p. 74; Scott, *Epidemic Disease in Ghana*, p. 91.

Note: [a]Fifteen months.

TABLE 19

Streptococcus - Related Conditions: Cases

1936-8; 1953-5

Year

Condition	1936	1937	1938	1953	1953	1955
scarlet fever	6	2	0	0	272	62
pharyngitis	-	-	-	260	494	399
erysipelas	28	22	18	83	29	26
infections of skin	-	-	-	19155	10694	9437
otitis media[a]	3444	3774	3549	2756	2720	2154
rheumatic fever	-	-	-	2743	2436	854
rheumatic heart dis.						
cases	-	-	-	513	262	99
deaths	-	-	-	2	2	5
glomerulonephritis[b]						
cases	547	554	517	990	1061	1058
deaths	57	58	66	169	52	35

Sources: M.D.A.R., R.M.H.

Notes: [a]Infections of middle ear and mastoid sinus.
[b]Acute and chronic, includes Bright's disease.

TABLE 20

Whooping Cough (Pertussis) and Measles, Cases Treated and Hospital Deaths, 1902-1955

Year	Whooping Cough Cases[a]	Whooping Cough Deaths	Measles Cases[a]	Measles Deaths	Year	Whooping Cough Cases[a]	Whooping Cough Deaths	Measles Cases[a]	Measles Deaths
1902[b]	0		6		1929-30	1,151	0	421	
1903	0		1		1930-1	1,451	1	607	
1904	0		16		1931-2	1,511	2	778	
1905	0		1		1932-3	815	1	264	
1906	1		0		1933-4	989	2	324	
1907	0		1		1934	913	3	163	
1908	0		0		1935	1,012	0	320	
1909	0		0		1936	1,430	2	440	
1910	0		35	1	1937	1,010	6	191	
1911	12		4		1938	433	0	277	3
1912	3		45		1939	1,079	2	714	1
1913	95		1		1940	1,328	2	546	
1914	44		22		1941	897	0	248	
1915	77		22		1942	968	4	812	
1916	161		0		1943	1,543	6	927	6
1917	262		82		1944	1,337	2	862	0
1918	120		78		1945	1,290	6	786	1
1919	72		14		1946	1,060	1	747	1
1920	126		149		1947	2,138	0	1,071	2
1921	118		19		1948	2,747	1	1,590	3
1922-3[c]	409	1	217		1949	1,791	0	1,477	2
1923-4	193		88		1950	3,941	4	1,833	2
1924-5	35		22		1951	2,330	0	2,503	2
1925-6	107		32	1	1952	22,463	4	25,108	8
1926-7	102		44		1953	5,567	7	8,567	25
1927-8	116		53		1954	1,717	6	2,483	14
1928-9	998	1	429		1955	1,617	9	1,316	24

Sources: M.D.A.R., R.M.H.

Notes: [a]Virtually all patients were treated as out-patients.
[b]Returns for 1902-1906 are very incomplete. See Table 6.
[c]Fifteen months, Jan. 1922 - Mar. 1923.

TABLE 21

Smallpox Notifications and Vaccinations, 1899-1955

Year	Cases Notified	Vaccinations (in thousands)	Year	Cases Notified	Vaccinations (in thousands)
1899	189		1926-7	172	244
1900	519		1927-8	34	232
1901	893		1928-9	76	275
1902	244	at least 9	1929-30	230	414
1903	37		1930-1	600	377
1904	62		1931-2	201	374
1905	25		1932-3	5	372
1906	34		1933-4	46	378
1907	4	1	1934	48	338
1908	89	7	1935	0	353
1909	217	14	1936	59	455
1910	165	25	1937	43	343
1911	130	28	1938	123	365
1912	221	23	1939	167	367
1913	163	16	1940	77	336
1914	23	8	1941	1,470	606
1915	12	10	1942	1,649	643
1916	4	10	1943	161	285
1917	358	21	1944	143	323
1918	5	15	1945	702	447
1919	23	21	1946	1,646	549
1920	298	221	1947	848	614
1921	9	87	1948	1,269	1,583
1922-3[a]	14	123	1949	91	509
1923-4	8	82	1950	353	1,060
1924-5	406	103	1951	474	602
1925-6	1,948	312	1952	695	1,161
			1953	865	475
			1954	79	1,042
			1955	14	n.a.

Sources: M.D.A.R., Scott, Epidemic Disease in Ghana, p. 67.

Note: [a]Fifteen months.

TABLE 22

Leprosy Cases Treated and Deaths, 1902-1955

Year	Male Cases	Female Cases	Total[a] Cases	Deaths	Year	Male Cases	Female Cases	Total Cases	Deaths
1902[b]			7	3	1929-30			1,404	4
1903			2	2	1930-1			3,148	6
1904			0	0	1931-2			1,160	6
1905			2	0	1932-3			848	8
1906			2	0	1933-4			735	9
1907			21	0	1934			786	9
1908			20	1	1935			1,034	25
1909			24	0	1936			1,090	21
1910			40	0	1937			845	26
1911			43	0	1938			813	19
1912			34	0	1939			841	31
1913			64	1	1940			714	25
1914			45	0	1941			673	43
1915			42	2	1942	515	227	742	38
1916			15	1	1943	434	194	628	45
1917			20	9	1944	415	193	608	41
1918			15	1	1945	487	315	802	38
1919			19	0	1946	525	300	825	41
1920			8	2	1947	717	361	1,078	37
1921			12	0	1948	1,342	798	2,140	49
1922-3[c]			52	0	1949	1,304	881	2,185	48
1923-4			145	0	1950	5,699	4,680	10,379	20
1924-5			96	1	1951	7,608	6,761	14,369	65
1925-6			445	2	1952	2,482	2,028	4,510	23
1926-7			667	1	1953	1,534	1,118	2,652	4
1927-8			753	1	1954	1,136	981	2,117	3
1928-9			1,427	1	1955	615	553	1,168	0

Sources: M.D.A.R., R.M.H.

Notes: [a]The large majority of cases were treated as out-patients in any given year.
[b]Returns for 1902-1906 are very incomplete. See Table 6.
[c]Fifteen months.

TABLE 23

Venereal Diseases Cases Treated 1902 - 1955

Year	Syphilis				Gonorrhea			Syphilis & Gonorrhea as % of all cases treated
	Males[a]	Females[a]	Total Cases[b]	Hospital Deaths	Males[a]	Females[a]	Total Cases[b]	
1902[c]			20	3			10	
1903			9	1			27	
1904			17	0			18	
1905			7	0			22	
1906			11	2			22	
1907			274	0			427	2.1
1908			340	1			544	2.4
1909			278	1			596	1.9
1910			378	1			621	2.3
1911			373	2			562	2.2
1912			544	1	631	21	697	2.7
1913	281	102	412	2	714	34	700	2.2
1914	233	119	387	2			808	2.3
1915			459	1			850	2.7
1916			287	3			854	2.4
1917			308	3			1197	2.9
1918			416	4			1196	2.7
1919			365	4			1328	2.9
1920			475	3			1224	2.9
1921			271	1			892	2.1
1922-3[d]			746	7			1807	2.8
1923-4			1308	3			1958	4.2
1924-5			2291	10			2461	5.8
1925-6			2206	4			3356	5.7
1926-7	790	529	1503	8	2333	1128	3760	5.0
1927-8	967	661	1789	7	2654	403	3347	3.9
1928-9	1886	1365	3454	12	2971	1386	4578	3.7
1929-30	895	490	1574	18	2582	612	3437	2.0
1930-1	648	307	1105	13	2742	547	3580	1.7
1931-2	384	172	681	17	2261	326	2867	1.4
1932-3	439	221	791	12	2569	500	3325	1.7
1933-4	342	162	640	14	2538	374	3211	1.6
1934	441	215	811	14	2992	376	3687	1.7
1935	384	212	715	13	2989	291	3598	1.6
1936	481	263	856	28	3562	477	4416	1.7
1937	480	274	866	18	3262	422	3946	1.5
1938	501	226	834	11	3988	533	4842	1.8
1939	393	178	611	12	4356	752	5526	1.9
1940	371	209	695	15	5561	1021	7336	2.4
1941	462	197	755	19	5209	887	7304	2.1
1942	664	215	879	7	7317	1518	8835	2.4
1943	688	238	926	18	7224	1906	9130	2.0
1944	606	180	786	19	7405	1475	8880	2.0
1945	608	231	839	9	7702	1724	9426	2.0
1946	910	361	1271	7	9111	1793	10,904	2.3
1947	1281	367	1648	16	12,082	2957	15,039	2.8
1948	2056	560	2616	9	15,890	4237	20,127	2.8
1949	1446	701	2147	6	14,390	4180	18,570	2.5
1950	1368	453	1821	10	13,137	4328	17,465	2.4
1951	1555	803	2358	15	11,629	4043	15,672	2.2
1952	1306	679	1985	4	10,235	2713	12,948	1.4
1953	1793	687	2480	3	14,639	2733	17,372	2.4
1954	1061	710	1771	3	6332	2262	8594	1.9
1955	803	236	1039	4	10,454	1757	12,211	2.8

Sources: M.D.A.R., R.M.H.

Notes: [a]Cases by sex are for out-patient only until 1942.
[b]the vast majority of cases were treated as out-patients.
[c]returns are very incomplete for 1902-1906, See Table 6.
[d]fifteen months.

TABLE 24

Yaws Cases Treated, 1902 - 1955

Year	Male[a] Cases	Female[a] Cases	Total[b] Cases	Yaws Cases as % of all Cases Treated
1902[c]			1	
1903			0	
1904			6	
1905			10	
1906			4	
1907			409	1.2
1908			437	1.2
1909			592	1.3
1910			507	1.2
1911			535	1.3
1912			627	1.4
1913	504	116	634	1.3
1914	432	170	613	1.2
1915			529	1.1
1916			463	1.0
1917			362	0.7
1918			440	0.8
1919			477	0.8
1920			531	0.9
1921			487	0.9
1922-3[d]			1,845	2.0
1923-4			5,310	6.9
1924-5			6,119	7.5
1925-6			9,576	9.8
1926-7	10,339	7,744	18,255	17.4
1927-8	15,283	10,568	26,081	19.7
1928-9	30,430	23,776	54,456	25.4
1929-30	30,862	21,757	52,945	21.3
1930-1	39,915	29,419	69,785	25.9
1931-2	34,931	27,329	62,524	24.2
1932-3	34,544	27,653	62,529	26.1
1933-4	32,190	27,931	60,374	24.2
1934	36,930	28,498	65,784	25.8
1935	37,261	29,142	66,691	24.6
1936	43,716	33,732	77,713	25.1
1937	46,827	36,555	83,666	25.5
1938	42,768	32,447	75,497	23.5
1939	37,046	27,529	64,891	20.3
1940	39,489	29,215	68,976	20.2
1941	47,584	30,954	78,808	20.1
1942	54,693	41,222	95,915	24.0
1943	79,745	63,572	143,317	29.1
1944	79,771	64,011	143,782	28.9
1945	84,209	70,835	155,044	29.3
1946	85,907	47,960	133,867	26.2
1947	81,453	62,967	144,420	23.6
1948	81,325	62,464	143,789	18.1
1949	78,740	64,521	143,261	17.2
1950	83,821	56,250	140,071	17.4
1951	67,142	48,223	115,365	14.3
1952	90,492	61,845	152,337	14.7
1953	77,131	51,590	128,721	15.5
1954	28,305	19,682	47,987	9.1
1955	17,670	7,790	48,090	10.1

Sources: M.D.A.R., R.M.H.

Notes: [a]Data by sex available only for out-patients until 1942.
[b]The vast prepondernace of victims were seen as out-patients.
[c]Returns for 1902-1906 are very incomplete. See Table 6.
[d]Fifteen months.

TABLE 25

Tropical Ulcer Cases Treated 1902-1938; 1953-1955.

Year	Cases[a]	Tropical ulcer as % of all cases treated	Year	Cases[a]	Tropical ulcer as % of all cases treated
1902[b]	66		1931-2	12,477	4.8
1903	165		1932-3	10,657	4.5
1904	120		1933-4	12,299	4.9
1905	218		1934	13,399	5.3
1906	194		1935	14,262	5.3
1907	3,688	11.1	1936	16,520	5.3
1908	3,575	9.6	1937	14,604	4.5
1909	5,308	11.3	1938	15,836	4.9
1910	5,512	12.6	1939-1952[d]	n.a.	-
1911	3,681	8.7	1953	51,205	6.1
1912	4,252	9.2	1954	23,451	4.5
1913-15	n.a.	-	1955	25,218	5.3
1916	4,269	8.9			
1917	5,851	11.2			
1918	4,968	8.5			
1919	5,301	9.1			
1920	5,018	8.6			
1921	5,318	9.3			
1922-3[c]	8,172	9.0			
1923-4	6,520	8.4			
1924-5	11,574	14.1			
1925-6	8,227	8.4			
1926-7	n.a.	-			
1927-8	8,724	6.6			
1928-9	10,118	4.7			
1929-30	13,276	5.3			
1930-1	15,243	5.6			

Sources: M.D.A.R., R.M.H.

Notes: [a]The overwhelming majority of cases were treated as out-patients.
[b]Returns for 1902-1906 are very incomplete. See Table 6.
[c]Fifteen months.
[d]Lumped with many other conditions under the heading, "Diseases of the Skin, Cellular Tissue, Bones, and Organs of Locomotion."

TABLE 26

Tetanus Cases Treated and Deaths, 1902 - 1955

Year	Cases[a]	Hospital Deaths	Case-Mortality Rate-%[b]	Year	Cases[a]	Hospital Deaths	Case-Mortality Rate-%[b]
1902[c]	5	3		1929-30	95	22	42.3
1903	0	0		1930-1	116	24	41.4
1904	3	2		1931-2	61	20	63.0
1905	1	0		1932-3	93	16	35.6
1906	1	0		1933-4	85	18	40.0
1907	4	1		1934	56	16	48.5
1908	8	3		1935	103	36	57.1
1909	7	2		1936	77	26	54.2
1910	6	4		1937	102	27	45.8
1911	5	2		1938	99	26	40.6
1912	1	1		1939	97	26	47.3
1913	7	3		1940	127	33	50.0
1914	12	5		1941	188	25	41.0
1915	9	5		1942	143	40	50.0
1916	7	1		1943	155	48	55.8
1917	12	2		1944	222	49	40.1
1918	26	1		1945	251	51	37.0
1919	19	6		1946	191	45	44.1
1920	12	4		1947	262	62	47.0
1921	13	8		1948	335	72	39.6
1922-3[d]	21	9		1949	584	75	32.6
1923-4	31	9		1950	400	85	37.3
1924-5	22	9		1951	480	82	31.9
1925-6	25	7		1952	523	78	38.4
1926-7	44	15	75.0	1953	412	97	35.7
1927-8	36	10	45.5	1954	546	121	32.4
1928-9	96	11	57.9	1955	437	130	36.9

Sources: M.D.A.R., R.M.H.

Notes: [a]A preponderance of cases were treated in hospitals.

[b]Case-Mortality is for hospitalized patients only.

[c]Returns for 1902-1906 are very incomplete. See Table 6.

[d]Fifteen months.

TABLE 27

Cancer Patients Treated, 1945-55

Year	In-patients	Deaths	Out-patients	Total Treated
1945	70	17	94	164
1946	113	19	66	179
1947	92	24	100	192
1948	57	16	93	150
1949	100	27	211	311
1950	128	102	362	490
1951	144	17	421	565
1952	142	14	405	547
1953	707	35	867	1574
1954	1230	71	1314	2544
1955	720	56	1427	2147

Sources: Cancer Patients Treated, 1945-55. 1945-51, "Cancer and other tumours, malignant." "Undetermined tumours and non-tumourous cancers" not included. 1953-5, "Malignant Neoplasms." _M.D.A.R._, _R.M.H._

TABLE 28

Injuries Due to External Causes

Cases Treated and Hospital Deaths, 1907 - 1955

Year	Cases Treated	As % of all Cases Treated	Hospital Deaths	Year	Cases Treated	As % of all cases Treated	Hospital Deaths
1907	5,509	16.5	10	1934	16,425	6.5	123
1908	5,633	15.1	21	1935	16,865	6.2	186
1909	6,827	14.5	24	1936	17,965	5.8	179
1910	6,023	13.7	15	1937	17,686	5.4	179
1911	6,610	15.6	12	1938	22,699	7.1	178
1912	6,771	14.7	20	1939	21,346	6.7	188
1913	8,351	16.9	26	1940	18,144	5.3	139
1914	6,420	12.4	39	1941	32,392	8.2	174
1915	6,034	12.5	21	1942	13,923	3.5	115
1916	5,840	12.2	34	1943	13,155	2.7	128
1917	-	-	-	1944	14,280	2.9	138
1918	6,131	10.5	23	1945	14,832	2.8	146
1919	8,232	14.2	45	1946	16,433	3.2	154
1920	7,780	13.3	54	1947	27,069	4.4	167
1921	7,632	13.3	36	1948	33,379	4.2	219
1922-3[a]	12,153	13.3	55	1949	35,898	4.3	282
1923-4	9,985	12.9	51	1950	37,356	4.6	234
1924-5	9,567	11.7	30	1951	44,796	5.6	159
1925-6	10,823	11.1	72	1952	30,785	3.0	201
1926-7	9,949	9.5	103	1953	44,201	5.3	342
1927-8	10,608	8.0	170	1954	63,315	12.0	345
1928-9	15,384	7.2	149	1955	63,683	13.3	376
1929-30	14,660	5.9	152				
1930-1	16,057	5.9	177				
1931-2	12,820	5.0	115				
1932-3	14,734	6.2	130				
1933-4	15,500	6.2	153				

Sources: M.D.A.R., R.M.H.

Note: [a]Fifteen months

TABLE 29

Traumatic Injuries - 1953-55

Cause	1953 Injuries	1953 Deaths	1954 Injuries	1954 Deaths	1955 Injuries	1955 Deaths
Motor Vehicle and transport accidents	14,106	202	19,205	174	22,642	196
Assaults	3,415	9	2,396	8	4,708	11

TABLE 30

Estimated Population by Regions (In Thousands)

Year[a]	Colony[a]	Ashanti	Northern Territories[a]	Total Gold Coast[a]
1901	1,067	---	---	1,894
1911	1,237	---	---	1,966
1921	1,396	450	698	2,550
1931	1,699	579	886	3,164
1948	2,381	877	1,154	4,412
1960	3,741	1,698	1,289	6,727
1970	---	---	---	8,637

Sources: 1901, 1911, 1921; Kuczynski, as corrected in G.B. Kay, The Political Economy of Colonialism in Ghana: A Collection of Documents and Statistics 1900-1960 (Cambridge, U.K. 1972), p. 310.

1931; Census.

1948; Caldwell, in Birmingham, ed., vol. II, p. 82, assumption "C". Presumed excess due to undeclared aliens (294,000) assigned to the three regions on the basis of their percentage of the total census count (4,118,000). This doubtlessly assigns too many migrants to the N.T.s at the expense of Ashanti and the Colony.

1960; Census.

1970; U.N. mid-year estimate, based on 1970 census. U.N. Statistical Yearbook, 1973, p. 67.

Note: [a]Includes attached portions of Togo from 1921.

TABLE 31

Approximate Population of Ghana - In Thousands

Year	Estimated Population	Year	Estimated Population
1901	1894	1929	3041
1902	1901	1930	3103
1903	1908	1931	3164
1904	1916	1932	3237
1905	1923	1933	3311
1906	1930	1934	3384
1907	1937	1935	3458
1908	1944	1936	3531
1909	1952	1937	3604
1910	1959	1938	3678
1911	1966	1939	3751
1912	2024	1940	3825
1913	2083	1941	3898
1914	2141	1942	3972
1915	2200	1943	4045
1916	2258	1944	4118
1917	2316	1945	4192
1918	2375	1946	4265
1919	2433	1947	4339
1920	2492	1948	4412
1921	2550	1949	4605
1922	2611	1950	4798
1923	2673	1951	4991
1924	2734	1952	5184
1925	2796	1953	5377
1926	2857	1954	5569
1927	2918	1955	5762
1928	2980		

TABLE 32

Average Annual Intercensal Growth Rates

Period	Colony[a]	Ashanti	Northern Territories[a]	Total Gold Coast & Togo[a]
1901-11	1.5	---	---	1.3
1911-21	1.2	---	---	2.6
1921-31	2.0	2.5	2.4	2.2
1931-48	1.9	2.4	1.6	2.0
1948-60	3.8	5.5	0.9	3.5
1901-60	2.1	---	---	2.2

Source: Calculated from data of Table 1, using the continuous growth formula $P_2/P_1 = e^{rn}$, where P_2 = second population, P_1 = first population, e = base of natural logarithms, r = growth rate, n = interval in years.

Note: [a]Includes attached portions of Togo from 1921.

TABLE 33

Foreign-born Africans

Year	Number	Change	% of Total Population
1931	199,438	---	6.3
1948	194,000	-4,438	4.4
1960	660,000	+466,000	9.8

Sources: 1931; Kuczynski, Demographic Survey, p. 413; 1948 and 1960; Caldwell, in Birmingham, ed., vol. II, p. 82, column "C". Foreign-born Africans were not counted separately until 1931.

TABLE 34

Births, Stillbirths, and Infant Mortality in Registration Areas

Year	Live Births	Official[a] Crude Birth Rate	Revised Crude Birth Rate	Stillbirths[c]	Infant Deaths[d]	Infant Mortality Rate[e]
1913	1,331			76		
1914	1,984			n.a.		
1915	2,199			n.a.		
1916	2,103			n.a.		
1917	2,031			102		
1918	2,045			103		
1919	1,927			102		
1920	2,075			95		
1921	2,963	24.2		153		
Jan-Mar. 1922	759	----		42		
1922-3	2,988	23.2		149		
1923-4	2,941	21.9		117		
1924-5	3,011	21.3		124		
1925-6	2,914	20.6		142		
Apr-Dec. 1926	3,672	----		140		
1927	5,574	22.8		216	679	122
1928	5,539	24.3[f]		218	764	138
1929	7,476	30.9[f]		280	851	114
1930	8,054	28.6[f]		320	936	116
1931	8,239	31.5		343	936	114
1932	9,376	34.7	34.1	392	954	102
1933	9,614	34.2	33.3		957	100
1934	9,637	32.9	31.8		1,017	106
1935	10,106	31.8	31.9	432	1,285	127
1936	11,222	34.5	33.9	501	1,203	107
1937	11,234	33.7	32.6	590	1,310	117
1938	11,265	33.1	31.4	559	1,146	102
1939	12,621	36.2	33.8	568	1,382	110
1940	13,548	38.1	35.0	645	1,491	110
1941	12,627	35.5	31.5	685	1,388	110
1942	12,560	35.3	30.3	709	1,482	118
1943	12,983	36.5	30.3	881	1,670	129
1944	13,526	38.0	30.6	904	1,694	125
1945	13,615	38.3	29.8	959	1,622	119
1946	14,454	40.6	30.7	980	1,589	110
1947	14,714	41.4	30.4	1,067	1,728	117
1948	14,634	29.4		1,274	1,764	121
1949	15,634	30.6	30.8	1,295	1,954	125
1950	14,787	29.3	28.7	1,309	1,804	122
1951	15,335	29.7	29.2	1,313	1,803	117
1952	15,878	30.0	29.8	1,237	1,978	125
1953	18,181	35.3	33.5	1,327	2,061	113
1954	19,600	37.0	35.6	1,529	2,328	119
1955	22,445	42.0	40.1	1,568	2,452	109
1960	33,676	55.8		n.a.	3,808	113

Sources: R.R.B.D.; M.D.A.R., R.M.H., United Nations Demographic Yearbook, 1961, p. 121.

Notes: [a]Live births per 1000 population. Because of poor population data, there were no estimates prior to 1920.

[b]Based on revised population estimates for registration areas, Table 36.

[c]Babies born dead. Calculated from published rates for 1953-5.

[d]Deaths of children less than one year old, excluding stillbirths. The Registrar, recognizing poor reporting in many areas, made no overall tabulation until 1927.

[e]Infant deaths per 1000 live births.

[f]Data from fifteen registration areas only, with 4990 births in 1928, 6497 in 1929, and 6111 in 1930. See Table 36 for population estimates.

TABLE 35

Age Composition

	Census			
Age Group	1921[a]	1931[b]	1948	1960
under 16	44.1	39.6	43.0	46.3
16-45	42.3	48.3	43.2	42.1
46 and over	13.6	12.1	13.8	11.8

Sources: 1921, 1948, 1960; Caldwell, in Birmingham, ed., vol. II, p. 41; 1931; Kuczynski, p. 436.

Notes: [a]Colony and Ashanti only.
[b]1931--0-14; 15-44, 45 and over.

TABLE 36

Deaths and Crude Death Rates in Registration Areas

Year	Deaths[a] Male	Female	Total	Official[b] Population Estimate	Official[c] Crude Death Rate	Revised[d] Population Estimate	Revised Crude Death Rate
1913			2,335				
1914			2,597				
1915			2,692				
1916			3,050				
1917			3,164				
1918	2,994	2,089	5,083				
1919	1,487	1,037	2,524				
1920	1,909	1,314	3,223				
1921	1,708	1,208	2,916	122,518	23.8		
Jan.-Mar. 1922	422	278	700	127,881	-		
1922-3	1,987	1,296	3,283	128,774	25.5		
1923-4	1,991	1,294	3,285	134,314	24.5		
1924-5	2,164	1,427	3,591	141,643	25.4		
1925-6	2,240	1,574	3,814	150,529	25.3		
Apr.-Dec. 1926	2,260	1,376	3,636	208,755			
1927	3,093	1,791	4,884	244,822	19.9		
1928	3,139	2,043	5,182	205,380[e]	19.9		
1929	3,454	1,997	5,451	210,107[e]	19.4		
1930	3,752	2,220	5,972	213,454[e]	20.4		
1931	3,765	2,207	5,972	261,198	22.9		
1932	3,687	2,218	5,905	270,357	21.8	275,155	21.5
1933	3,981	2,283	6,264	280,847	22.3	289,112	21.7
1934	4,025	2,525	6,550	292,666	22.4	303,069	21.6
1935	4,827	3,004	7,831	317,837	24.6	317,026	24.7
1936	4,972	3,030	8,002	325,433	24.6	330,983	24.2
1937	5,257	3,174	8,431	333,159	25.3	344,940	24.4
1938	4,789	2,741	7,530	340,600	22.1	358,897	21.0
1939			8,079	348,190	23.2	372,854	21.7
1940			7,894	355,780	22.2	386,811	20.4
1941			8,467	355,780	23.8	400,768	21.1
1942			9,441	355,780	26.5	414,725	22.8
1943			10,449	355,780	29.4	428,682	24.4
1944			10,093	355,780	28.4	442,639	22.8
1945			9,506	355,780	26.7	456,596	20.8
1946			9,294	355,780	26.1	470,553	19.8
1947			10,224	355,780	28.7	484,510	21.1
1948			10,681	498,466	21.4		
1949			10,873	510,122	21.3	507,235	21.4
1950	5,969	4,137	10,106	504,658	20.0	516,004	19.6
1951	5,856	4,144	10,000	516,533	19.4	524,773	19.1
1952	6,245	4,535	10,780	529,924	20.3	533,542	20.2
1953	6,167	4,553	10,720	515,200	20.8	542,211	19.8
1954	6,395	4,630	11,025	529,707	21.1	551,080	20.0
1955	6,623	5,007	11,639	534,461	21.8	559,849	20.8

Sources: R.R.B.D., M.D.A.R., R.M.H.

Notes: [a]Excludes stillbirths.

[b]1921, 1931 and 1948; Census of the African population; 1922-30, estimates based on 1911-1921 growth rates; 1932-1940, estimates based on 1921-31 growth rates and on the proclamation of new registration areas in 1936. The 1950 figure may be a clerical error. 1949-1955, calculated from 1931-48 growth rates, except 1953, which I have calculated from published crude birth and death rates.

[c]Deaths per 1000 population; corrected for computational errors in a few cases.

[d]Assuming steady arithmetic increase between 1931 and 1960; ignores small increase due to expansion of registration areas from 29 (1931) to 36 (1942).

[e]Data from fifteen registration areas only, with 4094 deaths in 1928, 4074 in 1929, and 4,335 in 1930.

TABLE 36a

Male Deaths By Age, As Percentage of All Male Deaths, 1920-38; 1950-55

Year	0-24 Hours	24 Hours - 1 Year	1-5 Years	5-15 Years	15-25 Years	25-45 Years	45-65 Years	over 65
1920	4.5	9.9	11.1	5.4	7.7	36.1	15.3	10.0
1921	2.7	11.3	13.3	4.3	10.0	37.9	11.6	8.8
1922-3	4.7	12.3	9.7	5.7	10.1	34.3	13.2	10.0
1923-4	3.8	11.1	10.8	4.8	12.7	36.6	12.4	7.8
1924-5	3.4	10.0	8.7	3.7	13.4	40.9	13.6	6.4
1925-6	4.0	12.1	12.5	3.9	8.2	38.3	13.2	7.8
1926	3.9	11.3	8.6	3.0	13.1	42.0	10.8	7.4
1927	3.0	11.9	9.4	3.4	13.0	39.5	12.8	7.0
1928	3.7	12.5	10.7	4.4	10.8	36.1	14.1	7.6
1929	4.6	15.2	9.4	3.9	10.6	34.9	14.2	7.3
1930	2.5	15.6	10.7	3.9	9.5	38.5	12.4	6.9
1931	1.5	12.1	9.5	5.0	10.0	40.2	13.9	7.8
1932	1.1	12.9	10.3	4.9	9.5	37.0	14.4	9.8
1933	1.4	12.0	9.5	4.8	10.1	38.9	15.1	9.2
1934	1.5	12.5	10.2	4.5	8.2	39.3	14.7	9.1
1935	1.0	12.9	10.5	4.8	8.5	39.5	12.9	9.9
1936	1.0	11.7	10.8	5.8	9.7	36.6	15.1	9.7
1937	0.9	12.9	9.5	5.4	8.8	37.8	14.8	9.9
1938	1.0	12.0	8.7	4.9	10.4	37.8	15.0	10.2
1950	1.3	14.9	12.7	6.1	8.4	30.9	14.3	11.5
1951	0.9	15.5	14.3	5.9	9.0	28.1	14.3	12.1
1952	1.1	16.2	14.9	5.8	7.1	27.6	12.4	15.0
1953	2.2	15.5	15.7	5.4	7.3	27.6	12.9	13.4
1954	2.2	17.7	15.9	5.9	7.1	27.1	13.0	11.0
1955	1.7	18.3	16.9	6.5	6.7	24.4	14.1	11.4

TABLE 36b

Female Deaths By Age, As Percentage of All Female Deaths, 1920-38; 1950-55

Year	0-24 Hours	24 Hours - 1 Year	1-5 Years	5-15 Years	15-25 Years	25-45 Years	45-65 Years	over 65
1920	5.7	17.4	17.5	5.9	6.3	17.3	11.9	17.9
1921	3.1	12.6	16.0	5.6	7.0	20.9	12.3	22.6
1922-3	5.6	16.7	12.9	6.9	9.7	17.7	12.7	17.8
1923-4	5.0	18.5	13.1	8.2	7.8	18.4	13.2	15.8
1924-5	4.8	11.5	13.4	8.2	7.7	21.3	11.5	21.5
1925-6	4.7	15.8	20.0	7.1	8.5	16.1	11.6	16.2
1926	5.2	17.7	14.1	8.1	8.3	20.4	10.2	15.9
1927	4.3	16.7	12.6	5.9	12.1	16.6	12.2	19.5
1928	3.5	14.2	15.7	7.6	9.0	19.9	11.6	18.6
1929	5.2	19.0	12.6	7.1	11.2	16.9	11.6	16.3
1930	2.9	18.3	13.0	5.9	10.4	20.9	13.3	15.2
1931	1.1	18.1	15.8	7.6	9.3	21.3	12.1	14.7
1932	1.5	18.2	14.7	6.7	9.2	20.7	10.8	18.1
1933	1.5	17.2	16.6	7.0	10.4	18.9	11.7	16.6
1934	1.7	16.3	16.1	5.9	9.9	21.2	11.0	17.8
1935	1.7	18.7	14.9	7.8	8.0	19.7	11.2	18.1
1936	1.4	17.4	15.9	7.4	9.5	20.3	11.4	16.7
1937	0.8	17.6	15.1	7.6	9.4	19.8	10.8	19.0
1938	1.2	17.8	14.6	6.3	9.0	20.6	11.0	19.3
1950	1.5	18.8	17.0	6.8	10.6	20.1	8.5	16.7
1951	1.3	19.0	17.1	7.8	10.5	19.1	8.7	16.5
1952	1.1	18.8	19.0	7.9	8.8	20.6	8.3	16.3
1953	1.4	20.0	17.3	6.1	9.4	19.7	7.5	18.6
1954	2.4	20.5	17.9	7.0	9.9	17.6	8.4	16.4
1955	1.5	21.1	20.4	6.9	8.6	18.2	8.0	15.3

TABLE 37

Ratio of Male/Female Deaths by Age Group, 1920-1938, 1950-1955

Year	0-24 hrs.	24 hrs.- 1 yr.	1-5 yrs.	5-15 yrs.	15-25 yrs.	25-45 yrs.	45-65 yrs.	over 65 yrs.	All Deaths
1920[a]	1.07	.84	.93	1.34	1.79	3.08	1.90	.82	1.47
1921	1.24	1.27	1.18	1.08	2.02	2.56	1.34	.55	1.41
1922-3	1.29	1.14	1.17	1.26	1.61	3.01	1.61	.87	1.55
1923-4	1.21	.97	1.33	.94	2.63	3.19	1.51	.79	1.60
1924-5	1.06	1.29	.97	.68	2.58	2.86	1.76	.44	1.49
1925-6	1.22	1.09	.90	.80	1.37	3.40	1.62	.69	1.43
1926	1.44	1.22	1.16	.70	3.02	3.94	2.03	.89	1.92
1927	1.18	1.22	1.28	1.00	1.85	4.08	1.80	.61	1.72
1928	1.48	1.23	.95	.81	1.67	2.53	1.70	.57	1.39
1929	1.33	1.19	1.12	.81	1.40	3.07	1.82	.67	1.49
1930	1.27	1.23	1.19	.96	1.32	2.66	1.35	.66	1.45
1931[b]	2.20	1.14	1.03	1.13	1.83	3.22	1.97	.91	1.71
1932	1.18	1.18	1.16	1.23	1.71	2.97	2.22	.91	1.66
1933	1.54	1.22	1.00	1.19	1.69	3.50	2.25	.97	1.74
1934	1.40	1.22	1.01	1.21	1.32	2.96	2.12	.82	1.59
1935	1.00	1.19	1.13	1.00	1.72	3.21	1.86	.88	1.61
1936	1.17	1.11	1.07	1.28	1.67	2.96	2.18	.96	1.64
1937	2.04	1.22	1.05	1.18	1.55	3.15	2.28	.86	1.66
1938	1.44	1.17	1.04	1.35	2.02	3.20	2.38	.92	1.75
1939-49	n.a.	n.a	n.a.	n.a.	n.a	n.a.	n.a.	n.a.	n.a.
1950	1.19	1.14	1.08	1.31	1.14	2.22	2.43	.99	1.44
1951	.91	1.15	1.18	1.08	1.21	2.07	2.33	1.03	1.41
1952	1.32	1.19	1.08	1.11	1.11	1.85	2.06	1.27	1.38
1953	2.14	1.05	1.23	1.21	1.05	1.91	2.32	.97	1.35
1954	1.27	1.19	1.23	1.16	.99	2.13	2.14	.93	1.38
1955	1.53	1.14	1.10	1.25	1.03	1.78	2.33	.98	1.32

Sources: R.R.B.D., M.D.A.R., R.M.H.

Notes: [a]1920-30 data are for Accra, Cape Coast, and Sekondi only.

[b]1931-8 and 1950-55 data are for all registration areas.

TABLE 38

Pregnancy, Childbrith, and Diseases of the Puerperal State

Cases Treated and Hospital Deaths, 1920 - 1935

Year	In-Patients	Deaths	Case-Mortality Rate-percent[a]	Out-Patients	Total Patients
1920		4			70
1921		8			85
Jan.Mar. 1922		2			30
1922-3		4			87
1923-4		9			118
1924-5		11			124
1925-6		15			155
1926-7	122	19	15.6	226	348
1927-8	138	29	21.0	190	328
1928-9	316	30	9.5	3,895	4,211
1929-30	654	75	11.5	15,453	16,107
1930-1	1,092	65	5.6	13,721	14,813
1931-2	1,307	56	4.3	14,421	15,728
1932-3	1,813	73	4.0	16,638	18,451
1933-4	1,891	70	3.7	14,315	16,206
1934	2,163	115	5.3	8,729	10,892
1935	2,343	102	4.4	14,777	17,120
1936	2,232	137	6.1	18,836	21,068
1937	2,355	167	7.1	23,275	25,630
1938	2,444	139	5.7	22,189	24,633
1939	2,255	144	6.4	24,029	26,284
1940	2,316	126	5.4	25,911	28,227
1941	2,424	143	5.9	42,845	45,269
1942	3,005	147	4.9	54,641	57,646
1943	3,486	168	4.8	62,978	66,464
1944	3,811	162	4.3	43,668	47,479
1945	4,186	221	5.3	37,129	41,315
1946	4,620	233	5.0	34,323	38,943
1947	5,217	306	5.9	48,169	53,386
1948	6,365	243	3.8	86,045	92,410
1949	6,762	400	5.9	63,874	70,636
1950	7,991	256	3.2	64,295	72,286
1951	8,071	362	4.5	43,047	51,064
1952	8,592	257	3.0	56,488	65,080
1953	11,134	277	2.5	14,209	25,343
1954	12,397	277	2.2	10,059	22,456
1955	10,332	272	2.6	4,355	14,687

Sources: M.D.A.R., R.M.H.

Note: [a]Percentage of hospitalized patients who died.

TABLE 39

Infant Mortality, Stillbirths, and Child Mortality; Special Surveys

Year of Survey	Place	Live Births	Still-births	Infant Deaths	Infant[a] Mortality	Child Deaths	Total Deaths Infant & Children
1924	Koforidua	3,666	422	924	252		
1931	Eastern Prov., Colony	10,222	1,046	1,624	159	1,648[b]	3,272
1931	Central Prov., Colony	2,643	325	453	171	747[b]	1,200
1931	Western Prov., Colony	3,942	316	584	148	1,225[b]	1,809
1931	Ashanti	6,049	563	875	145	1,450[b]	2,325
1931	Northern Terr.	8,295	514	1,779	214	2,060[b]	3,839
1939	Northern Terr.	2,693	183	646	240	586[c]	1,232
1939	Akim	2,338	145	246	105	687[c]	933
1950	Kwansakrom	162					75
1954	Tema	337	48				118
1968-9	Ghana				133		
1968-9	urban				98		
1968-9	rural				148		
1968-9	Accra				53		
1968-9	Upper Region - rural				208		

Sources: 1924: "A Report on the Birth Rate and Infant Mortality in the Koforidua District," by J. M. O'Brien, M.D.A.R., 1924-5, Appendix E, p. 70.

1931: Cardinall, The Gold Coast, 1931, p. 213. Some urban areas are included.

1939: ADM 11/1294, "Diet and Nutrition Surveys, Gold Coast, Final Report - 1940," p. 82; p. 112.

1950: Colbourne, et al., "Medical Survey," p. 174.

1954: Henry Richards, "Child Loss in Tema, Gold Coast," W.A.M.J., m.s., IV(1955), pp 154-5.

1968-9: S.K. Gaishie, "Levels and Patterns of Infant and Child Mortality in Ghana," Demography, 12(1975), p. 29.

Notes: [a]Per 1,000 live births; not a true I.M.R., as the data do not refer to any specific year.

[b]"Deaths before puberty."

[c]Undefined and may include stillbirths; in any case high child mortality is suggested.

TABLE 40

Four Major Causes of Deaths in Registration Areas

1920 - 1954, 1967

Year	Tuberculosis all forms Deaths	Tuberculosis all forms Mortality[a] Rate	Pneumonia[b] and Bronchitis Deaths	Pneumonia[b] and Bronchitis Mortality[a] Rate	Malaria[c] Deaths	Malaria[c] Mortality[a] Rate	Dysentary, Diarrhea, Enteritis, Typhoid Paratyphoid Deaths	Dysentary, Diarrhea, Enteritis, Typhoid Paratyphoid Mortality[a] Rate
1920[d]	160	268	301	504	57	95	351	588
1921	126	200	349	554	68	108	245	389
Apr. 1922 - Apr. 1923	134	202	321	485	61	92	233	352
1923-4	160	230	328	473	77	111	226	326
1924-5	149	205	277	381	58	80	183	252
1925-6	184	242	340	448	69	91	213	281
1926	197	249	358	452	73	92	217	274
1927	189	229	270	328	66	80	199	242
1928	157	183	346	404	49	57	226	264
1929	182	205	322	362	74	83	196	221
1930[d]	178	193	303	329	71	77	225	244
1931[e]	639	245	954	365	383	147	614	235
1932								
1933	705	244						
1934	695	229						
1935	887	280						
1936	853	258						
1937	846	245						
1938	825	230						
1939	866[f]	232	1,233[g]	331	604	162	848[h]	227
1940	792	205	1,141	295	614	159	749	194
1941	935	233	1,091	272	665	166	710	177
1942	1,062	256	1,120	270	880	212	801	193
1943	1,094	264	1,435	346	1,081	261	810	195
1944	1,048	237	1,259	284	1,109	251	697	157
1945	944	207	1,177	258	838	184	616	135
1946	940	200	1,091	232	789	168.	551	117
1947	927	191	1,209	250	1,051	217	766	158
1948	893	179	1,261	253	1,084	217	812	163
1949	789	156	1,162	229	1,252	247	789	156
1950	747	145	1,023	198	1,245	241	681	132
1951	759	145	969	185	1,300	248	825	157
1952[i]	694	130	1,117	209	1,535	288	805	151
1953[i]	674	124	1,179	217	1,297	239	943	174
1954[j]	665	121	1,202	218	1,334	242	992	180
1967[j]	179	-	841	-	704	-	-	-

Sources: R.R.B.D., M.D.A.R., R.M.H., Annual Report of the Medical Services of Ghana, 1967.

Notes:

[a]Cause-specific mortality per 100,000 population. Population bases for 1920-30 determined by arithmetic interpolation from 1921 and 1931 census results for Accra, Sekondi, and Cape Coast; for later years, see Table 36.

[b]All forms, including bronchopneumonia.

[c]Includes blackwater fever.

[d]1920-1930; Accra, Cape Coast, and Sekondi only.

[e]1931-1954: all registration areas.

[f]Respiratory tuberculosis only from 1939. In previous years, non-respiratory tuberculosis accounted for twelve percent or less of all tuberculosis deaths.

[g]From 1939, data are for "All Other Respiratory Diseases." In previous years over ninety percent of all deaths caused by respiratory diseases other than tuberculosis were assigned to bronchitis and various forms of pneumonia.

[h]From 1939, data are for "Intestinal Diseases." Based on previous reports, conditions other than those lised at the head of the column probably accounted for less than ten percent of total deaths.

[i]Deaths calculated from published figures for percent of total deaths.

[j]All registration areas.

TABLE 41

Animal Protein Imported 1921-1938, in Thousands of Pounds

Year	Meat	Fish	Total	Pounds per capita
1921	986	1,481	2,467	1.0
1922	2,335	1,879	4,214	1.6
1923	5,059	5,440	10,499	3.9
1924	7,510	7,848	15,358	5.6
1925	8,820	7,623	16,443	5.9
1926	8,016	7,016	15,032	5.3
1927	15,842	9,195	25,037	8.6
1928	16,953	10,816	27,769	9.3
1929	11,720	11,587	23,307	7.7
1930	9,797	13,093	22,890	7.4
1931	6,540	8,888	15,428	4.9
1932	6,133	7,558	13,691	4.2
1933	n.a.	n.a.		
1934	n.a.	n.a.		
1935	n.a.	n.a.		
1936	8,237	13,116	21,353	6.0
1937	10,379	16,992	27,371	7.6
1938	6,493	13,454	19,947	5.4

Sources: V.D.A.R., 1930-1; 1932-3; Gold Coast Colony Blue Book.

Note: Includes smoked, canned, bottled, salted, pickled, dried, frozen, and fresh meat and fish.

NOTES

PREFACE

1. K. David Patterson and Gerald W. Hartwig, "An Introductory Overview," in Hartwig and Patterson, eds., *Disease in African History: An Introductory Survey and Case Studies* (Durham, N.C., 1978).

2. Patterson, "River Blindness in Northern Ghana, 1900-1950" (see note 1 above); "The Influenza Epidemic of 1918-19 in the Gold Coast," *Transactions of the Historical Society of Ghana*, 16 (1977); "Health in Urban Ghana: The Case of Accra, 1900-1940," *Social Science and Medicine*, 13B (1979), pp. 251-68; "The Veterinary Department and the Animal Industry in the Gold Coast, 1909-1955," *International Journal of African Historical Studies*, 13 (1980), pp. 457-91.

3. Marc Dawson, Ph.D. dissertation in progress, University of Wisconsin; Rita Headrick, Ph.D. dissertation in progress, University of Chicago.

CHAPTER 1–THE CHANGING HUMAN ENVIRONMENT: AN OVERVIEW

1. For general discussions of disease ecology and the impact of epidemic diseases on previously unexposed populations, see William H. McNeill, *Plagues and Peoples* (New York, 1976); F. M. Burnett and D. O. White, *Natural History of Infectious Disease* (Cambridge, 1972); René Dubos, *Man Adapting* (New Haven, 1965); Alfred W. Crosby, "Virgin Soil Epidemics as a Factor in the Aboriginal Depopulation in America," *The William and Mary Quarterly*, 33 (1976), pp. 289-99; Charles C. Hughes and John M. Hunter, "Disease and Development in Africa," *Social Science and Medicine*, III (1970), pp. 443-93; and the introductory chapter in Gerald W. Hartwig and K. David Patterson, eds., *Disease in African History* (Durham, N.C., 1978).

2. J. W. S. Macfie, "Prevalent Diseases of the Gold Coast," *T.R.S.T.M.H.*, 16 (1922), pp. 156-61; T. Edward Bowdich, *Mission from Cape Coast Castle to Ashantee* (1819; 3rd ed. London, 1966), pp. 370-80. These observations were made by Henry Tedlie, the surgeon who accompanied Bowdich.

3. F. B. Livingstone, "Anthropological Implications of Sickle Cell Gene Distribution in West Africa," *American Anthropologist*, 60 (1958), pp. 533-62; Stephen L. Weisenfeld, "Sickle-Cell Trait in Human Biological and Cultural Evolution," *Science*, 157 (1967), pp. 1134-40.

4. See, for example, Willem Bosman, *A New and Accurate Description of the Coast of Guinea* (1705; reprinted, London, 1967), pp. 108, 110. The topic of disease introductions as a result of European trade needs much closer examination, as discussed in K. David Patterson, "The Vanishing Mpongwe: European Contact and Demographic Change in the Gabon River," *J.A.H.*, 16 (1975), pp. 237-38.

5. Hartwig and Patterson, eds., *Disease in African History*, introduction; James W. Brown, "Increased Intercommunication and Epidemic Disease in Early Colonial Ashanti" (in Hartwig and Patterson, *Disease in African History*).

6. The following discussion is based on Kwamina B. Dickson, *A Historical Geography of*

Ghana (Cambridge, 1971), pp. 221-29, 329-32; and Peter R. Gould, *The Development of the Transportation Pattern in Ghana* (Evanston, 1960), pp. 40-48, and maps on pages 14, 39, 41, 67, 69, 101, 103-5, 107-9.

7. The number of motor vehicle licenses rose from 3,287 in 1923 to over 10,000 in 1938. G. B. Kay, *The Political Economy of Colonialism in Ghana: A Collection of Documents and Statistics, 1900-1960* (Cambridge, 1972), pp. 398-99.

8. Dickson, *Historical Geography*, pp. 229-34; Gould, *Transportation Pattern*, pp. 23-24.

9. Kay, *Documents and Statistics*, p. 390.

10. Gould, *Transportation Pattern*, p. 27.

11. Kay, *Documents and Statistics*, pp. 394-95.

12. Ibid., p. 315; N. O. Addo, "Some Demographic Aspects of Urbanization in Ghana, 1931-1960," *Ghana Social Science J.*, 1 (1970), pp. 57, 63.

13. For the origins of migrant labor, see Roger G. Thomas, "Forced Labour in British West Africa: The Case of the Northern Territories of the Gold Coast," *J.A.H.*, 14 (1973), pp. 79-108.

14. *Annual Report, Eastern Region of Ashanti*, 1930-31, p. 17.

15. *M.D.A.R.*, 1929-30, pp. 43-44; *M.D.A.R.*, 1940, p. 5. The impact of labor migration on northern agriculture deserves study, but seasonal drought and, in many places, rapid population growth and land shortage seem to have been much more significant constraints. For case studies of other regions, see Meredith Turshen, "The Impact of Colonialism on Health and Health Services in Tanzania," *Int. J. of Health Services*, 7 (1977), pp. 7-35; and Leroy Vail, "Ecology and History: The Example of Eastern Zambia," *Journal of Southern African Studies*, 3 (1977), pp. 129-55.

16. Polly Hill, *The Migrant Cocoa Farmers of Southern Ghana: A Study in Rural Capitalism* (Cambridge, 1963), especially pp. 219-38.

17. Kay, *Documents and Statistics*, pp. 416-17.

18. Ibid.

19. W. E. Masters, "A Model Mining Village in the Tropics," *J.T.M.H.*, 22 (1919), pp. 89-93; *M.D.A.R.*, 1936, p. 99; *M.D.A.R.*, 1938, pp. 112-13. Dissertations on mine labor now being prepared by James W. Silver (University of Sussex) and Jeffery Crisp (University of Birmingham) will provide valuable information on public health in mining areas.

20. *M.D.A.R.*, 1937, p. 104.

21. Kay, *Documents and Statistics*, p. 313; Robert R. Kuczynski, *Demographic Survey of the British Colonial Empire* (London, 1948), vol. I, p. 418, 441; Gold Coast, *Census of Population: 1948; Report and Tables* (London, 1950), p. 83, table 16.

22. A. I. Asiwaju, "Migrations as Revolt: The Example of the Ivory Coast and the Upper Volta before 1945," *J.A.H.*, 17 (1976), pp. 577-94.

23. J. C. Caldwell, "Population Change," in Walter Birmingham, I. Neustadt, and E. N. Omaboe, eds., *A Study of Contemporary Ghana* (London, 1967), vol. II, p. 82.

24. Caldwell, "Migration and Urbanization," p. 121 (see note 23 above). The country was divided into its present regions, except that the present Western and Central Regions were combined, as were the Northern and Upper Regions.

25. Dickson, *Historical Geography*, pp. 337-43.

26. Hughes and Hunter, "Disease and 'Development'," pp. 456-58.

27. Roger G. Thomas, "Education in Northern Ghana, 1906-1940: A Study in Colonial Paradox," *I.J.A.H.S.*, 7 (1974), pp. 427-67.

28. Philip Foster, *Education and Social Change in Ghana* (London, 1965), is a good survey.

29. Gold Coast, Education Department, "Village Health: A Pamphlet for Teachers" (Accra, 1932).

CHAPTER 2–THE DEVELOPMENT AND RECEPTION OF MODERN MEDICAL SERVICES

1. The name of the department was changed from time to time, and there were numerous administrative rearrangements and changes of title which are of little relevance for this

study. Perhaps most significant were the creation and eventual suppression of special administrators for Ashanti, the Northern Territories, and the three provinces of the Colony. High turnover rates in top positions may have discouraged innovation. *Report of the Commission of Enquiry into the Health Needs of the Gold Coast* (S.P.V. of 1952), p. 9. For the Veterinary Department, see K. David Patterson, "The Veterinary Department and the Animal Industry in the Gold Coast, 1909-1954," *IJAHS*, 13 (1980), pp. 457-91.

2. Thomas S. Gale, "Official Medical Policy in British West Africa," unpublished Ph.D. dissertation (University of London, S.O.A.S., 1973), pp. 277-317; British Medical Association, "Colonial Medical Service," *Brit. Med. J.*, supplement, 2 (1931), pp. 1-6.

3. Gale, "Medical Policy," pp. 368-70; Ralph Furse, *Aucuparius, Recollections of a Recruiting Officer* (London, 1962), p. 241.

4. Gale, "Medical Policy," pp. 310-11; Raymond E. Dumett, "The Campaign Against Malaria and the Expansion of Scientific Medical and Sanitary Services in British West Africa, 1898-1910," *Af. Hist. St.*, I (1968), pp. 191; interview with Dr. B. B. Waddy, London, 7 Oct. 1977. Fees were still a problem in 1952 (*Commission of Enquiry*, pp. 47-49).

5. ADM 14/2/1, *Legislative Council Debates*, 1 Dec. 1914, p. 61, Statement by Lt. Col. W. H. Grey.

6. *M.D.A.R.*, 1907, p. 9; *M.D.A.R.*, 1910, p. 6.

7. Gale, "Medical Policy," pp. 321-22.

8. ADM 1/2/217, no. 683, Governor to Secretary of State, 6 Dec. 1935, and encl., D.M.S.S. to C.S., 7 Nov. 1935.

9. ADM 14/2/12, *Legislative Council Debates*, 22 Feb. 1926, p. 163, Governor's Budget Speech.

10. *M.D.A.R.*, 1930-31, p. 9.

11. *M.D.A.R*, 1931-32, p. 4; *M.D.A.R.*, 1932-33, p. 5.

12. *M.D.A.R.*, 1948, pp. 5, 18.

13. ADM 1/2/312, no. 1259, Governor to Secretary of State, 8 July 1949.

14. Dumett, "Campaign Against Malaria," p. 170.

15. British Medical Association, "Colonial Medical Service," p. 12.

16. ADM 1/2/116, no. 376, Governor to Secretary of State, 11 June 1917, and encl., Minute by T. E. Rice, 11 June 1917.

17. Dumett, "Campaign Against Malaria," p. 195; Robert Rene Kuczynski, *Demographic Survey of the British Colonial Empire. Vol. I. West Africa* (London, 1948), pp. 15-17, 540.

18. Gale, "Medical Policy," p. 364, 366.

19. ADM 1/2/59, no. 204, Governor to Secretary of State, 15 June 1903.

20. ADM 1/2/81, no. 573, Governor to Secretary of State, 20 Aug. 1912. The *Bulletin* first appeared in 1911.

21. ADM 1/2/226, no. 760, 20 Dec. 1930, encl., "Human Nutrition in the Gold Coast," p. B. 1.

22. *M.D.A.R.*, 1923-24, p. 20; Jane C. Wright, "Survey of Medical Conditions in Ghana in 1957," *J. National Medical Association*, 53 (1961), p. 315.

23. Gale, "Medical Policy," pp. 280-310; Ralph Schram, *A History of the Nigerian Health Services* (Ibadan, 1971), pp. 130-34; David Kimble, *A Political History of Ghana* (London, 1963), pp. 93-105.

24. For example, *Gold Coast Leader*, 11 Feb. 1913, p. 3; *Gold Coast Independent*, 23 Aug. 1924, p. 670; *Gold Coast Independent*, 17 Nov. 1934, p. 1094.

25. *Gold Coast Leader*, 7 Dec. 1912, pp. 3-4.

26. ADM 14/2/11, *Legislative Council Debates*, 1925, p. 241, Question of Nana Essandoah III.

27. Gale, "Medical Policy," pp. 376, 380.

28. Gale, "Sir Gordon Guggisberg and his African Critics," *Trans. Hist. Soc. Ghana*, 14 (1973), p. 273.

29. *Gold Coast Leader*, 29 Sept. 1923, pp. 5-6.

30. ADM 1/2/159, no. 876, Governor to Secretary of State, 7 Nov. 1924. Guggisberg may have been overly influenced by the failure of one of his first African appointees (Gale, "Medical Policy," p. 381).

31. *Gold Coast Leader*, 28 Mar. 1925, p. 7.

32. Gale, "Guggisberg," p. 275, n. 12.

33. ADM 14/2/18, *Legislative Council Debates*, 14 June 1930, pp. 321-23, Questions of J. Glover-Addo and J. E. Casely Hayford.

34. ADM 1/2/246, no. 62, Governor to Secretary of State, 25 Jan. 1939.

35. ADM 1/2/213, no. 344, Governor to Secretary of State, 15 June 1935.

36. C.S.O. 11/1, 1292/30, D.M.S.S. to C.S., 2 Aug. 1930; "Terms of Appointment of Medical Women to the Gold Coast," petition of June 1930.

37. Ibid., D.M.S.S. to C.S., 30 July 1930.

38. Ibid., C.S. to Governor, 31 Oct. 1930.

39. Ibid., D.M.S.S. to C.S., 20 Apr. 1931.

40. Ibid., C. D. Williams to D.D.H.S., 13 Sept. 1932.

41. Ibid., Ag. D.M.S.S. to C.S., 3 Oct. 1932; Governor to C.S., 19 July 1935.

42. *Gold Coast Leader*, 14 Oct. 1916, p. 3.

43. Gale, "Medical Policy," p. 355, n. 4; *Gold Coast Leader*, 6 Sept. 1924, p. 5.

44. *Gold Coast Independent*, 20 May 1939, p. 471.

45. Ibid., 11 Nov. 1922, p. 525.

46. Ibid., 12 Oct. 1929, p. 1295. See also K. David Patterson, "Health in Urban Ghana: The Case of Accra, 1900-1940," *Social Science and Medicine*, 13B (1979), pp. 251-68.

47. NAG–Tamale, TNA-1-496, "Annual Report of Navrongo Sub-District of Mamprusi for the Year 1935-6," p. 43.

48. *M.D.A.R.*, 1936, p. 98.

49. Ibid., 1931-32, p. 5; *Commission of Enquiry*, p. 45. For the role of missionary medicine in Nigeria, see Schram, *History of Nigerian Health Services*, pp. 143-56, 170-80, 217-29.

50. *A.R.G.C.*, 1935-36, p. 13.

51. ADM 14/2/20, *Legislative Council Debates*, 14 Mar. 1934, p. 17, Statement of D.M.S.S.

52. *R.M.H.*, 1953, p. 4

53. In 1969, 67 of the 81 private practitioners in Ghana were in either Accra or Kumasi, and 6 more were in Sekondi-Takoradi. There were none in Ashanti outside Kumasi, none in the Volta, Upper or Brong-Ahafo Regions, and only one in the Northern Region. See M. J. Sharpston, "Uneven Geographical Distribution of Medical Care: A Ghanaian Case Study," *J. of Development Studies*, 8 (1972), pp. 207-8.

54. ADM 1/2/116, no. 376, Governor to Secretary of State, 11 June 1917, and encl., Minute by P.M.O. Rice.

55. ADM 14/1/16, *Report by Dr. P. S. Selwyn-Clarke on the Yellow Fever Conference at Dakar, 1928*, S.P. VII of 1929-30, p. 16. Peggy R. Sabatier, " 'Elite' Education in French West Africa: The Era of Limits, 1903-1945," *IJAHS*, 11 (1978), pp. 252-3265.

56. Gale, "Guggisberg," p. 174.

57. ADM 5/3/26, *Report on the Establishment in British West Africa of a College for Medical Practitioners and Assistants*, 1928, by W. J. D. Innes, D.M.S.S., Gold Coast, pp. 54-55, Governor to Secretary of State, 25 Feb. 1926.

58. Ibid., *Proceedings of the Third Conference of the Senior Members of the West African Medical Staff from the Colonies of Nigeria, the Gold Coast, Sierra Leone, and the Gambia*, Dec. 1925, pp. 56-57.

59. *College for Medical Practitioners*, pp. 6, 8, 37-39.

60. ADM 14/1/27, *Dispatch from the Secretary of State Relating to the Proposal to Establish a Medical College in the Gold Coast*, S.P. XVI of 1930-31, pp. 3-8. A medical school was established in 1964.

61. ADM 14/1/27, *Correspondence Relating to a Scheme for Extending the System of Village Dispensaries and Improving the Training of African Nursing and Dispensing Staff*, S.P. XV of 1930-31, pp. 3-10.

62. *M.D.A.R.*, 1935, p. 35.

63. *M.D.A.R.*, 1941, p. 7; *M.D.A.R.*, 1948, pp. 9, 18; B. B. Waddy, "Organization and Work of the Gold Coast Medical Field Units," *T.R.S.T.M.H.*, 50 (1956), pp. 334-35; *Commission of Enquiry*, p. 6.

64. Docia A. N. Kissieh, "Developments in Nursing in Ghana," *Intern. J. Nursing Studies*, 5 (1968), pp. 206-7; *R.M.H.*, 1953, p. 4; *Commission of Enquiry*, pp. 33-34.

65. ADM 1/2/233, no. 607, encl. 2, "Development of the Education of Women and Their Employment in Health Work in the Gold Coast," by D. Duff, D.M.S., 10 May 1937.

66. *R.M.H.*, 1953, p. 4.

67. *M.D.A.R.*, 1931-32, p. 5.

68. B. F. 3989, "Memorandum onsthe Type of Department Which will be Necessary to Implement a Policy of Preventive Medicine in the Gold Coast," by J. Balfour Kirk, 5 July 1943.

69. Ibid., D.M.S. (Kirk) to C.S., 14 Mar. 1944.

70. *Commission of Enquiry*, pp. 21-22 and end map.

71. *R.M.H.*, 1954, p. 32.

72. Sharpston, "Uneven Distribution," pp. 205-22.

73. C.S.O. 11/1, 153/37, Circular of D.M.S., 16 July 1936.

74. B. B. Waddy, personal communication, 1 Jan. 1976.

75. Maurice King, *Medical Care in Developing Countries: A Primer on the Medicine of Poverty* (London, 1966), pp. 2:6-2:8; Gary W. S. Shannon and G. E. Alan Dever, *Health Care Delivery and Spatial Perspectives* (New York, 1973), pp. 98-100.

76. F. T. Sai, "Ghana," in Ian Douglas-Wilson and G. McLachan, *Health Care Prospects: An International Survey* (London, 1973), p. 139.

77. *Gold Coast Leader*, 5 Dec. 1925, p. 4; *Gold Coast Leader*, 18 May 1929; ADM 14/2/22, *Legislative Council Debates*, 18 Feb. 1936, Statements by K. A. Korsah (pp. 100-101), Togbi Sri II (p. 105), Nana Tsibu Darku IX (p. 108), and Kojo Thompson (p. 118).

78. E. G., *Gold Coast Independent*, 13 Feb. 1932, p. 182; *Gold Coast Independent*, 26 Aug. 1933, p. 803; B. F. 3460, Yaw Sapong, Omanhene, New Juaben, to C.E.P., 17 July 1942.

79. *M.D.A.R.*, 1942, p. 1; *M.D.A.R.*, p. 1.

80. *Gold Coast Leader*, 21 Nov. 1923, p. 5.

81. E.g., *M.D.A.R.*, 1938, p. 43. These figures were remarkably consistent over the years.

82. *Gold Coast Leader*, 19 Jan. 1924, pp. 3-4. ADM 1/2/144, no. 170, encl., C. V. LeFanu and A. J. R. O'Brien to Prin. M.O., 23 Jan. 1922.

83. C.S.O. 11/5, 113/36, Sr. M.O., Cape Coast, to D.M.S., 11 July 1936; Governor to Secretary of State, 7 Nov. 1936.

84. ADM 56/1/405, P. D. Oakley to D.M.S.S., 20 Dec. 1927.

85. Ibid., Ag. D.M.S.S. to C.C.N.T., 3 May 1932; C.S.O. 11/6, 726/32, Governor to C.S., 6 May 1929.

86. C.S.O. 11/1, 153/37, D.M.S. to Governor, 2 Apr. 1937.

87. Ibid., J. D. Reid to Asst. D.M.S., Kumasi, 18 Feb. 1937.

88. Ibid., F. M. McKernan to Asst. D.M.S., Kumasi, 16 Feb. and 26 Feb. 1937.

89. Ibid., "Note of an Interview with His Excellency, 15 Apr. 1937," by D.M.S.

90. Rhodes House Library, Mss. Afr., s1368, "Diary of Dr. J. B. Kirk, 5 Jan. 1942-15 June 1943," pp. 14, 55, 57.

91. Rhodes House Library, Mss. Afr., s.1402 (1) "Some General Considerations Arising Out of Tours of Certain Parts of the Gold Coast, Made by the Director of Medical Services between January 5th and September 23, 1942," by J. B. Kirk, 10 Oct. 1942, pp. 17, 13.

92. *Commission of Enquiry*, p. 20.

93. *M.D.A.R.*, 1944, p. 7; *M.D.A.R.*, 1948, pp. 5, 18.

94. *Commission of Enquiry*, p. 19; *Statement by the Gold Coast Government on the Report of the Commission of Enquiry into the Health Needs of the Gold Coast* (Accra, Government Printer, 1955), p. 1.

95. E.g., *M.D.A.R.*, 1924-25, p. 28; *M.D.A.R.*, 1938, p. 49.

96. Allister MacMillan, *The Red Book of West Africa* (1920, reprinted London, 1968), p. 210.

97. ADM 1/2/163, no. 384, Ag. Gov. to Secretary of State, 4 June 1925.

98. *M.D.A.R.*, 1926-27, p. 42; *Gold Coast Independent*, 13 Mar. 1929, p. 5.

99. Ag. Gov. to Secretary of State, 4 June 1925.

100. Gale, "Medical Policy," p. 233.

101. Ibid., p. 396.

102. ADM 39/1/582, D. C. Keta to C.E.P., 13 July 1939.

103. C.S.O. 11/14, 454/32, Ag. D.D.H.S. to D.M.S.S., 12 Mar. 1932.

104. Ibid., Ag. C.C.P. to C.S., 6 Sept. 1932.

105. Ibid., C.C.N.T. to C.S., 18 July 1932.

106. Ibid., C.C.A. to C.S., 24 Sept. 1932.

107. George Rosen, *A History of Public Health* (New York, 1958), p. 224, citing an editorial in the *Times*.

108. C.S.O. 11/6, 736/32, C.S. to Governor, 27 June 1932; ADM 1/2/198, no. 610, Governor to Secretary of State, 5 Aug. 1932.

109. Kirk, "Some General Considerations," p. 43.

110. "Diary of Dr. J. B. Kirk," 15 Jan. 1942; Kirk, "Some General Considerations," p. 20.

111. Charles Tettey, "A Brief History of the Medical Research Institute and Laboratory Service of the Gold Coast, 1908-1957," *W.A.M.J.*, n.s., 9 (1960): 73-74; ADM 1/2/136, no. 1131, Governor to Secretary of State, 29 Nov. 1920.

112. ADM 1/2/167, no. 80, Governor to Secretary of State, 27 Jan. 1926.

113. Tettey, "Brief History," p. 76; *Commission of Enquiry*, p. 7.

114. Tettey, "Brief History," pp. 77, 83; *Gold Coast Independent*, 12 Mar. 1932, pp. 286-87.

115. Andrew Balfour and Henry Harold Scott, *Health Problems of the Empire: Past, Present, and Future* (New York, 1924), p. 83.

116. *Gold Coast Independent*, 18 Nov. 1944, p. 178. Purcell also complained that the Medical Department was too autocratic and too subservient to the political service.

117. Rhodes House Library, Mss. Afr., s. 1402(4), "Memorandum on Certain Aspects of Medical Service in the Gold Coast," by J. Balfour Kirk, p. 1.

118. ADM 1/2/312, no. 1259, Governor to Secretary of State, 8 July 1949.

119. ADM 1/2/302, S.T. 1424, Governor to Secretary of State, 10 Aug. 1948.

120. B. B. Waddy, personal communication, 17 Aug. 1976; interview, London, 7 Oct. 1977.

121. Tettey, "Brief History," p. 84.

122. Acc. no. 1763/58, B.P. 249, "Report of the Committee on Infant Mortality in Accra," 31 Aug. 1917.

123. Ibid., Governor to Secretary of State, 17 Mar. 1919.

124. Ibid., "Conference on Infant Mortality in the Gold Coast," 14 Sept. 1920.

125. *R.R.B.D.*, 1921, p. 7.

126. ADM 1/2/144, no. 169, Governor to Secretary of State, 1 Apr. 1922, and encl. 1, "Conference on School M.O.s," 17 May 1921.

127. Acc. no. 2763/58, B.P. 249, Dr. J. G. Pirie to D.D.S.S., 31 Dec. 1923; and Governor's Remarks on Dr. Pirie's Memorandum, 18 Mar. 1924.

128. *M.D.A.R.*, 1924-25, pp. 9, 10, 23; Acc. no. 2763/58, B.P. 249, D.D.H.S. to D.M.S.S., 17 June 1924.

129. ADM 14/2/12, *Legislative Council Debates*, 22 Feb. 1926, pp. 153-55, Governor's Budget Speech.

130. *Gold Coast Leader*, 28 Feb. 1925, p. 4; ADM 14/2/14, *Legislative Council Debates*, 1 Mar. 1928, p. 49, Speech of Governor Slater. Lady Slater was President of the Organization.

131. *Togo Report*, 1924, pp. 58-60; *Togo Report*, 1925, pp. 64-65; *Togo Report*, 1929, p. 49; *Togo Report*, 1930, p. 55.

132. C.S.O. 11/6, 976/32, Ag. D.M.S. to C.C.N.T., 26 Oct. 1932; Ag. C.S. to C.C.N.T., 27 Nov. 1932.

133. ADM 14/2/14, *Legislative Council Debates*, 3 Mar. 1928, p. 260, Speech of Ag. Governor Thomas.

134. C.S.O. 11/6, 736/32, Memorandum of D.M.S.S., 14 June 1932.

135. Ibid., C.S. to Governor, 17 June 1932.

136. Ibid., D. E. Stewart, W.M.O., to M.O.H., Koforidua, 21 Sept. 1931; C. D. Williams, W.M.O., to D.D.H.S., 24 Mar. 1932; Dr. W. M. Howells, Sr. S.O., to D.D.H.S., 25 Apr. 1932.

137. Ibid., Ag. Governor to Secretary of State, 5 Aug. 1932.

138. C. D. Williams, "Maternal and Child Health in Kumasi in 1935," *J. Trop. Pediatrics*, 2 (1956), pp. 142-46; Kirk, "Some General Considerations," pp. 26-28.

139. *Gold Coast Independent*, 26 Mar. 1932, pp. 351-52; ADM 39/1/265, C.S. to C.E.P., 15 Dec. 1930, Aid for a mission-run center at Dsoje, Keta District, was refused, despite the fact that the villagers had raised £100 themselves.

140. C.S.O. 11/6, 149/32, "Petition of the Unofficial Members of the Town Council of Cape Coast and Other Inhabitants," 10 Feb. 1932.

141. C.S.O. 11/6, 1028/31, s.f. I, "Petition of the Women-Folk of Sekondi," encl. in African Members of the Sekondi Maternity and Child Welfare League to Lady Slater, 13 Feb. 1932.

142. Ibid., African Members to Lady Slater, 25 Jan. 1932.

143. P. S. Selwyn-Clarke, "The British Red Cross Society on the Gold Coast," *W.A.M.J.*, 7 (1934), pp. 117-19.

144. C.S.O. 11/6, 252/32, Ag. Governor to Secretary of State, 5 Aug. 1932; *Gold Coast Independent*, 21 Jan. 1933, p. 60; *Gold Coast Independent*, 11 Feb. 1933, p. 133; *Gold Coast Independent*, 1 Apr. 1933, p. 29.

145. *M.D.A.R.*, 1945, pp. 5-6, 13.

146. Williams, "Maternal and Child Health," p. 143.

147. C.S.O. 11/6, 3581, "Report of the Visiting Committee Held on the Infant Welfare Clinic, Kumasi, on 8 November 1943."

148. *Togo Report*, 1924, pp. 50-51; 1925, p. 57.

149. *M.D.A.R.*, 1931-32, p. 39.

150. *M.D.A.R.*, 1928-29, p. 42.

151. *M.D.A.R.*, 1930-31, pp. 142-48; "Report on the Traveling Dispensary."

152. *M.D.A.R.*, 1931-32, p. 39.

153. John McKelvey, Jr., *Man Against Tsetse: Struggle for Africa* (Ithaca, N.Y., 1973), pp. 126-32.

154. ADM 1/2/304, S.T. 2059, Governor to Secretary of State, 23 Nov. 1948.

155. ADM 1/2/311, S.T. 1796, Governor to Secretary of State, 26 Sept. 1949.

156. Waddy, "Medical Field Units," pp. 313-14; interviews, London, 7 Oct. and 14 Oct. 1977; *R.M.H.*, 1955, p. 28.

157. Waddy, interviews, 7 Oct. and 14 Oct. 1977. There is a file on this subject in NAG-Tamale which I could not consult because of the thirty-year rule.

158. Waddy, "Medical Field Units," p. 337, comments by Dr. A. Duggan.

159. K. David Patterson, "River Blindness in Northern Ghana, 1900-1950," in Gerald W. Hartwig and K. David Patterson, eds., *Disease in African History: An Introductory Survey and Case Studies* (Durham, N.C., 1978).

160. B. B. Waddy, "Rural Health Services in the Tropics, and the Training of Medical Auxilliaries for Them," *T.R.S.T.M.H.*, 57 (1963), p. 385.

161. J. L. McLetchie, "Medical Field Units in Nigeria," *T.R.S.T.M.H.*, 48 (1954), pp. 156-82; Waddy, "Medical Field Units," pp. 320-21.

162. King, *Medical Care in Developing Countries*; Sai, "Ghana"; John Bryant, *Health and the Developing World* (Ithaca, N.Y., 1969).

163. This point was emphasized by the first two directors of the M.F.U.s, both of whom volunteered the word "paternalism." Waddy, interview 14 Oct. 1977; David Scott, interview, Accra, 4 Nov. 1977. For details of training, see Waddy, "Medical Field Units," pp. 318-19; "Rural Health Services," pp. 388-91.

164. Waddy, "Medical Field Units," pp. 315-18.

165. Scott (interview, 4 Nov. 1977) stressed the high quality of the staff. See also comments of Dr. G. MacDonald and Dr. W. E. Kershaw, in Waddy, "Medical Field Units," pp. 340-41. Favorable official views are given in *Commission of Enquiry*, pp. 17-18; and *Statement of Government*, p. 1.

166. Scott, interview, 4 Nov. 1977; Waddy, interviews, 7 Oct. and 14 Oct. 1977.

167. Sai, "Ghana," p. 128.

168. Colin Baker, "The Government Medical Service in Malawi: An Administrative History, 1891-1974," *Medical History*, 20 (1976), pp. 302-3; Ann Beck, *A History of the British Medical Administration of East Africa, 1900-1950* (Cambridge, Mass., 1970), pp. 216-22.

27. *M.D.A.R.*, 1945, p. 3.

28. L. G. Eddey, "Spray-Killing of Mosquitoes in Houses–A Contribution to Malaria Control on the Gold Coast," *T.R.S.T.M.H.*, 38 (1944), pp. 167-97.

29. L. G. Eddey, "Destruction of Adult Mosquitoes by Residual DDT Methods," *T.R.S.T.M.H.*, 40 (1947), pp. 567-88.

30. *M.D.A.R., 1933-34, p. 19; M.D.A.R.*, 1937, p. 14; ADM 1/2/258, encl. 1 in no. 333 of 16 June 1940, "Malaria and Anti-Malaria Measures," memorandum by the D.M.S.

31. *M.D.A.R.*, 1937, p. 14.

32. Faust, Russell, and Jung, *Clinical Parasitology*, p. 210; Charles Wilcocks and P. E. C. Manson-Bahr, *Manson's Tropical Diseases* (17th ed., London, 1972), pp. 53, 57.

33. CSO 11/10, 3721, s. f. 9, Memorandum of D.M.S., 2 Feb. 1943. For similar frustrations in another colony, see J. Storey, "A Review of Malaria Work in Sierra Leone 1900 to 1964," *W.A.M.J.*, n.s., 21 (1972), pp. 57-68.

34. Russell, "Malaria among Children," pp. 238-42; C. D. Williams, "Quinine in Treatment of Malaria in Children," *W.A.M.J.*, 7 (1933), pp. 105-6.

35. M. J. Colbourne, "The Effect of Malaria Suppression in a Group of Accra School Children," *T.R.S.T.M.H.*, 49 (1955), pp. 356-69; M. Colbourne and F. Wright, "Malaria on the Gold Coast, Pt. I," *W.A.M.J.*, n.s., 4 (1955), pp. 2-11.

36. Colbourne and Wright, "Malaria on the Gold Coast, I," pp. 13-17.

37. Ibid., part II, pp. 161-65.

38. Ibid., pp. 170-72.

39. Michael James Colbourne, *Malaria in Africa* (London, 1966), pp. 7, 31, 36.

40. W. A. Chinery, "Mosquito Control in an Urban Environment, with Reference to the Anti-Mosquito Operations in Accra and Tema," *Ghana Med. J.*, 7 (1968), pp. 205-9; Chinery, "A Survey of Mosquito Breeding in Accra, Ghana, During a Two-Year Period of Larval Mosquito Control: II. The Breeding of *Culex pipiens fatigans* Weidemann and *Anopheles* (cellia) *gambiae* Giles in Accra," *Ghana Med. J.*, 9 (1970), pp. 109-16.

41. The existence of yellow fever in monkeys in Ghana was confirmed by 1936. *M.D.A.R.*, 1935, p. 5; *M.D.A.R.*, 1936, p. 6.

42. See, for example, John Duffy, *Sword of Pestilence: The New Orleans Yellow Fever Epidemic of 1853* (Baton Rouge, 1966).

43. E.g., ADM 1/2/90, encl. 1 in no. 60 of 28 Jan. 1914, "Medical Report on the Illness and Death of Captain W. Swire." Captain Swire, D.C. of Tumu, suffered for eight days before dying; his ghost was reported in the area for many years. B. B. Waddy, "World Health Notes," *The Practicioner*, 212 (1974), pp. 307-8.

44. Wilcocks and Manson-Bahr, *Manson's Tropical Diseases*, p. 374.

45. Henry Beeuwkes and A. F. Mahaffy, "The Past Incidence and Distribution of Yellow Fever in West Africa as Indicated by Protection Test Surveys," *T.R.S.T.M.H.*, 28 (1934), pp. 39-76.

46. David Scott, *Epidemic Disease in Ghana, 1901-1960* (London, 1965), pp. 37-39.

47. Ibid., pp. 29, 41.

48. ADM 5/3/4, *Report on Certain Outbreaks of Yellow Fever in 1910 and 1911*, 1913, pp. 12-22.

49. *Gold Coast Leader*, 5 Aug. 1911, pp. 2-3, "The Yellow Fever Scare."

50. Raymond E. Dumett, "The Campaign Against Malaria and the Expansion of Scientific Medical and Sanitary Services in British West Africa, 1898-1910," *Af. Hist. St.*, 1 (1960)8), pp. 170-72; Leo Spitzer, "The Mosquito and Segregation in Sierra Leone," *Can. J. Af. St.*, 2 (1968), pp. 52, 56.

51. Thomas S. Gale, "Official Medical Policy in British West Africa, 1870-1930," unpublished Ph.D. dissertation, University of London, S.O.A.S. (1973), pp. 262-66.

52. *Gold Coast Leader*, 4-11 Feb. 1922, p. 4.

53. *M.D.A.R.*, 1934, p. 15.

54. *M.D.A.R.*, 1939, p. 3

55. *Gold Coast Leader*, 21 Jan. 1903, p. 4.

56. *Gold Coast Leader*, 20 July 1912, p. 4.

57. *Gold Coast Leader*, 31 Aug. 1912, p. 4.
58. *Gold Coast Leader*, 12-26 Aug. 1911, p. 3.
59. *Gold Coast Leader*, 20 July 1912, p. 5.
60. *Gold Coast Independent*, 24 July 1926, p. 800.
61. *Gold Coast Independent* 18 Jan. 1930, p. 81.
62. Figures were tabulated in the *M.D.A.R.* and the *Municipal Annual Reports*.
63. Indexes were reported in the sources cited in n. 62 above.
64. ADM 14/1/20, *Report of the Medical Officer of Health, Accra*, 1922, S. P. VIII of 1923-24, p. 4.
65. Rockefeller Archive Center, 495, West Africa, Box 52, folder 329, A. M. Walcott to H. Beeuwkes, 4 Nov. 1925.
66. C.S.O. 11/10, 1141/30, D.D.H.S. to Ag. D.M.S.S., 8 July 1930; C.S. to All Department Heads, 13 Aug. 1930.
67. Rockefeller Archive Center (see note 65 above), "Report of an Epidemic of West African Yellow Fever which Occurred at Asamankese, Gold Coast, During the Spring and Summer of 1926," by Henry Beeuwkes.
68. The Rockefeller Commission estimated 123-178 deaths; a somewhat lower figure was suggested in *M.D.A.R.*, 1926-27, pp. 19-21.
69. ADM 1/2/174, encl. 1 in no 324 of 25 Apr. 1927, "Yellow Fever–Asamankese and Suhum," by W. A. Young.
70. ADM 1/2/179, encl. in no. 426, D.M.S.S. to C.S., 31 May 1928.
71. Scott, *Epidemic Disease*, p. 55; B. B. Waddy, "Organization and Work of the Gold Coast Medical Field Units," *T.R.S.T.M.H.*, 50 (1956), p. 327.
72. *M.D.A.R.*, 1913, p. 9; *M.D.A.R.*, 1918, p. 40.
73. *M.D.A.R.*, 1931-32, p. 19.
74. *M.D.A.R.*, 1933-34, p. 22.
75. *M.D.A.R.*, 1936, p. 19; *M.D.A.R.*, 1937, p. 18.
76. J. W. S. Macfie and A. Ingram, "The Domestic Mosquitoes of Accra," *Bull. Ent. Res.*, 7 (1916), p. 162; Ingram and Macfie, "The Mosquitoes of Accra," *Ann. Trop. Med. Parasit.*, 18 (1924), p. 264; Chinery, "Mosquito Breeding in Accra," p. 109.
77. *M.D.A.R.*, 1906, p. 29; *M.D.A.R.*, 1937, p. 18.
78. *M.D.A.R.*, 1932-33, p. 18.
79. John M. Hunter, "River Blindness in Nangodi, Northern Ghana: A Hypothesis of Cyclical Advance and Retreat," *Geographical Review*, 56 (1966), pp. 398-416; K. David Patterson, "River Blindness in Northern Ghana, 1900-1950," in Gerald W. Hartwig and K. David Patterson, eds., *Disease in African History: An Introductory Survey and Case Studies* (Durham, N.C., 1978), pp. 88-117.
80. B. B. Waddy, "Some Reminiscences of the Western Northern Territories of the Gold Coast," *The Nigerian Field*, 22 (1957), p. 84.
81. Patterson, "River Blindness," p. 109.
82. *M.D.A.R.*, 1930-31, p. 24.
83. J. W. S. Macfie and J. F. Corson, "A New Species of Filaria Larva Found in the Skin of Natives in the Gold Coast," *Ann. Trop. Med. Parasit.*, 16 (1922), pp. 465-71. The parasite, which was assigned the now superseded generic name *Agamofilaria*, was detected in 22 out of 50 adult males selected "at random" in Accra.
84. Colbourne, Edington, and Hughes, "Medical Survey," p. 280; *M.D.A.R.*, 1911, p. 56.
85. Compiled from *Reports of the Ministry of Health*.
86. Faust, Russell, and Jung, *Clinical Parasitology*, p. 105; Scott, *Epidemic Disease*, p. 147.
87. Faust, Russell, and Jung, *Clinical Parasitology*, pp. 104-5. For an excellent general study of trypanosomiasis in Africa, see J. Ford, *The Role of the Trypanosomiases in African Ecology: A Study of the Tsetse Fly Problem* (London, 1971).
88. K. R. S. Morris, "The Ecology of Epidemic Sleeping Sickness. I. The Significance of Location," *Bull. Ent. Res.*, 42 (1951), pp. 429-31.
89. *M.D.A.R.*, 1925-26, pp. 61-63, appendix E, "Report on the Incidence of Sleeping Sickness in the Lawra District, October, 1924."

90. ADM 1/2/59, no. 206, Governor to Secretary of State, 13 June 1903.

91. *M.D.A.R.*, 1904, p. 26.

92. Scott, *Epidemic Disease*, p. 141.

93. ADM 56/1/9 9, "Medical Report on a Tour Through the Centre and West of the Gonja District with Special Reference to Sleeping Sickness," by F. J. A. Beringer, 10 Mar. 1910.

94. ADM 1/2/89, encl. 2 in no. 769 of 16 Oct. 1913, "A Report on Human Trypanosomiasis in the Western Province of Ashanti," by W. M. Wade, 25 June 1913.

95. ADM 1/2/175, no. 611, Ag. Governor to Secretary of State, 19 Sept. 1910.

96. ADM 14/1/24, *Despatches and Reports on the Subject of Tsetse Fly Investigation*, 31 Dec. 1925, Reports of Dr. W. A. Young, 12 Mar. 1924 and 1 Sept. 1925, S. P. VI of 1926-27.

97. ADM 1/2/170, encl. in no. 545, "Investigation of the Prevalence of *Glossina spp.* and of Human Trypanosomiasis in the Oda District. Nov. 16-Dec. 8, 1925," by C. M. Ingolby.

98. *M.D.A.R.*, 1928-29, p. 22.

99. *M.D.A.R.*, 1931-32, p. 6.

100. *M.D.A.R.*, 1932-33, pp. 6-7.

101. G. F. T. Saunders and K. R. S. Morris, "The Distribution of Human Trypanosomiasis," *W.A.M.J.*, 5 (1932), pp. 40-41, 44. Scott (*Epidemic Disease*, pp. 140-41), however, considers this unlikely.

102. ADM 11/560, "Trypanosomiasis and Anti-Tsetse Clearings in the Northern Territories," 6 June 1935, by V. E. Whitman, appendix, p. 2.

103. CSO 11/11, 2090/30, s. f. 2, D.M.S.S. to Ag. C.S., 23 May 1932; Governor to Governor-General, French West Africa, 21 June 1932.

104. ADM 1/2/196, no. 101, Governor to Secretary of State, 6 Feb. 1932. Enclosure 1, a memo by the Senior Pathologist, praised Pomeroy's work, especially his studies on bovine trypanosomiasis.

105. ADM 1/2/217, no. 727, Governor to Secretary of State, 29 Dec. 1935.

106. Scott, *Epidemic Disease*, pp. 145-47.

107. K. R. S. Morris, "The Ecology of Epidemic Sleeping Sickness. I," pp. 430, 434; Morris, "The Ecology of Epidemic Sleeping Sickness. II. The Effects of an Epidemic," *Bull. Ent. Res.*, 43 (1952), pp. 377-78, 384-87.

108. *M.D.A.R.*, 1925-26, pp. 61-71. Scott considers the diagnosis incorrect. David Scott, "Human Trypanosomiasis in Northern Ghana, 1950-56: An Epidemiological Review," *W.A.M.J.*, n.s., 8 (1959), p. 170.

109. ADM 5/3/28, *Report of the Committee on Human Trypanosomiasis*, 1935, p. 2.

110. Ibid., p. 21, "Meeting of the Northern Sub-Committee."

111. Ibid., p. 22.

112. Ibid., pp. 3-6. Prophylaxis was considered impractical because the population was so mobile, and it was only used for small special groups, like the inmates of a leper colony (Scott, *Epidemic Disease*, p. 181).

113. Scott, *Epidemic Disease*, pp. 178-79.

114. ADM 57/5/2, *Bawku District Diary*, 18 Nov. 1936.

115. ADM 1/2/232, no. 521, Governor to Secretary of State, 20 Aug. 1937, and encls. 1 and 2, memos by D.M.S. of 20 Apr. 1937 and 26 May 1937.

116. ADM 1/2/235, no. 852, Governor to Secretary of State, 30 Dec. 1937; ADM 1/2/237, no. 203, Governor to Secretary of State, 23 Mar. 1938.

117. *M.D.A.R.*, 1938, pp. 104-7, Sleeping Sickness Survey. Entomologist's Quarterly Report, Jan.-March 1938.

118. ADM 1/2/248, encl. 2 in no. 217 of 30 Mar. 1939, "Trypanosomiasis Campaign Progress Report," by G. Saunders.

119. Ibid., Governor to Secretary of State, 30 Mar. 1939 and encl. 1, "Minutes of a Conference on Trypanosomiasis held on 7 July 1938."

120. Scott, "Human Trypanosomiasis," pp. 175-77.

121. Morris's plans and activities are outlined in ADM 1/2/248, encl. 1 in no. 217, "Minutes of a Conference"; ADM 1/2/249, no. 415, Governor to Secretary of State, 14 June 1939; ADM 1/2/278, encl. 1 in no. 278 of 20 Jan. 1945, "Proposals for the Control of Human and Bovine

Trypanosomiasis by the Eradication of Tsetse," 8 Aug. 1944. Enclosure 2 is a very favorable evaluation of Morris's work by Dr. P. A. Buxton. See also Morris, "Planning the Control of Sleeping Sickness," *T.R.S.T.M.H.*, 43 (1949), pp. 165-98.

122. Patterson, "River Blindness," pp. 99-100.

123. ADM 1/2/313, no. 2282, Governor to Secretary of State, 5 Dec. 1949.

124. E. Akwei, "Planning the Control of Sleeping Sickness: A Sequel," *T.R.S.T.M.H.*, 46 (1952), pp. 437-48.

125. Scott, *Epidemic Disease*, pp. 161-63.

126. Scott, "A Note on Sleeping Sickness Control in North-West Ashanti (Gold Coast," *T.R.S.T.M.H.*, 47 (1953), pp. 408-9.

127. Scott, *Epidemic Disease*, pp. 161-62.

128. Scott, "Human Trypanosomiasis," p. 182.

129. Ibid., p. 179; Waddy, "Medical Field Units," p. 327; Scott, *Epidemic Disease*, pp. 166-67.

130. Scott, *Epidemic Disease*, p. 158.

131. Ibid., pp. 4-6.

132. *Gold Coast Leader*, 25 Jan. 1908, p. 2.

133. Ibid., 1 Feb. 1908, p. 2.

134. Scott, *Epidemic Disease*, pp. 8-9.

135. Great Britain, Parliamentary Papers, 1909, LXI, Cmd. 4718, *Report by Professor W. J. Simpson on Sanitary Matters in Various West African Colonies and the Outbreak of Plague in the Gold Coast*, p. 7.

136. Scott, *Epidemic Disease*, pp. 6-7.

137. Ibid., pp. 8, 11.

138. Simpson Report, p. 4.

139. ADM 56/1/171, M. O. Salaga to Prov. M. O., 25 Aug. 1913. Mortality in Kawlaw had previously been ascribed to trypanosomiasis. See Beringer report cited in n. 93 above.

140. Ibid., M. O. Salaga to Prov. M.O., 7 June 1914.

141. Ibid., 25 Aug. 1913. Possibly the disease was anthrax, but this was familiar to M.O.s and probably would have been diagnosed.

142. Scott, *Epidemic Disease*, pp. 14-15; *M.D.A.R.*, 1919, p. 14.

143. Scott, *Epidemic Disease*, pp. 16-17.

144. *Gold Coast Leader*, 19 Apr. 1924, p. 7.

145. Scott, *Epidemic Disease*, p. 20.

146. James W. Brown, "Increased Intercommunication and Epidemic Disease in Early Colonial Ashanti," in Hartwig and Patterson, eds., *Disease in African History*, pp. 180-206; *Report on the Outbreak of Plague in Kumasi, Ashanti, by P. S. Selwyn-Clarke, Medical Officer of Health, Kumasi*, S.P. XI of 1925-26, p. 33.

147. Selwyn-Clarke Report, p. 30.

148. Scott, *Epidemic Disease*, pp. 19-20.

149. Charles M. Good, "Man, Milieu, and the Disease Factor: Tick-Borne Relapsing Fever in East Africa," in Hartwig and Patterson, eds., *Disease in African History*, pp. 46-87.

150. Gerald W. Hartwig, "Louse-borne Relapsing Fever in Sudan, 1908-1951," in Hartwig and Patterson, eds., *Disease in African History*, pp. 46-87.

151. *Accra Municipal A. R.*, 1923, pp. 8-9; P. S. Selwyn-Clarke, G. E. H. Le Fanu, and A. Ingram, "Relapsing Fever in the Gold Coast," *Ann. Trop. Med. Parasit.*, 17 (1923), pp. 390-93.

152. ADM 1/2/151, no. 614, Ag. Governor to Secretary of State, 13 Aug. 1923.

153. Ibid., encls., D.M.S.S. to C.S., 9 Aug. 1923; M.O.H. to D.D.S.S., 14 July 1923; A. Ingram to D.D.H.S., 31 July 1923.

154. Scott, *Epidemic Disease*, pp. 128-29.

155. Brown, "Epidemic Disease in Ashanti," pp. 193-98.

156. *M.D.A.R.*, 1931-32, p. 21.

157. *M.D.A.R.*, 1932-33, p. 21.

158. Scott, *Epidemic Disease*, pp. 127-28; Selwyn-Clarke, Le Fanu, and Ingram, "Relapsing Fever," pp. 391-92.

159. N. A. Dyce-Sharp, "Epidemic Disease in West Africa: The Menace of the Future," *T.R.S.T.M.H.*, 19 (1925), p. 259.

160. *M.D.A.R.*, 1936, pp. 9, 81.

161. *M.D.A.R.*, 1938, p. 9; G. M. Findlay and G. T. L. Archer, "The Occurrence of Tick-borne Typhus in West Africa," *T.R.S.T.M.H.*, 41 (1948), pp. 815-18.

CHAPTER 4–DISEASES SPREAD IN CONTAMINATED WATER, FOOD, AND SOIL

1. *M.D.A.R.*, 1924-25, p. 7.
2. *M.D.A.R.*, 1935, p. 18.
3. *M.D.A.R.*, 1929-30, p. 13.
4. Ernest C. Faust, Paul F. Russell, and Rodney C. Jung, *Craig and Faust's Clinical Parasitology* (8th ed., Philadelphia, 1970), p. 151.
5. M. H. Hughes, "Bacillary Dysentery in Accra, Gold Coast," *West African Medical Journal*, n.s., 4 (1955), pp. 73-77.
6. *M.D.A.R.*, 1920, p. 13.
7. *M.D.A.R.*, 1928-29, p. 23.
8. *M.D.A.R.*, 1926-27, p. 22; N. A. Dyce-Sharp, "Epidemic Disease in West Africa: The Menace of the Future," *T.R.S.T.M.H.*, 19 (1925), p. 22.
9. Kwame Mayer Kwafie, "A Spatio-Temporal Analysis of Cholera Diffusion in Western Africa," *Economic Geography*, 52 (1976), pp. 127-32; Robert F. Stock, *Cholera in Africa* (London, 1976), pp. 21-22.
10. F. M. Burnett and D. O. White, *Natural History of Infectious Disease* (4th ed., Cambridge, 1972), pp. 91-96.
11. *R.M.H.*, 1953, p. 19; *R.M.H.*, 1954, p. 26.
12. David Scott, *Epidemic Disease in Ghana, 1901-1960* (London, 1965), p. viii.
13. Willem Bosman, *A New and Accurate Description of the Coast of Guinea* (4th ed., reprinted, London, 1967, 1st ed., 1705), pp. 108-9; C. E. Reindorf, "Influence of Fifty Years of Scientific Medicine on Beliefs and Customs in the Gold Coast," *W.A.M.J.*, n.s., 3 (1954), p. 116; J. W. S. Macfie, "Intravenous Injections of Tartar Emetic in Guinea-Worm Infections," *Lancet*, 198 (1920), p. 654.
14. *R.M.H.*, 1955, p. 55; D. W. Belcher, F. K. Wurapa, W. B. Ward, and I. M. Lourie, "Guinea Worm in Southern Ghana: The Epidemiology and Impact on Agricultural Productivity," *Am. J. T. M. H.*, 24 (1975), p. 248.
15. W. H. Graham, "Report on Guinea-Worm," *J.T.M.H.*, 11 (1908), pp. 353-54.
16. Robert T. Leiper, "Note on the Seasonal Incidence of Dracontiasis on the Gold Coast," *J.T.M.H.*, 14 (1911), pp. 211-12.
17. *M.D.A.R.*, 1938, p. 27.
18. *A.R.N.T.*, 1923-24, p. 12.
19. *Annual Report on Togo*, 1923-24, p. 31.
20. *M.D.A.R.*, 1931-32, p. 9; *M.D.A.R.*, 1932-33, p. 9.
21. *Annual Report on the Gold Coast*, 1917, p. 42.
22. *M.D.A.R.*, 1926-27, p. 27; *M.D.A.R.*, 1928-29, p. 27; *Togo Report*, 1927, p. 42.
23. *M.D.A.R.*, 1931-32, p. 24.
24. D. W. A. Nugent, D. Scott, and B. B. Waddy, "Effect of Water-Point Treatment with DDT on the Incidence of Guinea Worm Infection," *T.R.S.T.M.H.*, 49 (1955), pp. 476-77.
25. Macfie, "Intravenous Injections," pp. 654-55.
26. *M.D.A.R.*, 1921, appendix B, p. 53.
27. *Togo Report*, 1923-24, p. 31.
28. *M.D.A.R.*, 1928-29, p. 14.
29. *M.D.A.R.*, 1930-31, p. 32.
30. *M.D.A.R.*, 1933-34, p. 9; *M.D.A.R.*, 1938, p. 28.
31. M. J. Colbourne, G. M. Edington, and M. H. Hughes, "A Medical Survey in a Gold Coast Village," *T.R.S.T.M.H.*, 44 (1950), p. 281.
32. *R.M.H.*, 1955, p. 33.

33. Nugent, Scott, and Waddy, "Effect of Water-Point Treatment," p. 476.

34. B. B. Waddy, "Organization and Work of the Gold Coast Medical Field Units," *T.R.S.T.M.H.*, 50 (1956), p. 331.

35. *M.D.A.R.*, 1926-27, p. 26; *M.D.A.R.*, 1930-31, p. 32.

36. *M.D.A.R.*, 1938, p. 27.

37. *R.M.H.*, 1955, p. 22.

38. *M.D.A.R.*, 1911, p. 78; *M.D.A.R.*, 1912, p. 107; *M.D.A.R.*, 1913, p. 67; *M.D.A.R.*, 1914, p. 85.

39. *M.D.A.R.*, 1911, p. 78; *M.D.A.R.*, 1912, p. 107; *M.D.A.R.*, 1913, p. 67; *M.D.A.R.*, 1914, p. 85.

40. Colbourne, Edington, and Hughes, "Medical Survey," p. 280.

41. *M.D.A.R.*, 1933-34, p. 27.

42. *M.D.A.R.*, 1938, p. 27.

43. *M.D.A.R.*, 1932-33, p. 9.

44. *M.D.A.R.*, 1929-30, p. 15.

45. *M.D.A.R.*, 1931-32, p. 9.

46. *M.D.A.R.*, 1950, p. 20; Colbourne, Edington, and Hughes, "Medical Survey," p. 280.

47. ADM 1/2/90, encl. in no. 71 of 31 Jan. 1914, minute by Ag. Prin. M.O., 22 Jan. 1914.

48. Acc. No. 2529/58, B.P. 1, "Ankylostomiasis–Prevalence of and Measures Against in the Gold Coast," by J. M. Dalziel, 29 April 1921. Also in ADM 1/2/139, encl. in no. 534 of 26 May 1921.

49. ADM 1/2/90, no. 15, Governor to Secretary of State, 6 Jan. 1914 and enclosures.

50. ADM 1/2/90, no. 71, Governor to Secretary of State, 30 Jan. 1914.

51. Acc. No. 2529/58, B.P. 1, "Report on the Prevalence of Ankylostomiasis in the Cocoa Districts of Akwapim," by G. E. H. Le Fanu, 21 Feb. 1914. *Ascaris* was found in 23 persons (31 percent) and *T. trichiura* in 9 (11.6 percent).

52. Ibid., Secretary of State to Governor, 16 Dec. 1920; Ankylostomiasis report by Dalziel.

53. E.g., *M.D.A.R.*, 1929-30, p. 15.

54. *M.D.A.R.*, 1938, p. 8.

55. *M.D.A.R.*, 1938, p. 27; *M.D.A.R.*, 1936, "A Report on the Western Province, With Special Reference to Mining Areas," p. 102.

56. C.S.O., B.F. 4822, D.M.S. to C.S., 11 June 1945.

57. Colbourne, Edington, and Hughes, "Medical Survey," p. 280; *M.D.A.R.*, 1950, p. 20.

58. Fergus S. McCullough, "The Distribution of Human Schistosomiasis and the Potential Snail Hosts in Ghana," *W.A.M.J.*, n.s., 6 (1957), p. 90.

59. Ibid., p. 92. The nomenclature and taxonomy of snail hosts is complex, and other species may be involved.

60. J. W. S. Macfie, "The Occurrence of Lateral-Spined Bilharzia Eggs (*Schistosomium mansoni*) in Urine," *J.T.M.H.*, 23 (1920), pp. 45-46.

61. *R.M.H.*, 1954, p. 72.

62. F. R. Sandbach, "The History of Schistosomiasis Research and Policy for Its Control," *Medical History*, 20 (1976), p. 168.

63. A. Ingram, "Notes on a Possible Intermediate Host of *Schistosoma haematobium* in the Gold Coast," *Annals of Tropical Medicine and Parasitology*, 18 (1924), pp. 265-66.

64. *M.D.A.R.*, 1920, pp. 19, 55.

65. Ibid., p. 19.

66. ADM 57/5/2, *Bawku District Diary*, 9 Sept. 1935; *Togo Report,* 1936, p. 63.

67. *M.D.A.R.*, 1930-31, pp. 32-33.

68. *M.D.A.R.*, 1935, p. 21.

69. *M.D.A.R.*, 1945, p. 9.

70. *M.D.A.R.*, 1935, p. 21.

71. *R.M.H.*, 1953, p. 36.

72. *R.M.H.*, 1954, p. 72.

73. G. M. Edington, "Schistosomiasis in Ghana, with Special Reference to Its Pathology," *W.A.M.J.*, n.s., 66 (1957), p. 46; McCullough, "Distribution of Schistosomiasis," pp. 92-95.

74. Edington, "Schistosomiasis," p. 48.

75. McCullough, "Distribution of Schistosomiasis," pp. 95, 97.

76. Edington, "Schistosomiasis," p. 56.

77. Sandbach, "History of Schistosomiasis Research," p. 271.

78. Charles C. Hughes and John M. Hunter, "Disease and 'Development' in Africa," *Social Science and Medicine*, 13B (1979), pp. 251-68.

79. *M.D.A.R.*, 1939, p. 5.

80. Stanley Shallof, "The Gold Coast Water Rate Controversy, 1909-1938," *Institute of African Studies Research Review* [Legon], 8 (1972), pp. 21-34.

81. David Brokensha, *Social Change at Larteh, Ghana* (Oxford, 1966), pp. 66-68; John Dunn and A. F. Robertson, *Dependence and Opportunity: Political Change in Ahafo* (Cambridge, 1973), pp. 117-19.

82. K. David Patterson, "Health in Urban Ghana: The Case of Accra, 1900-1940," *Social Science and Medicine*, 13 (1979), pp. 251-68.

83. *Annual Report on Ashanti*, 1910, p. 13.

84. *Annual Report on Ashanti*, 1914, p. 20; *Annual Report on Ashanti*, 1920, p. 16.

85. Annual Report on Ashanti, 1921, p. 12.

86. ADM 1/2/170, encl. 2 in no. 605 of 10 Aug. 1926, report by Dr. J. H. Mathews.

87. *M.D.A.R.*, 1933-34, p. 37.

88. *Togo Report*, 1928, p. 41; *Togo Report*, 1930, p. 53.

89. *Togo Report*, 1937, p. 55.

90. ADM 56/1/99, "Medical Report on a Tour Through the Centre and West of the Gonja District, With Special Reference to Sleeping Sickness," by F. J. A. Berringer, 14 March 1910; Meyer Fortes, *The Dynamics of Kinship Among the Tallensi* (Oxford, 1945), p. 8; *Annual Report on the Northern Territories*, 1910, p. 11.

91. ADM 1/2/211, no. 191, Governor to Secretary of State, 12 Apr. 1935.

92. *M.D.A.R.*, 1938, p. 36.

93. *M.D.A.R.*, 1935, p. 27.

94. E.g., *Annual Report, Eastern Province of Ashanti*, 1930-31, pp. 18-19; *Annual Report, Western Province of Ashanti*, 1930-31, p. 41.

95. ADM 39/1/326, Five Queen Mothers of the Ho Division to the D.C., Ho, 10 May 1946; D.C., Ho, to C.E.P., 25 Apr. 1946.

96. ADM 1/2/284, no. 162, Governor to Secretary of State, 30 May 1946.

97. For example, 440 new wells were sunk in 1948, and many existing wells were improved (*M.D.A.R.*, 1948, p. 15).

98. *Report of the Commission of Enquiry Into the Health Needs of the Gold Coast*, S.P. V of 1952, p. 42.

99. F. T. Sai, "Ghana," in Ian Douglas-Wilson and G. McLachan, eds., *Health Service Prospects: An International Survey* (London, 1973), p. 143.

CHAPTER 5–DISEASES TRANSMITTED BY THE RESPIRATORY ROUTE

1. *Annual Report on Togo*, 1928, p. 38; *M.D.A.R.*, 1938, pp. 4, 7.

2. *M.D.A.R.*, 1928-29, p. 12.

3. *M.D.A.R.*, 1938, p. 26.

4. Ibid, pp. 7, 45.

5. Penicillin was first used in Ghana in late 1944. *M.D.A.R.*, 1945, p. 14.

6. *M.D.A.R.*, 1941, p. 4.

7. K. David Patterson, "The Influenza Epidemic of 1918-1919 in the Gold Coast," *Transactions of the Historical Society of Ghana*, 16 (1977), pp. 187-212.

8. A. J. Murray and J. A. Crocket, *Report on Silicosis and Tuberculosis Among Mine Workers in the Gold Coast* (Accra, 1946), p. 48; Frederick Heaf, "Tuberculosis in British West Africa," *W.A.M.J.*, n.s., 2 (1953), p. 8.

9. *M.D.A.R.*, 1920, p. 19.

10. *M.D.A.R.*, 1923-24, p. 14; *M.D.A.R.*, 1940, p. 3.

11. *M.D.A.R.*, 1930-31, pp. 13, 29.
12. *M.D.A.R.*, 1927-28, p. 16.
13. *M.D.A.R.*, 1926-27, p. 25.
14. C.S.O. 11/1, 772/32, s. f. 1, Ag. D.M.S.S. to C.S., 30 June 1934.
15. *M.D.A.R.*, 1925-26, p. 8.
16. *M.D.A.R.*, 1928-29, appendix C, p. 122.
17. *M.D.A.R.*, 1949, p. 5.
18. F. M. Burnet and D. O. White, *Natural History of Infectious Disease* (4th ed., Cambridge, 1972), p. 219; René Dubos, *Man Adapting* (New Haven, 1965), pp. 165-66, p. 175.
19. Roger G. Thomas, "Forced Labour in British West Africa: The Case of the Northern Territories of the Gold Coast," *J.A.H.*, 14 (1973), pp. 79-103.
20. Acc. No. 3016/58, B.P. 538, P.M.O. to C.S., 10 Jan. 1918; and Senior Sanitary Officer to P.M.O., 23 Feb. 1920.
21. W. E. Masters, "A Model Mining Village in the Tropics," *J.T.M.H.*, 22 (1919), pp. 89-93.
22. ADM 1/2/149, sub-encl. 2 to encl. 1, in no. 240 of 21 March 1923, M.O. Tarquah to D.D.H.S., 9 Jan. 1923 and encl. 3, Ordinance.
23. Acc. No. 3016/58, B. P. 538, Senior Sanitary Officer to P.M.O., 2 Apr. 1917.
24. ADM 1/2/153, encl. 2 in no. 840 of 9 Nov. 1923, "Report of the Committee on Discharged Mine Labourers."
25. Ibid., sub-encl. 2, M. Schwartz, M. O. Abontiakoon Mines Ltd. to J. R. Harley, 9 March 1923.
26. Ibid., Governor to Secretary of State, 9 Nov. 1923.
27. ADM 14/1/22, *Preliminary Report by Sir W. J. Simpson on an Investigation Regarding the High Death-Rate of Mine Labourers* (S. P. IV of 1925-26), pp. 1-9.
28. *M.D.A.R.*, 1934, p. 22.
29. ADM 1/2/246, encl. 2 in no. 57 of 23 Jan. 1939, D.D.H.S. to D.M.S., 12 Jan. 1939.
30. Murray and Crocket, *Silicosis and Tuberculosis*, pp. 11-12.
31. Ibid., p. 24.
32. *M.D.A.R.*, 1923-24, p. 14.
33. ADM 14/1/20, *Report of the Medical Officer of Health, Accra*, 1922 (S. P. VIII of 1923-24), pp. 58-59; *Annual Report of the Accra Town Council*, 1937-38, p. 14; *M.D.A.R.*, 1938, pp. 7, 25.
34. See table 40 (page 152).
35. *M.D.A.R.*, 1932-33, pp. 83-84.
36. *M.D.A.R.*, 1930-31, p. 20; Murray and Crocket, *Silicosis and Tuberculosis*, comments by W. M. Howells, Ag. D.M.S., p. 3.
37. E. Roelsgaard, E. Iverson, and C. Blocker, "Tuberculosis in Tropical Africa: An Epidemiological Study," *Bull. W.H.O.*, 30 (1964), p. 460; *M.D.A.R.*, 1931-32, p. 8; Heaf, "Tuberculosis," p. 7.
38. As, for example, Yendi. *Togo Report*, 1938, p. 59.
39. K. W. Todd, "A Gold Coast Tuberculosis Survey, 1947," *Tubercule*, 29 (1948), pp. 198-207.
40. Roelsgaard, Iverson, and Blocher, "Tuberculosis in Tropical Africa," pp. 463, 476-81.
41. *M.D.A.R.*, 1922-23, p. 46. The authorities were convinced that compulsory isolation would cause concealment of cases and would further discourage hospital attendance.
42. *M.D.A.R.*, 1928-29, pp. 123-24.
43. Murray and Crocket, *Silicosis and Tuberculosis*, p. 54; *M.D.A.R.*, 1948, p. 7.
44. Murray and Crocket, *Silicosis and Tuberculosis*, p. 56; Heaf, "Tuberculosis," p. 3.
45. For good general treatments, see B. B. Waddy, "Cerebro-Spinal Meningitis in the Gold Coast, 1900-1950," Tenth Langley Memorial Prize Essay, 1954, 69 pp., copy at London School of Hygiene and Tropical Medicine; and "African Epidemic Cerebro-Spinal Meningitis," *J.T.M.H.*, 60 (1957), pp. 179-89, 218-23.
46. David Scott, *Epidemic Disease in Ghana, 1901-1960* (London, 1965), p. 115.

47. Waddy, "Cerebro-Spinal Meningitis in the Gold Coast," p. 5; ADM 1/2/54, no. 491, Governor to Secretary of State, 29 Nov. 1900.

48. Waddy, "Cerebro-Spinal Meningitis in the Gold Coast," pp. 10-11; A. E. Horn, "An Investigation of Cerebro-Spinal Fever in the Northern Territories of the Gold Coast in 1908," *T.R.S.T.M.H.*, 2 (1908), pp. 2-9. A. M. Watherston, the C.C.N.T., estimated that 20,000 people died in 1906 alone; this guess is probably too high (see Scott, *Epidemic Disease*, p. 97).

49. Waddy, "Cerebro-Spinal Meningitis in the Gold Coast," p. 15.

50. ADM 66/5/6, *Tumu District Diary*, 31 March 1919; ADM 66/5/2, *Wa District Information Book*, p. 74.

51. ADM 14/1/17, *Cerebro-Spinal Fever in the Northern Territories of the Gold Coast and Ashanti* (S. P. VI of 1919-1920), pp. 1-25.

52. *M.D.A.R.*, 1920, p. 81; Scott, *Epidemic Disease*, p. 91.

53. ADM 5/3/56, *Report of an Outbreak of Cerebro-Spinal Meningitis in the Western Northern Territories, 1st January-21st March, 1945* (Accra, 1946), p. 3; M. P. Brown, B. B. Waddy, and R. W. Tudor, "Cerebrospinal Meningitis in the Gold Coast," *Lancet* i (1947), pp. 741-43.

54. Waddy, "Cerebro-Spinal Meningitis in the Gold Coast," p. 22.

55. *M.D.A.R.*, 1947, p. 5.

56. Scott, *Epidemic Disease*, p. 103.

57. M. J. Colbourne, "Cerebrospinal Meningitis in Kusasi, 1948," *J.T.M.H.*, 54 (1951), p. 4.

58. Ibid., p. 3.

59. Robert Cruickshank, "Streptococcal Infections and Sequelae," in Robert Cruickshank, Kenneth L. Standard, and Hugh B. L. Russell, eds., *Epidemiology and Community Health in Warm Climate Countries* (London, 1976), p. 50.

60. *M.D.A.R.*, 1906, p. 34; *M.D.A.R.*, 1930-31, pp. 31, 63.

61. *M.D.A.R.*, 1935, p. 43.

62. Ibid., p. 18.

63. M. H. Hughes, "Diphtheria in West Africa," *W.A.M.J.*, n.s., 4 (1955), p. 156.

64. *M.D.A.R.*, 1930-31, p. 177.

65. *R.M.H.*, 1954, p. 26.

66. Ibid., p. 27; J. W. S. Macfie, "Prevalent Diseases of the Gold Coast," *T.R.S.T.M.H.*, 16 (1922), p. 158.

67. Scott, *Epidemic Disease*, p. viii. See also *Annual Report of the Medical Services of Ghana, 1967*, pp. 9, 31. For 1970-72, see J. M. Blankson, "Measles and Its Problems as seen in Ghana," *Ghana Med. J.*, 13 (June 1974), pp. 134-40.

68. David Morley, "Measles and Whooping Cough," in Cruickshank, Standard, and Russell, eds., *Epidemiology and Community Health*, pp. 63-66.

69. ADM 56/1/171, Prov. M.O. to C.C.N.T., 18 June 1918.

70. Ibid., Prov. M.O. to C.C.N.T., 19 June 1918.

71. ADM 68/5/1, *Zuarungu District Diary*, pp. 299-300; entries for 25, 26, 28, 29, 30 May 1918 and 2 June 1918.

72. *A.R.N.T.*, 1918, p. 12.

73. *M.D.A.R.*, 1905, p. 11; ADM 1/2/117, encl. in no. 570 of 11 Sept. 1917, "Report on Sanitary Work in Accra, 1916."

74. F. M. Purcell, *Diet and Ill Health in the Forest Country of the Gold Coast* (London, 1939), p. 57.

75. William H. Foege, J. D. Miller, and D. A. Henderson, "Smallpox Eradication in West and Central Africa," *Bull. W.H.O.*, 52 (1975), pp. 209-22; Donald A. Henderson, "The Eradication of Smallpox," *Scientific American*, 235 (Oct. 1976), pp. 25-33.

76. Willem Bosman, *A New and Accurate Description of the Coast of Guinea* (4th ed., London, 1967; 1st published 1705), p. 108.

77. James W. Brown, "Increased Intercommunication and Epidemic Disease in Early Colonial Ashanti," in Gerald W. Hartwig and K. David Patterson, eds., *Disease in African*

History: An Introductory Survey and Case Studies (Durham, N.C., 1978); R. S. Rattray, *The Tribes of the Ashanti Hinterland* (London, 1932), vol. II, pp. 341, 475.

78. Eugenia W. Herbert, "Smallpox Innoculation in Africa," *J.A.H.*, 16 (1975), pp. 539-59.

79. Rattray, *Ashanti Hinterland*, vol. I, p. 55; vol. II, p. 514.

80. *Medical Report on the Northern Territories*, 1910, in *M.D.A.R.*, 1910, p. 37.

81. Acc. No. 1578/58, B. P. 388, Petition of the Executive Committee of the Axim Branch of the Aborigines' Rights Protection Society, 16 Sept. 1901.

82. Brown, "Increased Intercommunication," p. 190.

83. *M.D.A.R.*, 1911, p. 12; *A.R.N.T.*, 1916, p. 11.

84. Scott, *Epidemic Disease*, p. 83.

85. *M.D.A.R.*, 1930-31, p. 11.

86. For example, one M.O. claimed that 95 percent of smallpox cases in northwestern Ghana resulted from innoculation. Acc. No. 3060/58, B. P. 593, "Report on Smallpox in Wa and Lorha Districts," by R. Whyte, 18 Mar. 1918.

87. Scott, *Epidemic Disease*, p. 71. Another problem was that smallpox and chickenpox were easily confused (*M.D.A.R.*, 1924-25, p. 8), sometimes with tragic consequences (in B. B. Waddy, personal communication, 19 Oct. 1975).

88. Foege, Miller, and Henderson, "Smallpox Eradication," p. 211.

89. Scott, *Epidemic Disease*, pp. 78-81.

90. Acc. No. 1578/58, B. P. 388, King Codjoe Abbey of Prampram to D.C., 20 Nov. 1901.

91. Ibid., Herbert Lamptey, Public Vaccinator, to P.M.O., 3 March 1901.

92. C. E. Reindorf, "Influence of Fifty Years of Scientific Medicine on Beliefs and Customs in the Gold Coast," *W.A.M.J.*, n.s., 3 (1954), p. 117.

93. Lamptey to P.M.O., 3 March 1901.

94. Acc. No. 1578/58, B. P. 388, Ag. P.M.O. to Ag. C.S., 24 Sept. 1901; ADM 1/2/56, no. 506, Governor to Secretary of State, 25 Oct. 1901.

95. *M.D.A.R.*, 1910, p. 51.

96. ADM 1/2/175, no. 478, Governor to Secretary of State, 26 July 1910.

97. ADM 1/2/89, no. 821, Governor to Secretary of State, 4 March 1913.

98. "Report on Smallpox in Wa and Lorha Districts," by R. Whyte, 1918.

99. Scott, *Epidemic Disease*, p. 83; ADM 1/2/83, no. 116, encl. 1, P.M.O. to C.S., 24 Feb. 1913. The Germans had similar failures in Togo; see ADM 1/2/103, no. 744, encl. 1, "Smallpox in Togoland," by G. E. H. Le Fanu, 4 Aug. 1915.

100. Acc. No. 3060/58, B. P. 593, C.S. to Crown Agents, 16 Jan. 1922.

101. Acc. No. 3061/58, B. P. 594, Governor to Secretary of State, 25 Feb. 1926, and Secretary of State to Governor, 31 Jan. 1928; *M.D.A.R.*, 1938, p. 22.

102. ADM 1/2/103, no. 738, Ag. Governor to Secretary of State, 7 Sept. 1915.

103. *M.D.A.R.*, 1920, pp. 16-17; *Report of the Medical Officer of Health, Accra*, 1921 (S. P. XVI of 1922-23), pp. 10-11.

104. Acc. No. 2981/58, B. P. 499, Sr. Sanitary Officer to P.M.O., 3 Nov. 1920.

105. Copy in ibid.

106. E.g., ADM 66/5/8, *Wa District Diary*, 19, 20, 22, 23, 25 July 1924, 20 Aug. 1924, and 11 Sept. 1924.

107. *M.D.A.R.*, 1947, p. 4.

CHAPTER 6–OTHER INFECTIOUS AND NON-INFECTIOUS DISEASES

1. *Gold Coast Leader*, 17 Aug. 1912, p. 2; *Gold Coast Independent*, 12 Mar. 1938, p. 253.

2. ADM 56/1/162, P.C.N.E.P. to D.C.s, 27 Sept. 1913 and 12 Nov. 1913; ADM 56/1/392, C.C.N.T. to Ag. C.S.P., 10 Mar. 1914.

3. ADM 56/1/162, D.C. Bawku to P.C.N.E.P., 10 Nov. 1913; D. C. Gambaga to P.C.N.E.P., 25 Nov. 1913.

4. Ibid., P.C.N.E.P. to C.C.N.T., 27 Dec. 1913; ADM 56/1/392, D. C. Salaga to C.S.P., 30 Mar. 1914.

5. ADM 56/1/162, D. C. Zuarungu to P.C.N.E.P., 23 Dec. 1913.

6. Ibid., C.C.N.T. to C.N.P., 1 Sept. 1925.

7. Ibid., D. C. Southern Mamprussi to C.N.P., 19 Sept. 1925; D.C. Bawku to C.N.P., 26 Sept. 1925; ADM 56/1/392, D.C. Western Gonja to C.S.P., 12 Sept. 1925.

8. ADM 56/1/162, D.C. Northern Mamprussi to C.N.P., Sept. 1925.

9. Ibid., D.C. Lawra-Tumu to C.N.P., 26 Sept. 1925; D.C. Wa to C.N.P., 26 Sept. 1925.

10. D.C. Wa to C.N.P., 26 Sept. 1925.

11. ADM 56/1/392, D.C. Eastern Dagomba to C.S.P., 12 Sept. 1925; M.O. Yendi to D.C. E. Dagomba, 11 Sept. 1925; D.C. E. Dagomba to C.S.P., 13 Nov. 1925.

12. ADM 1/2/166, no. 878, Governor to Secretary of State, 30 Nov. 1925.

13. F. H. Cooke, "Leprosy in the British Mandated Territory of Togoland," *T.R.S.T.M.H.*, 21 (1928), pp. 301-4; Cooke, "History of the Ho Leper Settlement," *Leprosy Review*, 2 (1931), pp. 8-11.

14. ADM 56/1/392, C.S. to C.C.N.T., 22 Mar. 1930; D.C. Yendi to C.S.P., 13 Sept. 1930; D.C. Kratchi to C.S.P., 23 Aug. 1930.

15. ADM 14/1/25, *Report by Dr. M. B. D. Dixey, Medical Secretary, British Empire Leprosy Relief Association (Gold Coast Branch) on Leprosy in the Gold Coast*, S.P. XXV of 1930-31.

16. C.S.O. 11/9, 2099/30, M.O. Dixey to D.M.S.S., 15 Aug. 1929; D.M.S.S. to C.S., 13 Mar. 1930.

17. Ibid., s.f. 7, Secretary of State to Governor, 14 Jan. 1936; Ag. D.M.S. to Dr. E. Muir, 5 Feb. 1936.

18. E. Muir, "Leprosy in the Gold Coast: A Short Report on Anti-Leprosy Work in the Gold Coast, With Suggestions for Its Further Development," *Leprosy Review*, 7 (1936), pp. 182-90.

19. Rhodes House Library, Mss. Afr., 1402 (1), "Some General Considerations Arising Out of Tours of Certain Parts of the Gold Coast, Made by the Director of Medical Services Between January 5th and September 23rd 1942," by J. B. Kirk, p. 38.

20. *M.D.A.R.*, 1948, p. 8.

21. B. B. Waddy, "Organization and Work of the Gold Coast Medical Field Units," *T.R.S.T.M.H.*, 50 (1956), p. 331.

22. *Annual Report of the Medical Services of Ghana*, 1967, p. 69.

23. Quentin N. Myrvik, Nancy N. Pearsall, and Russell S. Weiser, *Fundamentals of Medical Bacteriology and Mycology for Students of Medicine and Related Sciences* (Philadelphia, 1974), p. 399.

24. R. R. Willcox, "Prevalence of Veneral Disease in British West Africa," *W.A.M.J.*, n.s., 5 (1956), p. 106.

25. *M.D.A.R.*, 1914, p. 36.

26. *M.D.A.R.*, 1906, pp. 9-10.

27. *M.D.A.R.*, 1904, p. 19.

28. *M.D.A.R.*, 1920, p. 54.

29. *M.D.A.R.*, 1921, appendix C., pp. 54-55; C. E. Reindorf, "The Problem of Venereal Disease on the Gold Coast and Possibilities of Control," *W.A.M.J.*, 1 (1927), pp. 8-9.

30. *Gold Coast Independent*, 29 Jan. 1927, pp. 145-46.

31. ADM 1/2/148, encl. 1 in no. 3 of 3 Jan. 1923, D.M.S.S. to C.S.; ADM 1/2/151, encl. 1 in no. 567 of 30 July 1923, D.M.S.S. to C.S.

32. *Annual Report on Togoland*, 1922, p. 16; *Annual Report on Togoland*, 1923, p. 29.

33. Mrs. M. D. [Dr. Helen] Hendrie, "The Need for Antenatal Work Among the Women of the Outlying Districts of West Africa," *Health and Empire*, 8 (1933), p. 274.

34. *Togo Report*, 1923, pp. 33-34.

35. *Gold Coast Independent*, 1 Feb. 1930, p. 144.

36. ADM 27/5/3, *Tarkwah District Record Book*, 1939, p. 124. I am grateful to James W. Silver for showing me this document.

37. *Togo Report*, 1925, p. 78; *Togo Report*, 1928, p. 39; F. M. Purcell, "The Aetiology of Yaws," *W.A.M.J.*, 7 (1933), p. 96.

38. Purcell, "Yaws," p. 96.

39. *Togo Report*, 1937, pp. 50-52.

40. *M.D.A.R.*, 1928-29, p. 13.

41. *M.D.A.R.*, 1938, p. 8; *R.M.H.*, 1954, p. 24.

42. C.S.O. 11/11, 3967, s.f. 2, Ag. Sr. Health Officer Western Province to D.D.H.S., 2 July 1943; s.f. 1, D.M.S.S. to C.S., 4 Sept. 1943; R.R. Willcox, "Venereal Disease in British West Africa," *British J. of Venereal Diseases*, 22 (1946), pp. 65, 75; *Gold Coast Independent*, 23 Mar. 1946, p. 68.

43. Willcox, "Chancroid in Tropical Africa: Southern Rhodesia and the Gold Coast," *Bull. W.H.O.*, 4 (1951), p. 283.

44. *M.D.A.R.*, 1945, p. 8.

45. *R.M.H.*, 1954, p. 24.

46. Purcell, "Yaws," p. 96.

47. *M.D.A.R.*, 1928-29, p. 14; ADM 56/1/209, *Lorha District Diary*, entries for 22 Apr. and 15 June 1918.

48. ADM 1/2/170, encl. 2 in no. 605 of 10 Aug. 1926, D.M.R.I. to D.M.S., 25 June 1926.

49. *M.D.A.R.*, 1937, p. 21; *M.D.A.R.*, 1938, p. 24.

50. ADM 11/1294, *Diet and Nutrition Surveys, Gold Coast. Final Report–1940*, p. 192; B.F. 3327, "Extension of Medical Facilities, Sanitation, etc.," June 1943; *M.D.A.R.*, 1912, p. 9.

51. *M.D.A.R.*, 1922-23, appendix G, p. 79; C. E. Reindorf, "Influence of Fifty Years of Scientific Medicine on Beliefs and Customs in the Gold Coast," *W.A.M.J.*, n.s., 3 (1954), pp. 118-19.

52. *M.D.A.R.*, 1923-24, p. 7; *Togo Report*, 1923, pp. 30-31.

53. Leonard Goodman, "Obstetrics in a Primitive African Community," *American J. of Public Health*, 41 (Nov., pt. 2, 1951), p. 60; A. J. Hawe, "Looking Back," *Ghana Med. J.*, 1 (1962), p. 15.

54. Rockefeller Archive Center, 495, West Africa, Box 52, Folder 329, "Report on an Epidemic of West African Yellow Fever Which Occurred at Asamankese, Gold Coast, During the Spring and Summer of 1926," by Henry Beeuwkes; *A.R.N.T.*, 1925-26, pp. 11-12.

55. *M.D.A.R.*, 1925-26, appendix D, report of Dr. Helen Hendrie, pp. 59-60.

56. *M.D.A.R.*, 1926-27, pp. 25-26, 124-25; *M.D.A.R.*, 1928-29, p. 132.

57. CSO 11/11, 523/30, "Report–Yaws Clinic at Kumasi African Hospital," 14 Nov. 1930, by W. J. McClintock, Sr. M.O.

58. *M.D.A.R.*, 1930-31, p. iii; *M.D.A.R.*, 1931-32, p. 10.

59. *M.D.A.R.*, 1930-31, p. 31; *M.D.A.R.*, 1931-32, p. 21; *M.D.A.R.*, 1932-33, p. 21.

60. *M.D.A.R.*, 1937, p. 6.

61. *M.D.A.R.*, 1938, p. 7; *M.D.A.R.*, 1939, p. 3.

62. *M.D.A.R.*, 1940, p. 3.

63. *M.D.A.R.*, 1942, p. 3; *M.D.A.R.*, 1943, p. 4.

64. ADM 61/5/16, *Lawra District Diary*, entries for 8, 9, 13 June 1938, and 1, 13 Jan. 1939.

65. ADM 1/2/170, no. 100, Governor to Secretary of State, 29 Mar. 1943; *M.D.A.R.*, 1943, p. 2.

66. *M.D.A.R.*, 1944, p. 2; CSO 11/1, 3721, s.f. 4A, M.A. Cave, MOH, to Ag. C.C.N.T., 20 July 1944; C.C.N.T. to C.S., 19 Aug. 1944.

67. *M.D.A.R.*, 1945, pp. 4, 8.

68. ADM 1/2/284, no. 178, Governor to Secretary of State, 19 June 1946.

69. *M.D.A.R.*, 1948, p. 7.

70. *R.M.H.*, 1953, p. 33; *R.M.H.*, 1954, p. 52.

71. *M.D.A.R.*, 1944, p. 4.

72. *M.D.A.R.*, 1952, p. 7.

73. *R.M.H.*, 1954, p. 52.

74. Ibid.

75. *R.M.H.*, 1955, p. 32.

76. Waddy, "Medical Field Units," p. 325. In 1967, yaws cases numbered less than 0.2 percent of the population (*Annual Report of the Medical Services of Ghana*, 1967, p. 11).

77. *M.D.A.R.*, 1930-31, pp. 15-16.

78. C.S.O. 11/1, 0709, s.f. 3, D.M.S. to C.S., 20 Oct. 1943.

79. *A.R.N.T.*, 1915, p. 13; *M.D.A.R.*, 1947, p. 6.

80. *M.D.A.R.*, 1924-25, p. 6.

81. *M.D.A.R.*, 1929-30, p. 28.

82. *M.D.A.R.*, 1930-31, p. 52; F. M. Purcell, *Diet and Ill Health in the Forest Country of the Gold Coast* (London, 1939), pp. 28-29; ADM 11/1294, *Diet and Nutrition Surveys*, p. 163.

83. René Dubos, *Man Adapting* (New Haven, 1965), pp. 160-62.

84. Thomas McKeown, *The Modern Rise of Population* (New York, 1976), pp. 62, 143.

85. G. M. Edington, "Cardiovascular Disease as a Cause of Death in the Gold Coast African," *T.R.S.T.M.H.*, 48 (1954), pp. 419-20.

86. Ibid., p. 421. Edington ascribed them to yaws, but syphilis seems a more likely etiology.

87. B. Gampel, C. Slome, N. Scotch, and J. H. Abramson, "Urbanization and Hypertension Among Zulu Adults," *J. Chronic Diseases*, 15 (1962), pp. 67-70; Norman A. Scotch, "Sociocultural Factors in Zulu Hypertension," *American J. of Public Health*, 53 (1963), pp. 1205-13.

88. Edington, "Cardiovascular Disease," pp. 423-24; J. W. R. Sarkies, "Primary Glaucoma Amongst Gold Coast Africans," *Brit. J. Ophthalmology*, 37 (1953), pp. 616-17.

89. *R.M.H.*, 1954, p. 29.

90. Compiled from *R.M.H.*, 1953-55.

91. *A.R.G.C.*, 1892, p. 37; *A.R.G.C.*, 1901, p. 28.

92. *A.R.G.C.*, 1914, p. 31.

93. ADM 1/2/162, no. 292, Governor to Secretary of State, 23 Apr. 1925 and encl. 1, D.M.S.S. to C.S., 16 Jan. 1923.

94. Ibid., Governor to Secretary of State, 23 Apr. 1925; ADM 14/1/1, *Legislative Council Debates*, Governor's Budget Speech, 22 Feb. 1926, p. 162.

95. H. L. Mooney, "Lunacy Among West African Natives," *T.R.S.T.M.H.*, 19 (1925), p. 89.

96. Kirk, "Some General Considerations," pp. 39-40.

97. *M.D.A.R.*, 1951, p. 17.

98. *R.M.H.*, 1954, p. 80.

99. C.S.O. 11/1, 202/39, M.O.H. Accra to D.D.H.S., 16 June 1939; *Gold Coast Independent*, 2 Oct. 1937, p. 948. In Accra in March 1937, a demented person killed two children with a cutlass before he was killed by an angry mob. *Gold Coast Independent*, 17 Mar. 1937, p. 200; ADM 14/2/25, *Legislative Council Debates*, statement of Kojo Thompson, 23 Mar. 1937, p. 103.

100. Gustav Jahoda, "Traditional Healers and Other Institutions Concerned with Mental Illness in Ghana," *International Journal of Social Psychiatry*, 7 (1961), pp. 267-68; Marion Kilson, *African Urban Kinsmen: The Ga of Central Accra* (New York, 1974), pp. 89-95; and, especially, M. J. Field, *Search for Security: An Ethno-Psychiatric Study of Rural Ghana* (Evanston, Ill. 1960).

101. A. Romaniuk, "Infertility in Tropical Africa," in John C. Caldwell and Chukuka Okonjo, eds., *The Population of Tropical Africa* (New York, 1968), pp. 214-24.

CHAPTER 7–THE DEMOGRAPHIC CONSEQUENCES AND CAUSES OF THE CHANGING EPIDEMIOLOGICAL SITUATION

1. J. C. Caldwell, "Population: General Characteristics," in Walter Birmingham, I. Neustadt, and E. N. Omaboe, eds., *A Study of Contemporary Ghana*, vol. II (London, 1967), p. 74. Africanists are just beginning to recognize the crucial importance of demographic history. Our knowledge of population changes in Ghana and the rest of the continent is still rudimentary and, while there are serious methodological problems, the field has enormous potential. See, for example, R. P. Moss and R. J. A. R. Rathbone, eds., *The Population Factor in African*

Studies (London, 1975); K. David Patterson, "The Vanishing Mpongwe: European Contact and Demographic Change in the Gabon River," *J.A.H.*, 16 (1975), pp. 117-38; John Thornton, "Demography and History in the Kingdom of the Kongo, 1550-1750," *J.A.H.*, 17 (1976), pp. 507-30; and especially *African Historical Demography* (Centre of African Studies, University of Edinburgh, 1977).

2. Thomas McKeown, R. G. Record, and R. D. Turner, "An Interpretation of the Decline of Mortality in England and Wales During the Twentieth Century," *Population Studies*, 29 (1975), pp. 391-422; McKeown and Record, "Reasons for the Decline of Mortality in England and Wales During the Nineteenth Century," *Population Studies*, 16 (1962), pp. 94-122; Robert Higgs, "Mortality in Rural America, 1870-1920: Estimates and Conjectures," *Explorations in Economic History*, 10 (1973), pp. 177-95; Thomas McKeown, *The Modern Rise of Population* (London, 1976).

3. Kingsley Davis, "The Amazing Decline of Mortality in Underdeveloped Areas," *American Economic History Review*, 1956, pp. 305-18; I. O. Orubuloye and J. C. Caldwell, "The Impact of Public Health Services on Mortality: A Study of Mortality Differentials in a Rural Area of Nigeria," *Population Studies*, 29 (1975), pp. 259-72; Samuel S. Preston, "The Changing Relations Between Mortality and Level of Economic Development," *Population Studies*, 29 (1975), pp. 231-48; Jay R. Mandle, "The Decline in Mortality in British Guiana, 1911-1960," *Demography*, 7 (1970), pp. 301-15.

4. See, for example, P. Denoix, "Une prospection médicale de deux mois en Haute-Volta (octobre-novembre 1948)," *Bulletin de l'Institut National d'Hygiène*, 4 (1949), pp. 264-90; and Daniel Benoit, "Une étude démographique à partir des registres paroissaux en pays Gourounsi (Haute Volta)," *Cahiers O.R.S.T.O.M.*, sér. Sciences Humaines, 13 (1976), pp. 297-310.

5. Robert R. Kuczynski, *Demographic Survey of the British Colonial Empire*, vol. I (London, 1948), pp. 451-52, 462-63.

6. *United Nations Demographic Yearbook*, 1961, p. 121.

7. S. K. Gaisie and K. T. de Graft-Johnson, *The Population of Ghana* (Paris, 1976), p. 6; see also S. Ofosu-Amaah, "The Maternal and Child Health Centre in Action," *Ghana Medical Journal*, 6 (1967), p. 52.

8. Peter Laslett, *The World We Have Lost: England Before the Industrial Age* (New York, 1965), p. 235.

9. S. K. Gaishie, "Population Growth and Its Components," in J. C. Caldwell, ed., *Population Growth and Socioeconomic Change in West Africa* (New York, 1975), p. 346.

10. Caldwell, "Population: General Characteristics," p. 21.

11. ADM 5/2/3, Census of the Population, 1911, pp. 5-6.

12. ADM 56/1/96, District Commissioner Lorha-Tumu to C.C.N.T., 29 July 1921.

13. ADM 68/5/1, Zuarungu District Diary, 26 Sept. 1920.

14. ADM 5/2/5, Census Report, 1921, p. 5.

15. A. W. Cardinall, *The Gold Coast, 1931*, vol. I (Accra, 1932), p. 123.

16. ADM 56/1/96, Report on the Census of the North-Western Province, 1911, p. 4.

17. ADM 56/1/265, Census, Wa, 1921, p. 8.

18. Thomas E. Dow, Jr. and Eugene Benjamin, "Sierra Leone: Demographic Trends and Implications," in Caldwell, ed., *Population Growth*, p. 428,

19. P. O. Olusanya, "Population Growth and Its Components: The Nature and Direction of Population Change," in Caldwell, ed., *Population Growth*, p. 255.

20. S. P. Reyna and Christian Bouquet, "Chad," in Caldwell, ed., *Population Growth*, p. 575; B. Lacombe, B. Lamy, and J. Vaugelade, "Senegal," ibid., pp. 701-2; Louis Roussel, "Ivory Coast," ibid., p. 657.

21. Caldwell, "Population: General Characteristics," pp. 21-23.

22. Ibid., p. 21; Marion Johnson, "Census, Map, and Guestimates: The Past Population of the Accra Region," in *African Historical Demography*, p. 273.

23. Cardinall, *The Gold Coast*, pp. 151-53.

24. A. I. Asiwaju, "Migrations as Revolt: The Example of the Ivory Coast and Upper Volta Before 1945," *J.A.H.*, 17 (1976), pp. 577-94.

25. Caldwell, "Introduction," in Caldwell, ed., *Population Growth*, p. 4.

26. *R.R.B.D.*, 1920, p. 3; *R.R.B.D.*, 1922-23, p. 25; *R.R.B.D.*, 1927, p. 4; Kuczynski, *Demographic Survey*, pp. 522-27.

27. Kuczynski, *Demographic Survey*, p. 471.

28. *U.N. Demographic Yearbook*, 1969, p. 424.

29. *M.D.A.R.*, 1924-25, appendix E, "A Report on the Birth-Rate and Infant Mortality in the Koforidua District," by J. M. O'Brien, pp. 70-71.

30. Cardinall, *The Gold Coast*, pp. 212-17. If stillbirths were included, the 5,583 fertile women averaged 6.07 births.

31. ADM 11/1294, "Diet and Nutrition Survey-Gold Coast-Final Report-1940," p. 82; Donald J. Bogue, *Principles of Demography* (New York, 1969), p. 622.

32. M. Fortes, "A Note on Fertility Among the Tallensi of the Gold Coast," *Sociological Review*, 35 (1943), pp. 99-113.

33. "Final Report," p. 112.

34. Ibid., p. 135.

35. George W. Barclay, *Techniques of Population Analysis* (New York, 1958), pp. 180-82.

36. Caldwell, "Population Change," in Birmingham, Neustadt, and Omaboe, eds., *Contemporary Ghana*, p. 104. For stable population analysis, see D. Ian Pool, *African Historical Demography*, pp. 56-57, and references cited there. Interesting historical uses of this method include two works by John Thornton, "An Eighteenth Century Baptismal Register and the Demographic History of Manguenzo," *African Historical Demography*, pp. 405-15; and "Demography and History in the Kingdom of the Kongo."

37. Gaishie, "Population Growth and Its Components," pp. 339-40.

38. K. David Patterson, "Health in Urban Ghana: The Case of Accra, 1900-1940," *Social Science and Medicine*, 13B (1979), pp. 251-68.

39. N. O. Addo, "Some Demographic Aspects of Urbanization in Ghana, 1931-1960," *Ghana Soc. Sci. J.*, 1 (1970), p. 57. Registration covered most, but not all, of the places defined as "urban" in the census.

40. Caldwell, "Population Change," pp. 93-94.

41. Gaishie and DeGraft Johnson, *Population of Ghana*, p. 23.

42. McKeown, *Modern Rise of Population*; Higgs, " Mortality in Rural America."

43. *R.R.B.D.*, 1924-25, p. 3.

44. *R.R.B.D.*, 1929, p. 4.

45. McD. Hendrie, "The Need for Antenatal Work Among the Women of the Outlying Districts of West Africa," *Health and Empire*, 8 (1933), pp. 270-71; Leonard Goodman, "Obstetrics in a Primitive African Community," *Amer. J. Public Health*, 41, part 2 (1951), pp. 57-58.

46. Goodman, "Obstetrics," pp. 58, 61; *M.D.A.R.*, 1947, p. 4.

47. *M.D.A.R.*, 1938, p. 16.

48. S. N. Otoo, "Suggestions for the Re-Organization of the Maternal Health Services of Accra," *Ghana Med. J.*, 12 (1973), p. 81. However, only 9 percent of births in Accra were assisted by "traditional" attendants.

49. Kuczynski, *Demographic Survey*, pp. 523-24; *R.R.B.D.*, 1927, p. 6.

50. S. K. Gaishie, "Levels and Patterns of Infant and Child Mortality in Ghana," *Demography*, 12 (1975), pp. 32-33.

51. *M.D.A.R.*, 1924-25, appendix E, "Report on the Birth Rate and Infant Mortality in the Koforidua District," p. 72; *M.D.A.R.*, 1930-31, "Report on the Princess Marie Louise Hospital," pp. 177-81; Beatrice A. S. Russell, "Malnutrition in Children Under Three Years of Age in Ashanti, West Africa," *Arch. Dis. Childhood*, 21 (1946), p. 110; D. B. Jelliffe, "The African Child," *T.R.S.T.M.H.*, 46 (1952), pp. 14-33. D. B. Jelliffe, ed., *Child Health in the Tropics* (London, 4th ed., 1974), is a useful introduction to pediatric problems.

52. Nevin S. Scrimshaw and Moises Behar, "Malnutrition," in Edwin D. Kilbourne and Wilson G. Smillie, eds., *Human Ecology and Public Health* (4th ed., New York, 1969), pp. 296-97.

53. A. Thornton and A. J. Zuckerman, "The Virus of Acute Diarrhea," *Nature*, 254 (1975), pp. 557-58; Anon., "Rotaviruses of Man and Animals," *Lancet*, 1 (1975), pp. 257-59;

Albert Z. Kapikian, H. W. Kim, R. G. Wyatt, et al., "Human Reovirus-like Agent as the Main Pathogen Associated with 'Winter' Gastroenteritis in Hospitalized Infants and Young Children," *N. Eng. J. Med.*, 294, 18 (1976), pp. 965-72.

54. *M.D.A.R.*, 1931-32, appendix E, "Deficiency Diseases in Infants," by Cecily D. Williams, pp. 92-99; C. D. Williams, "Nutritional Diseases of Childhood Associated with Maize Diet," *Arch. Dis. Childhood*, 8 (1933), pp. 423-33; C. D. Williams, "Kwashiorkor; Nutritional Diseases of Children Associated with Maize Diet," *Lancet*, 229 (Nov. 16, 1935), pp. 1151-52.

55. C.S.O. 0709, s.f. 8, Ag. D.M.S. to C.S., 29 Jan. 1945; D.V.S. to C.S., 28 Feb. 1945.

56. H. F. Welbourn, "Bottle Feeding: A Problem of Modern Civilization," *J. Trop. Pediatrics*, 3 (1958), pp. 157-66; D. B. Jelliffe, "Urbanization and Child Nutrition in Africa," *Int. Child Welfare Rev.*, 16 (1962), pp. 68-72; D. B. Jelliffe and F. J. Bennett, "Aspects of Child Rearing in Africa," *J. African Studies*, 2 (1975), p. 379.

57. It has been argued that in Britain the greater availability of cows' milk in the nineteenth century had a positive impact on infant health despite the dangers of infection. From about 1890, measures against bovine tuberculosis and improvements in processing and transporting milk, notably pasteurization and refrigeration, sharply reduced the disease danger, thus contributing to a sharp decline in infant mortality. This hypothesis seems plausible for developed countries, where cows' milk is cheap and can be stored and prepared for use under sanitary conditions. See M. W. Beaver, "Population, Infant Mortality, and Milk," *Population Studies*, 27 (1973), pp. 243-54.

58. E.g., *Gold Coast Independent*, 24 Jan. 1925, pp. ii, 43.

59. C.S.O. 11/6, 98/32, C. D. Williams to D.D.H.S., 18 Jan. 1932; Gov. to C.S., 5 Feb. 1932. Dr. Williams had changed her views on bottle feeding by 1946. Welbourn, "Bottle Feeding," p. 157.

60. F. M. Purcell, *Diet and Ill Health in the Forest Country of the Gold Coast*, (London, 1939), pp. 15-16, 64.

61. J. E. Gordon, I. D. Chitkara, and J. B. Wyon, "Weanling Diarrhea," *Amer. J. Med. Sciences*, 245 (1963), pp. 347-48; J. E. Gordon, J. B. Wyon, and W. Ascoli, "The Second Year Death Rate in Less Developed Countries," *Amer. J. Med. Sciences*, 254 (1967), pp. 357-80.

62. S. Ofosu-Amaah, "The Maternal and Child Health Centre in Accra," *Ghana Med. J.*, 6, no. 2 (1967), p. 52.

63. Caldwell, "Population Change," pp. 105, 110.

64. *M.D.A.R.*, 1902, p. 17.

65. Caldwell, "Population Change," pp. 93-94.

66. McKeown, *Modern Rise of Population*, pp. 82-83.

67. Ibid., pp. 83-85.

68. "Record of Discussion," *African Historical Demography*, p. 6; Danielle Domergue, "La Côte d'Ivoire: essai de démographie historique (1905-1945)," in *African Historical Demography*, pp. 328-29; Catherine Coquery-Vidrovitch, "Population et démographie en Afrique Equatoriale Française dans le premier tiers du XXe siècle," in *African Historical Demography*, pp. 346-47; John Ford, *The Role of the Trypanosomiases in African Ecology* (London, 1971), pp. 337-39, 392. Helge Kjekshus, in *Ecology Control and Economic Development in East African History: The Case of Tanganyika, 1850-1950* (London, 1977), pp. 16-25, follows Kuczynski in arguing that the population of East Africa declined from c. 1890 to c. 1930. This is plausible and even likely, although his contention that population was stable or rising during the 1800-1890 period is questionable. See Gerald W. Hartwig, "Economic Consequences of Long-Distance Trade in East Africa: The Disease Factor," *African Studies Review*, XVIII, no. 2 (1975), pp. 63-73.

69. Caldwell, "Population: General Characteristics," p. 21; Johnson, "Census, Map, and Guesstimates," p. 273.

70. J. C. Caldwell, "Major Questions in African Demographic History," in *African Historical Demography*, pp. 12-13, 16.

71. Johnson, "Census, Map, and Guesstimates," p. 273.

72. Ivor Wilks, *Asante in the Nineteenth Century* (Cambridge, U.K., 1975), pp. 87-93.

73. Johnson, "Census, Map, and Guesstimates," p. 294.

74. T. E. Hilton, "Notes on the History of Kusasi," *Trans. Hist. Soc. Ghana.*, 6 (1962), p. 84.

75. J. J. Holden, "The Zabarima Conquest of North-West Ghana," *Trans. Hist. Soc. Ghana*, 8 (1965), pp. 66-86.

76. D. Ian Pool, "A Framework for the Analysis of West African Historical Demography," p. 54.

77. N. S. Scrimshaw, C. E. Taylor, and J. E. Gordon, *Interactions of Nutrition and Infection* (Geneva, 1968, W.H.O. Monograph Series, no. 57), p. 16; Charles Wilcocks and P. E. C. Manson-Bahr, *Manson's Tropical Diseases* (17th ed., London, 1972), pp. 738-39.

78. Scrimshaw et al., *Nutrition and Infection*, p. 27; N. S. Scrimshaw and M. Behar, "Malnutrition," p. 297.

79. Scrimshaw et al., *Nutrition and Infection*, pp. 64, 67; Jean Mayer, *Human Nutrition–Its Physiological, Medical, and Social Aspects* (Springfield, Ill., 1972), pp. 489-91.

80. Scrimshaw et al., *Nutrition and Infection*, pp. 30, 66; Mayer, *Human Nutrition*, pp. 485-87.

81. Scrimshaw et al., *Nutrition and Infection*, p. 75.

82. Mayer, *Human Nutrition*, p. 674.

83. Scrimshaw et al., *Nutrition and Infection*, pp. 13, 140.

84. Mayer, *Human Nutrition*, pp. 669-74. For a general discussion, see R. G. Hendrickse, "Some Observations on the Social Background to Malnutrition in Tropical Africa," *African Affairs*, 65 (1966), pp. 1-9.

85. CSO 11/1, 0709, s.f. 3, Secretary of State to Governor, 16 Aug. 1943; D.M.S. to C.S., 20 Oct. 1943.

86. *M.D.A.R.*, 1931-32, p. 33; *M.D.A.R.*, 1938, p. 37; *M.D.A.R.*, 1948, p. 15.

87. *M.D.A.R.*, 1920, p. 22.

88. E.g., *M.D.A.R.*, 1938, p. 37; *M.D.A.R.*, 1946, p. 10.

89. *M.D.A.R.*, 1945, p. 12.

90. E. B. Worthington, *Science in Africa: A Review of Scientific Research Relating to Tropical and South Africa* (London, 1938), p. 571; *Gold Coast Independent*, 5 Feb. 1938, p. 132.

91. ADM 1/2/221, no. 398, Governor's Deputy to Secretary of State, 11 July 1936, responding to Circular Dispatch of 18 Apr. 1936; G. M. Culwick, "Nutrition Work in British African Colonies Since 1939," *Africa*, 14 (1943), pp. 24-26.

92. ADM 1/2/231, no. 366, Governor's Deputy to Secretary of State, 5 June 1937, and encl. 1, Minutes of the Standing Committee on Nutrition.

93. ADM 11/1294, "Diet and Nutrition Survey-Gold Coast-Final Report, 1940." Purcell's draft, revised somewhat by the Committee, was accepted in 1941. See also D.M.S. to S.N.A., 1 May 1941, and Purcell to S.N.A., 5 July 1941.

94. F. M. Purcell, *Diet and Ill Health in the Forest Country*; ADM 11/1294, "Diet and Nutrition in Mamprusi," 26 Nov. 1939, 36 pp.

95. ADM 1/2/306, S.T. 337, Officer Administering the Government to Secretary of State, 21 Feb. 1949.

96. A. W. Cardinall, *The Natives of the Northern Territories of the Gold Coast: Their Customs, Religion, and Folklore* (London, 1920; reprinted Westport, Conn., 1969), p. 85.

97. M. Fortes and S. L. Fortes, "Food in the Domestic Economy of the Tallensi," *Africa*, 9 (1936), pp. 253-59; J. M. Hunter, "Seasonal Hunger in a Part of the West African Savanna: A Survey of Bodyweights in North-East Ghana," *Transactions of the Institute of British Geographers*, 41 (1967), pp. 167-85.

98. *M.D.A.R.*, 1931-32, p. 33; *M.D.A.R.*, 1940, p. 1.

99. Fortes and Fortes, "Tallensi," pp. 246-67.

100. Purcell, "Diet in Mamprusi," p. 14; "Final Report," p. 67.

101. Purcell, "Diet in Mamprusi," pp. 18, 26; "Final Report," p. 65. An active adult male requires about 2,600-2,900 calories per day. (Wilcocks and Manson-Bahr, *Manson's Tropical Diseases*, p. 738).

102. "Final Report," p. 79.

103. Ibid. Purcell emphasized the heavy disease burden in the region and stressed the necessity for radical agricultural improvements. His demographic data are discussed elsewhere in this chapter.

104. Purcell, *Diet and Ill Health in the Forest Country*, pp. 2-7.

105. Ibid., pp. 29-42, 59-64.

106. "Final Report," pp. 119, 137.

107. Ibid., p. 120; Purcell, *Diet and Ill Health in the Forest Country*, p. 14.

108. "Final Report," pp. 127-33.

109. Purcell, *Diet and Ill Health in the Forest Country*, pp. 10-14.

110. M. J. Colbourne, G. M. Edington, and M. H. Hughes, "A Medical Survey in a Gold Coast Village," *T.R.S.T.M.H.*, 44 (1950), pp. 275, 281-82.

111. Faye W. Grant, "Nutrition and Health of Gold Coast Children," *J. Amer. Dietetic Association*, 31 (1955), pp. 693, 685-87.

112. *V.D.A.R.*, 1931-32, p. 17.

113. *M.D.A.R.*, 1920, p. 22; *M.D.A.R.*, 1926-27, p. 34.

114. *M.D.A.R.*, 1926-27, p. 34; Purcell, *Diet and Ill Health in the Forest Country*, p. 16.

115. Purcell, *Diet and Ill Health in the Forest Country*, p. 16; *M.D.A.R.*, 1950, p. 11.

116. *V.D.A.R.*, 1931-32, p. 17.

117. See K. David Patterson, "The Veterinary Department and the Animal Industry in the Gold Coast, 1909-1950," *Int. J. Af. Hist. St.*, 13 (1980), pp. 457-91, for further information on local production and imports.

118. *V.D.A.R.*, 1948-49, p. 10.

119. *G.C.A.R.*, 1932-33, p. 26; Rowena M. Lawson and E. Kwei, *African Entrepreneurship and Economic Growth: A Case Study of the Fishing Industry of Ghana* (Accra, 1974), p. 25.

120. Lawson and Kwei, *African Entrepreneurship*, pp. 51, 69.

121. Claire C. Robertson, "Social and Economic Change in Twentieth Century Accra: Ga Women," (Ph.D. dissertation, University of Wisconsin, 1974), p. 245.

122. James W. Brown, "Kumasi, 1896-1923: Urban Africa During the Early Colonial Period," (Ph.D. dissertation, University of Wisconsin, 1972), pp. 86-87.

123. B. B. Waddy, "Onchocerciasis and Blindness in the Northern Territories of the Gold Coast," typescript, 1949, p. 10.

124. ADM 1/2/233, no. 571, Governor to Secretary of State, 16 Sept. 1936, and encl. 1, A. P. Brown to Governor, 2 Sept. 1936.

125. Lawson and Kwei, *African Entrepreneurship*, pp. 51-57.

126. Ibid., pp. 23-24, 45.

127. *G.C.A.R.*, 1932-33, pp. 23-24; Kwamina B. Dickson, *A Historical Geography of Ghana* (Cambridge, 1971), pp. 309-10; H. P. White, "Internal Exchange of Staple Foods in the Gold Coast," *Economic Geography*, 32 (1956), pp. 115-25.

128. Fortes and Fortes, "Tallensi," pp. 246, 252; Hunter, "Seasonal Hunger," pp. 171-73; White, "Internal Exchange," p. 119.

129. W. L. Langer, "American Food Crops and Europe's Population Growth, 1750-1850," *J. Social Hist.*, Winter (1975), pp. 51-66.

130. Walter Birmingham, "An Index of Real Wages of the Unskilled Labourer in Accra, 1939-1959," *Economic Bulletin of Ghana*, 4, no. 3 (1960), pp. 2-6; Robertson, "Social and Economic Change in Twentieth Century Accra," pp. 48-51, 355-56.

131. For data on Kumasi prior to 1923, see Brown, "Kumasi, 1896-1923," pp. 195-97, 259. Real wages declined during the First World War.

132. In addition to the sources cited in note 2, see T. McKeown, R. G. Brown, and R. G. Record, "An Interpretation of the Modern Rise of Population in Europe," *Population Studies*, 26 (1972), pp. 345-82; and E. A. Wrigley, *Population and History* (New York, 1969), pp. 168, 170, 172, 177.

133. Etienne Van de Walle, "Population and Development," in Caldwell, ed., *Population Growth*, p. 136.

134. Sir F. D. Lugard, *The Dual Mandate in British Tropical Africa* (3rd ed., Edinburgh and London, 1926), p. 92; Kuczynski, *Demographic Survey of the British Colonial Empire*, vols. I and II.

135. Lewis H. Gann and Peter Duignan, *Burden of Empire: An Appraisal of Western Colonialism in Africa South of the Sahara* (New York, 1967), p. 292.

136. Wrigley, *Population and History*, p. 165.

137. J. W. S. Macfie, "The Prevalent Diseases of the Gold Coast," *T.R.S.T.M.H.*, 16 (1922), pp. 156-61.

138. Kuczynski, *Demographic Survey*, p. 521.

139. Orubuloye and Caldwell, "The Impact of Public Health Services on Mortality," p. 272.

140. Mandle, "Mortality in British Guiana, 1911-1960," pp. 301-15.

141. See, for comparison, Alfred A. Buck, et al., *Health and Disease in Chad: Epidemiology, Culture, and Environment in Five Villages* (Baltimore, 1970).

142. For a probably over-optimistic view of a West Indian situation, see Burton A. Weisbrod et al., *Disease and Economic Development: The Impact of Parasitic Diseases in St. Lucia* (Madison, 1973).

INDEX

ABOUT THE AUTHOR

K. David Patterson is Professor of History at the University of North Carolina at Charlotte. He has been a Visiting Lecturer in the Department of Parasitology and Laboratory Practice at the School of Public Health, University of North Carolina, Chapel Hill, where he is a candidate for an M.S.P.H. degree. For the past several years his research and publications have been devoted to African medical and demographic history. Dr. Patterson is a member of the African Studies Association and the American Association for the History of Medicine.